RAINDROPS TO RAINBOWS
-
A STORY OF AWAKENING

by Yvonne Jevons

Raindrops to Rainbows - A Story of Awakening
© Yvonne Jevons

Published by Yvonne Jevons

Yvonne Jevons is hereby identified as the author of this work
in accordance with Section 77 of the Copyright, Designs and
Patent Act 1988. She asserts and gives   notice of her moral
right under this Act.

Cover design by Yvonne and Callum Jevons

Cover illustration by Natasha Probert

Typesetting and cover layout by Andrew Davis

Printed by MPG Biddles Ltd

ISBN
978-0-9570322-0-0

I dedicate this book to Eric.

A percentage of the profit from this book will go to
'One Generation Project'- a not for profit organisation
to support parents, mothers and children in a new vision
for humanity and generations to come.

Acknowlegements

To my Mum, who has been a true Earth Angel for me and my children.

To my two beautiful sons, whose own life experiences and love have helped me to grow and understand parts of myself I didn't know existed. Thank you for choosing me to be your Mum and your student.

To all the wondrous people I have been privileged to know -

Bill, for his unwavering support, love and guidance through some very tough times.

Chris Stormer-Fryer for her insights and for being at the other end of an email with consistent support.

Kiannaa for her patience, her teaching and her friendship.

Rae, for his support, his angelic healing and guidance.

To Callum for his help with the design of the cover.

To Natasha for her brilliant illustration of the cover design.

Special thanks to Joy, an inspirational teacher and friend. Thank you for waking me up before it was too late and helping me make the amazing connections I had yearned to find.

To all the friends who have come, gone and stayed with me on this path of self discovery - thank you for your love, no matter how brief the connection.

Thank you to all of you for helping me to begin to love myself.

Preface

For many years a number of people and friends have said to me that I should write a book. "A book about what?" I would say to myself. What have I got to say that's any more important or special than anything anyone else has to say?

As the years have gone by, I have come to realise that by telling my story, it has allowed others to tell theirs and share their experience, helping them to heal and to grow and become stronger. Living life in a much more joyous place of being.

So I write my life experiences in the hope that you too can share your experiences or begin to understand   yourself, begin to know yourself as the beautiful being that you are. Begin to live your life day by day with as much joy as you can possibly bring into yourself with every breathing moment.

I wrote this authors note in 2008, only a few days before the fifth anniversary of my father's passing. It was a time of reflection for me. More so than any other year since his death. My own personal and spiritual growth had tested my inner strength to the limit for a year and it was time for resting, reflection and gathering my thoughts so that I could finally get around to putting pen to paper.

I put off writing my story for so long, convinced that no-one would ever be that interested. Perhaps that will be the case. Perhaps you'll get a few pages through this book, put it down and never pick it up again. But perhaps you'll start reading and feel a connection with my story. And perhaps through reading this book you'll know that each one of us has a story to tell; that we are here to help each other, hold each other and share with each other so that we can feel the peace within our hearts.

I hope as you read, you'll know that you aren't alone and no matter what your life experience has been so far, you can pick yourself up and shine your light again.

Why is it that we strive to 'fit in', when in fact we fit perfectly into ourselves - we are each unique and special. To attempt to be like another isn't being who we are, where we feel at our very best.

Be yourself.

Shine YOUR special light into the world.

For there is no-one else quite like YOU in the whole world......

Light is the Key

Light is the key to all
Not darkness and gloom.
Surrounding, bathing, supporting -
Light is the key.

As each light is lit - more light comes in
Filling the dark scary places;
Banishing our demons;
Light is the key.

Dancing with the light;
Embracing its beauty;
Basking in its tranquillity.
Light is the key.

Clouds are vanishing;
Pain diminishing;
Growth more possible.
Light is the key.

We're only human – not perfect!
Mistakes are many on this Earth School!
But we are all special – all unique

Light is the key to all.

~ LIGHT IS LIFE ~

~ LIGHT IS LOVE ~

Yvonne Jevons
May 2005

Chapter One

My life has been little different to most people. I left school
having achieved good grades, but not quite good enough to
fulfill my childhood dream of becoming a doctor. Instead I
secured a place on a relatively new four year degree nursing
course. I was so excited that at least I would still be able to
work in the medical field.

The functioning of the human body had always held great
fascination for me, how self contained it is and the wondrous
interwoven workings of all its' systems and organs. We are all
walking around in such an incredible piece of biological art.

My first year at college went relatively well, but it was during
this year that my Dad left his job in Scotland and began to
work in Iraq for the United Nations as an engineer. He trained
groups of young men and women how to repair and maintain
air conditioning and refrigeration systems within hotels.

This was really hard for the family, as Mum, myself and my
younger sister stayed behind in Scotland. We only saw Dad
once or twice a year for two or three weeks and we all missed
him very much.

During my second year at college I was involved in a severe road accident on my way to a shift at a hospital outside Edinburgh. I had three other nursing students in my car as passengers and a car drove out in front of us from a closed off road and there was no way to avoid it.

I recall striking the other car and coming to moments later. My head had struck the steering wheel despite wearing a seat belt. My beloved old VW Beetle was a write off. There wasn't another car in sight and I thought I was losing my mind. There was my car in the middle of the road, no other car around and I recall seeing a dog wandering along the footpath some way off, thinking it rather strange that no-one was with the animal.

When the police and ambulance arrived we were told that we had been incredibly fortunate. I had the other car side-on as it crossed in front of us and the impact of the collision had folded the bodywork of the car onto the accelerator pedal. It had then careered across the carriageway, through a hedge and into someone's garden, embedding itself in the wall of a house. The occupant of the car was injured but would recover. We escaped serious injury and were able to go home after treatment at the hospital.

It was a weird time. I was in shock and had facial injuries from the crash. Something changed during the following few weeks. I lost my spark and felt very lost. I missed my Dad. I lost interest in college work, I'm not even sure why. Nothing seemed to feel right any more.

It came as no surprise that I failed an exam and had to sit it again during the summer, as well as complete the two weeks of the nursing placement I had missed because of the car accident.

My heart was no longer in my studies and I don't think I was aware that I had stopped enjoying the course, until I failed the re-sit. I couldn't return to re-sit my second year. I was devastated. I didn't know what else I wanted to do. I felt useless and a complete failure. I had wanted to enter medicine all my life and here I was excluded from it.

Mum had joined my Dad in Iraq a few weeks earlier and phone calls were sparse. For weeks I drifted through life, wondering where to turn next.

I was twenty years old and started looking at my other options, applying for other conventional nursing courses in Scotland and England only to find there were waiting lists of up to three years. A thought then struck me. I had always loved aircraft and flying - perhaps I could join the RAF and apply for the Queens Alexandra Nursing Corps instead?

I made some enquiries, filled out a variety of forms and waited. There was a waiting list of up to two years for entry to the QARANC. I remember sitting at home with all sorts of leaflets strewn around the floor from the Army, Navy and Air Force. I felt like nobody wanted me.

Then an idea formed. I went along to the recruiting office and asked what jobs they were currently recruiting for. They had some Air Traffic Control and technical roles available. Over the next few months I went through various tests, finding out that I had an aptitude for things I didn't know I was capable of.

This whole process was extremely laborious, with all sorts of checks required before I was accepted. There were medicals galore and more aptitude tests and interviews. While I waited for the process to be completed and a date for entry, I joined my parents in Iraq for my twenty-first birthday. It was an interesting experience living there for a few months and I even managed to find myself some part-time work for a little while.

My sister called in late November to tell me that I had been accepted into the RAF as an Electronics Technician and I needed to get home within the next two weeks. I was excited, but very nervous. Had I done the right thing?

I flew home a week later, leaving Mum and Dad in Iraq, and joined up. It was a surreal experience taking the oath to serve Queen and country one day and getting on a train the very next day in mid December to travel to the training camp. I had returned from an extremely hot climate and Britain in December felt like the arctic.

I somehow got through the six weeks of basic training, though ended up with frostbite in one of my toes. The whole experience was quite a shock to the system, but I had completed the gruelling basic training and I was proud of that achievement. I departed hours after the ceremony and travelled by bus with a few other recruits to the RAF base where I would be living. I had fifteen months of electronics training ahead of me.

This was a much more relaxed environment, yet exams came along almost every week throughout the whole course. I found that I had good skills for fault finding and I loved groveling about on the old aircraft in the hangars, 'fixing' the faults which were set by the training staff. I learned a variety of workshop skills, from soldering tiny components on electronic circuit boards to drilling and shaping perspex.

I had formed close bonds with the other members of the course. There were four girls including me and sixteen young men, which felt like having sixteen brothers.

Those months were quite an intense experience. Living and working so close to others on the course had its ups and downs. At times it was incredibly supportive, other times it was a challenge.

One of those challenges was the death of my uncle. A week before his death I awoke in the middle of the night in a complete panic, with a deep feeling of foreboding. I couldn't recall what I had dreamt, but I decided to phone home to see if everything was okay with my family. I was reassured that everyone was fine and I continued my week as usual until I received the call from home.

My uncle had taken his own life, on the same day as his sons sixteenth birthday. My head was reeling, I was so shocked. I requested some time off to attend his funeral and faced some difficulties as he wasn't considered to be close family. It took an immense amount of persuasion and explaining that he was my Godfather and he was close family to me.

I told my Commanding Officer that if I wasn't given permission to attend his funeral in Scotland I would go anyway and face the consequences on my return to the base. What I thought I was doing speaking to my senior officer in that way, I don't know, but I was determined to be at the service.

My Commanding Officer could see that I was deeply distressed, but he was concerned about the amount of work I would miss by being away. However he finally agreed to let me go and I drove the four hours from the RAF base to Edinburgh after classes finished at 5pm, attended the funeral the next day and drove back that night.

Suddenly the course didn't really seem that important anymore, but I persevered and my friends were very supportive during this time as I grieved for my family. It was hard being away from home at this time, as I was quite close to my cousins and the family had been deeply shocked by my uncle's suicide.

A few months later, one of my close friends came to speak to me one evening in my room. She was very upset. I thought that perhaps her father had taken ill again but when she began to tell me the reason for her distress I was stunned and began to get angry.

Someone had told her about a rumour which was circulating that she and I were lesbians. In one respect this was deeply hurtful, and yet in another it was highly amusing. I was secretly dating one of the male staff (this wasn't permitted because we were still in 'training') and Susan had just started dating one of the young men on our course, though this wasn't common knowledge. Perhaps because Susan and I were very close and spent time just talking and had visited each others parents during some weekends off, someone had jumped to the wrong conclusion.

We weren't sure what to do. We wondered who might have started this rumour. At the time, homosexuality was not accepted in the armed forces and we could potentially be discharged. Our careers over before they had even started. The rumour didn't bother me so much as the potential outcome.

We decided to visit the Padre to explain things to him in complete confidence. Our plan was that if anything did escalate, at least we would have him as some form of support. The meeting went well and we specifically requested that our conversation was to be kept in complete confidence. If we needed him to come forward on our behalf later we would ask.

Two days later, our whole course was called to the electrical engineering headquarters. No-one was sure what was going on, until Susan and I were called into the Commanders office. The moment he started to speak I knew what had happened. The Padre had spoken to our Commander without our permission and the whole story was now common knowledge at HQ.

Susan was very upset and we were questioned at length. The Commander believed us, much to our relief. It was an embarrassing experience and I was really angry.

We returned to the classroom, all our class mates were there looking at us. They could see how distressed we were, yet had no idea why. The Commander addressed everyone, expressing his disgust at the spiteful nature of the rumour and the potential affect on mine and Susan's career. He was very forthright and explained that if the others weren't able to support us, then everyone would be discharged except me and Susan. He was furious.

They were great, stunned that anyone would say these things about us. They knew how difficult it had been for me after my Uncles death and that Susan's father had been very unwell. They all knew we were close friends but certainly not intimately involved. A couple of the lads knew about me seeing the male member of staff and Susan dating one of their friends. It was all very messy, yet out of it came even stronger bonds within the group.

By the following week some of the lads had discovered who had started the rumours. It was Trevor, one of our course members who I hadn't particularly taken to. Trevor didn't like that my boyfriend was black and commented one day that, "No white man will ever touch you again".

He couldn't help his ignorance and he wasn't pleasant to be around with this attitude and I knew it wasn't worth my time and effort interacting with him at this level. Thankfully most of the other lads were extremely supportive and he was encouraged to stay away from me and keep his opinions to himself.

It was such an emotionally draining time. Apart from the rumours themselves, I felt completely betrayed by the Padre who had gone behind our backs to our Commanding Officer. Perhaps in hindsight it was the best way forward, to bring the whole silly situation out into the open. But I was less than impressed about the 'confidential' aspect having been completely ignored. My trust of others in authority was shattered and from then on I tended to keep things very much to myself.

At the end of the fifteen months training I passed the exams, attained a diploma in Aerospace Studies and was posted to a base in Northern Scotland.

Life changed again. There were new people to get to know and new ways of working. I felt a little out of my depth in those first months. I was there for over three years, during which time I became less and less happy. I couldn't put my finger on what was wrong, I just knew I didn't feel right.

My right knee had become extremely painful, possibly because I was small in stature yet had all the fitness regime of much larger men during the previous sixteen months. My knee was complaining at all the physical training and sometimes it had to be bandaged and splinted to minimise movement. It made life rather awkward for working and eventually I had a small knee operation done, which alleviated much of the pain and the restricted movement in the joint.

On top of my own physical problems a family member was struggling with an addiction. It wasn't an easy time. My younger cousin had been admitted to a psychiatric hospital. She had become involved with a man much older than she was who had introduced her to drugs. She was a mess. She was withdrawing from cocaine addiction and seeing all sorts of creatures crawling the walls. She had escaped from her ward one day after seeing tribesmen chasing her with spears. She tried to get out of the hospital grounds by climbing a wall and had fallen and broken her jaw.

I went to see her whenever I could and one day I bumped into one of the girls I had trained alongside during my time at nursing college. She was a staff nurse now working in the hospital and assured me they would do their best for my cousin. It was a long road for her, the treatment included ECT, an electric shock therapy. This was very unpleasant and she spoke to me years later of what that had felt like. It still gives me the shivers when I think about it.

It was a rocky time for me personally. Work wasn't going too well and I had been dumped by my boyfriend, with whom I was in love but unfortunately he didn't feel the same about me. My Mum had been unwell and during an operation she suffered heart failure and then experienced further complications following surgery. She had recovered well but I found it all very unsettling.

Everything in life seemed so negative and hard. I became quite low emotionally without noticing it myself. I was exasperated, yet didn't know what to do to improve things.

My previous experience with the Padre's 'confidential' talk had done nothing to encourage me to seek help and talk about my feelings. I wasn't willing to take that risk again. So I kept my feelings to myself, all the time becoming more and more withdrawn.

One night, feeling desperately low, I decided that I had had enough. I drove down to the car park in the local village overlooking the sea. I was emotionally exhausted, almost devoid of all feeling.

It was a dark night, black everywhere. As I stared out to sea, I began to take aspirins, forcing them down with a fizzy drink. I began to feel nauseous, I couldn't remember how many pills I had taken. I was staring out to sea, watching the light from the newly emerged moon glinting on the white tops of the waves as they rolled into shore.

Out of the sea appeared a figure. My heart was beating so fast, I was pinching myself to see if I had perhaps died without realising. The figure was my uncle. At that moment I experienced an overwhelming feeling of love and the word 'NO' popped into my head. I knew then I was doing the wrong thing. It wasn't my time.

I was panic stricken. Should I just drive back home? Should I seek help? I headed to the only person I trusted, Chris. I had babysat for him and his wife on many occasions and we were good friends. When I arrived at his house I told him what I'd done. I felt so stupid. He called for help and I was taken to the local hospital where I had my stomach pumped. That was a very unpleasant experience and not one I would recommend. After this I was taken back to the medical centre on the RAF base for overnight observation.

I felt more embarrassed than anything else. "How could I have let myself get so low?" I kept wondering. I spoke with the doctor the next morning and we agreed to set up some sessions for me to chat about my feelings. Much as I didn't trust him either, I had no other option.

Those weren't easy months. I hadn't wanted to draw attention to myself and yet my overdose was a cry for help from deep inside. The doctor encouraged me to attend a course in the south of England. This course was designed to help those nearing promotion to Corporal and it provided an opportunity to learn leadership qualities and man management. I wasn't sure it was for me. However a friend wanted to go, so we agreed that this would be a good opportunity for some much needed time away from the base and we might just learn something useful too.

A few weeks later we drove to the Armed Forces school. When we arrived we couldn't believe the setting. It was so beautiful. The school was an old mansion in the middle of the countryside set within lovely grounds. The five days I spent there were transformational. All the staff were friendly and if you wanted to attend the daily morning service you were welcome, but equally if it wasn't 'your thing', that was okay too.

Throughout the week we split into groups for a variety of activities. Some of these activities were designed to show others points of view and perspective on things. Some helped to teach us ways of assisting others with emotional difficulties. One of those activities involved our group being shown into a room. One of the padres, Bill, was sitting on a sofa watching the television. Some of the group tried to speak with him, but he didn't answer. I held back a little, not sure what was going on. Even though we knew it was an 'act' I became deeply unnerved.

He was acting out a scene where he had taken some drugs, was deeply depressed and attempting to kill himself, hoping to just drift away there on the sofa.

I couldn't be in the same room. I walked quietly to the door and tried to get out of the room, but the door wouldn't open. Surely they hadn't locked us inside? I began to feel rising panic. I had to get away from that scene. It was too familiar, my own similar experience was playing in my head.

One of the girls in our group came over and opened the door for me, following me out to make sure I was all right. Apparently I was ashen. I was trembling from head to foot. No dramatics, just trembling uncontrollably and I needed to sit down. I was surprised at my reaction, I hadn't felt like this before.

A member of staff brought me a glass of water and I gradually relaxed, feeling foolish at my reaction. They asked what was wrong and I told them about my uncle committing suicide a few years ago and that the scene had deeply upset me. In reality, it was my own experience which had set off this reaction, but I wasn't ready to share that with anyone.

Bill spoke to me later and said that he was sorry I had been so upset, but if I wanted to talk, he or any of the other Padres were around at any time to listen. There was something special about Bill and I trusted him. He was a real character and very much enjoyed a laugh, yet at the same time he was gentle and caring.

I knew that if I did decide to talk to anyone, it would be him.
I mulled things over in my mind, knowing that we were only
there for five days and this was day three already. I was so
scared of letting my stuff come out, scared that all the hurts and
confused emotions couldn't be contained once I started to talk.

However, on the fourth day I took the plunge, knocked on his
door and asked if I could speak to him. I spent four hours in his
office. My deepest darkest fears came tumbling out and I cried
and sobbed with the pain of the past few years of my life.

Bill listened and occasionally offered his intervention to help
me understand what was going on. I hadn't ever experienced
anything like this. Here was someone genuinely wanting
to help from their heart and letting me be 'me' without any
judgement.

Those four hours changed my life, at a time when it really
needed to change. At the end of that chat I felt more relaxed. I
had better insight into my personal experiences and felt happy
and content for the first time in ages. Bill and I became friends
over the next year. He was like a loving brother and I trusted
him with all my heart.

I settled back into life at my base following this course and
applied for a posting closer to my home in Edinburgh so that
I could support my Mum. She wasn't too well, physically and
emotionally and I felt we both needed to be closer. I moved to
a new base later that year, which made life much more pleasant
and six months later I was selected for promotion to Corporal.

This promotion involved attending a two week course, the

base was in Southern England and this was where I met Tom. At first I didn't take to him at all, especially once I found out that he was an RAF Policeman. During my time in the RAF I had been in a few minor scrapes with the RAF Police, nothing too serious, but I tended to be very wary. I kept my distance, despite him being in the same small group as myself, but as the first week wore on I realised that he wasn't all bad.

Tom was stationed in Germany, so wasn't going home that weekend and as I had quite a drive to get home to Scotland I was also staying. We agreed to share transport into town on Saturday and spent the day looking around, Tom got a haircut and we shared a meal together. On Sunday afternoon we met up in the unit club. I had really enjoyed the weekend. By mid week I found myself feeling very attracted to him and had no clue if we would stay in touch after the course was over.

On the final day of the course, we finished at midday and promised to meet up at the main gate to say goodbye and exchange our contact details. When I got back to my room I discovered I had padlocked my keys inside the wardrobe. I couldn't believe it.

So instead of meeting Tom, I spent the next forty minutes finding bolt cutters, packing to go home and hoping that I wouldn't miss him before he left to catch his train. When I got to the main gate I was too late, he had already left in a taxi for the station.

I sat in my car for a moment, wondering if I should drive home or drive to the station, just a few minutes away, to give him my phone number. Would he think I was too forward? My heart was pounding and feeling like a school girl, I decided to drive to the station. After all what did I have to lose? Maybe he would think I was crazy but I felt it was worth that risk.

I think he was surprised to see me on the platform and I handed him the piece of paper with my details on it.

"I would have found you through the RAF network," he said.

I hadn't thought of that. I was deeply embarrassed, so I gave him a quick kiss on the cheek and said goodbye. My face was bright with embarrassment and I'm sure it was possible to have toasted crumpets on it as I walked back to my car. I felt that I had just made a complete fool of myself and the day's events spun around in my head the whole way home.

A week or so later he called, true to his word. So began a long distance relationship by telephone and letter. I travelled to Germany to visit him several times and within just a few short months I was in love and found life rather dull when I wasn't with him.

He visited me in Scotland early in 1989, staying at my home for a week. He cooked meals ready for when I returned home from work, he made me laugh and feel so wonderful inside I couldn't imagine life without him. Tom proposed to me during that week and I couldn't believe he was serious after such a short time. However, our relationship felt right and I accepted his proposal. I was excited about the future and for the first time I felt loved by a man for who I was, warts and all. It was such a wonderful feeling.

We were married in September of 1989, a truly happy day for both of us. My friend Bill conducted the ceremony. The day went smoothly, we were happy and comfortable together and the vows we made were given and accepted from the heart.

We left two days later to spend our honeymoon in Corfu which was a fun filled week for us. I hadn't been on holiday with a boyfriend or lover before and here I was on holiday with my husband. It all felt surreal and yet not.

A few weeks after we returned home I was scheduled for an operation on my left knee. It had been quite painful and at times buckled beneath me. Tom was now stationed in Northern Ireland, I was still based in Scotland. I had to travel to England to a military hospital for the operation. It was a similar operation to the one I had two years previously on my right knee. That operation had gone well and I had no reason to suspect otherwise with this one.

Tom came to visit me whilst I was in the hospital, staying in the accommodation set aside for relatives. I was in extreme pain from the knee operation, but it had apparently gone well. I was told that I had been singing 'Edelweiss' from the Sound of Music when I returned to the ward, much to my embarrassment.

I returned to Scotland a few days later still using crutches. I set about exercising my leg as instructed but after two weeks of conscientiously following the exercise regime, my knee was getting worse and a lump the size of half an egg had formed over one of the incision sites. My knee seemed to have almost locked into position and after a quick visit to the medical centre I was sent back to the military hospital for some intensive physiotherapy.

That was a harrowing and painful experience. They set about 'breaking up' the scar tissue which had formed around the incision site. I was there for a week, my knee only improving slightly. It wasn't the outcome I had expected or wanted from a simple procedure.

I found many limitations to what I could do and spent around four months on crutches with frequent visits to doctors. I was later given a stick to help me walk, as without this aid I was in immense pain when weight bearing. The painkillers I had been given sent me to sleep, made me feel sick and did little for the pain. I couldn't be given anything stronger, the next step was morphine. I was disheartened and in despair. I was twenty-seven and didn't want to spend the rest of my life walking with the aid of a stick or having to take these drugs.

I came across a book called 'Drug Free Pain Relief' quite by accident and bought it, not knowing why. It described that you can use acupressure points at specific sites of the body to relieve pain, which was a completely new concept to me at the time. So I tried it out. The pressure points indicated were on the knee and this in itself was painful to apply, but I was so desperate to reduce the medication and be pain free that I persevered.

It really worked. I was stunned but overjoyed. At last I could do something for myself to help reduce my pain levels and not rely solely on the medication which made me feel so unwell.

I often collected Tom from the ferry port at Stranraer when he was off duty and I was finding driving very awkward. My knee sometimes locked and the clutch action was very painful to do. On one long journey my knee locked in position whilst pressing the clutch pedal in and I had to resort to kicking my foot off the pedal with my other foot. It frightened the life out of me and I decided I would have to sell my wonderful sports car and buy an automatic car for safety, as well as ease of driving. I wasn't happy at having to do this, I was a fit person and these restrictions on my life were purgatory.

I left the RAF in March of that year and we travelled to Northern Ireland, a whole new chapter in our relationship unfolding. I was still using a walking stick, our income had just halved with me leaving the RAF, I was in a completely new and bewildering environment and the job I had lined up at the local airport fell through because of my mobility problems. I was unable to take up the physically demanding job due to my knee problem and because of the situation in Ireland at the time I was unable to find other work.

This was a strange feeling for me. I had been employed almost all of my adult life and at twenty-eight it felt like a chasm. Housewifely duties were dull and boring in comparison, though I felt so very happy with Tom.

A few months later I felt the urge to start a family. This was bizarre, as I had never really considered having children and I couldn't quite understand why I felt this way. Tom and I discussed this and agreed that I stop taking the contraceptive pill. I bled heavily for a fortnight, so much so that I became extremely pale and started passing out. After visiting the GP I was whisked off to hospital. I was told that I would be examined and may require a simple procedure to be carried out.

About an hour later I was examined, only to find that all bleeding had stopped. I'm sure it must have been the fear of the 'simple procedure'. I spent the night in hospital and went home the next day.

The following month I discovered that I was pregnant. I was going to have a baby. I was going to be a mum. When I broke the news to Tom he was delighted. It felt right for us to have a baby together and we were both excited. I felt the flutterings of movement very early on in the pregnancy and even though

I was told that wasn't possible so early I knew that I had most definitely felt my baby moving around inside me.

I spent the following six months with morning sickness all day, every day. It was awful. The only respite was a few hours in the evening for some reason, but I was grateful for that. Surely pregnancy wasn't supposed to be like this?

I got bigger and bigger and felt like a barrage balloon. The baby's foot could often be seen on the right side of my belly just below my ribs, it could be so uncomfortable at times. But it was also fascinating to watch when my tummy was gently massaged where this tiny foot was placed, it would gradually disappear again. I laughed to myself whenever I was in a bath as baby seemed to enjoy the warmth of the water and was very active, so much so this movement created little waves in the bath water.

We made all the preparations for the birth, painting the second bedroom and gathering baby equipment. As the days wore on I began to wonder what the birth would be like. I had desperately wanted a water birth but there were no facilities for that in Ireland. I had to be content with a 'normal' birth, complicated by the fact that my knee mobility was still poor and I now walked with the aid of a hinged knee support.

I went into labour one Sunday afternoon in March 1991. By 7pm, when the contractions were just a few minutes apart, we phoned the hospital and were advised to go straight in. After an hour at the hospital the contractions had subsided. I wanted to go home but was advised to stay the night as I was already dilated, though my waters hadn't yet broken. I spent an uncomfortable night on a ward, having called my parents to let them know that hopefully, all going well, I would be a mum the following day.

The following morning it was decided that I should be induced and I was given medication. The contractions started again, with the back pain becoming intense. I didn't eat much that day, I felt very uncomfortable. Tom came in to see me that afternoon, contractions still regular and dilation progressing. I was taken to a delivery room, but yet again the contractions subsided.

"Was this baby ever going to make an appearance?!" I thought.

Tom went home and I tried to settle down for the evening, but for most of the night I was back and forward to the bathroom, my body clearing the way for baby. I was exhausted and hadn't eaten very much all day.

By morning all I wanted to do was sleep. I was advised that I would be placed on a drip to induce contractions and full dilation so that I could deliver my baby. I felt very nervous, but trusted it would soon be over and that I would be holding my baby.

When the drip was set up and the drugs circulated round my body, intense contractions began. I felt violently sick. I was given gas and air to reduce the pain and remember breathing it in and feeling wonderful, offering it to Tom to try.

"You should try this, it's AMAZING!!" I exclaimed to him.

And so the day went on...........contractions became more intense and I dilated, but still baby would not appear. Eventually the midwives could see the top of the head and I began to push. A doctor came in briefly at one point and said that I had to make more of an effort pushing and that they would be using forceps to aid the delivery.

By this time all modesty and inhibition were gone and I advised him that if he came anywhere near me with forceps I would stick them up his backside. Though I am sure I was much less polite. Tom was mortified. But I didn't want my babys head mushed with forceps nor my body assaulted any more than it already had been.

After a while it became evident that we just weren't getting anywhere and that baby was firmly stuck. Finally a midwife appeared. She told me that baby was wedged and even forceps wouldn't help at this stage. I required an emergency caesarian section which would be carried out very shortly. I was bereft, having wanted a natural birth. This was all wrong. However, I was exhausted, baby was firmly wedged and there was no other option.

I can vaguely remember coming round in the ward and told that I had a baby boy. Tom was there and baby Callum was on the bed beside me. I was so groggy I couldn't make out his face properly and was drifting in and out of consciousness. From the start of the contractions on the Sunday to delivery on the Tuesday evening, I had been in labour for a total of fifty-four hours. I was exhausted and the whole experience felt like it had happened to someone else. I wished it had. It was certainly not the delivery I had envisaged.

The following morning I was woken by two nurses and within minutes I was lifted unceremoniously up to a seated position. I nearly fainted with the pain of that move, never having had abdominal surgery of any kind. I was able to have a small amount of breakfast and after an hour or so I was allowed out of bed to visit my baby in the nursery. I slowly got out of bed and wandered through.

There were many cribs and I remember thinking, in a panic, that I didn't even know what he looked like. They could have given me anyone's baby. Eventually I found him by searching the name tags in the cribs. When I found him I thought he was so beautiful.

It was a very long week in the ward. My Mum, Dad and sister arrived later that week from Scotland. I was tearful and glad to see my Mum. I was allowed home after seven days and thankfully my family decided to stay another week to help me out at home during my recovery. It was all new and although breast feeding was going well, I was extremely tired.

Callum was a hungry baby and within six weeks I reverted to bottle feeding. He was consuming thirteen ounce bottles. No wonder he hadn't been sleeping or settled. Life improved a lot and we settled down to our new family life.

I think Tom found it quite hard, although playing computer games late into the night didn't help matters. Sometimes the noise from him playing games in the kitchen would waken me in the early hours of the morning. He would often be unaware that Callum was crying and on Tom's days off I would still be getting up during the night to feed and change our baby. This caused difficulties within the marriage, as Tom would often be tired from staying up so late playing these games. I couldn't see the fascination.

Callum was a clingy baby, not surprising after his stressed entry into the world I suppose and in those first eight months I often carryied him about in a sling on my front, even around the house. I loved him dearly, but got flashbacks of the difficult birth and found myself feeling quite overwhelmed at times. Nothing was ever diagnosed, but years later during a discussion with a health professional it was felt that I had experienced post natal depression after his birth which was never really noticed nor treated.

Living away from my family within our restricted environment left me feeling a little isolated and every couple of months I travelled home whilst Tom worked shifts. These visits rejuvenated me. In Ireland we had to check under the car for bombs each time we visited local towns and I found this was becoming more nerve wracking, perhaps because I was responsible for my baby too.

One day I was even followed from the base into Belfast. I watched the car following me all the way into the city and took a note of the number plate. I decided to keep driving and not stop in Belfast. When I returned to the base and reported it, the car registration turned out to be an IRA vehicle. I was very unnerved and well and truly ready to be posted elsewhere.

Callum was fifteen months old when we left Ireland and he was copying us by checking under the car each time we came back to it. Much as I loved the country, I was glad to be leaving.

We had requested specific bases we would like to be posted to and had served extra time in Ireland, promised a more 'exotic' posting if we stayed longer. Despite this we found ourselves posted to the North of Scotland. Not the posting we had hoped for after requesting Cyprus.

Life there was strange. Although back in Scotland, my life still seemed to be isolated. At least I could visit my family much more easily and there were no restrictions about where we could go.

Tom still spent many hours playing computer games and it was becoming tedious. He was often tired and sleeping late in the mornings when he was not at work. With a young child this wasn't an ideal situation. Sharing the parenting a little more would have been most welcome. I knew that Tom loved his son very much and did spend time with him, but he also managed to have a fair amount of time for himself, which I didn't seem to.

However, mother nature intervened and I felt the need to have another baby. Looking back this was a crazy idea given the circumstances but it felt right at the time. It was almost like I didn't have a choice, and I know how silly that may sound. We both wanted Callum to have a brother or sister, and no thought went into how I would cope with two children. Most of the time our life was really good and I tried not to dwell when life took a downturn.

What I didn't know then was that I had been under the influence of the 'baby blues', undiagnosed and untreated since the birth of my first child. Perhaps my grip on reality was less than strong. But I was still keen to have another baby and I discovered that I was pregnant in March 1993.

My sister Julie was getting married to Martin in May and she had asked me to be a bridesmaid. Part of me felt awful, as my pregnancy hadn't been planned to coincide with this wonderful event and I hoped that I wouldn't be too enormous for the wedding. When I look back now, I can laugh at my thought processes over this. What difference did it make whether I was pregnant or not? I hadn't planned to make things difficult and as it turned out I was barely showing on the day.

Julie's wedding was lovely and I felt so honoured to be her
bridesmaid. Callum was twenty-six months old and behaved so
well, having great fun at the evening reception playing with a
toy car with one of the guests.

We moved into a slightly better RAF quarter that summer,
close to the beach. It was a vast improvement on our previous
location. I much preferred living there and I would often go
for walks along the beach with Callum. He loved it. At times
it still felt weird being a 'mum' and not going out to work.
I had worked from the time I left school in various jobs or
training and occasionally I almost felt like I was playing truant.
Far from it with a young child. It dawned on me that despite
adoring my son I needed an outlet.

A friend suggested I accompany her to a talk at the 'Wives
Club' given by a local Aromatherapist. I wasn't keen as I didn't
know what it was and wasn't sure if I was even that interested.
However it got me out of the house for a little while, so I went
with her.

To my surprise it was very interesting and it captured my
imagination. The woman had a small local shop stocked with
candles, soaps and a variety of other items. I visited one day
and I spoke with her about a small patch of eczema on my
neck, for which I was always given a steroid cream by my GP.

I wasn't keen to use this cream whilst I was pregnant, though
the small amounts of steroids used wouldn't have made that big
an impact on my health. I asked if she perhaps had something
which might help to clear this patch of redness and itching.
She was helpful and very understanding. After I explained
about the condition, she disappeared into the back of the shop.
When she returned she had a small pot of cream which she had

made with essential oils, just for me. I paid her for the cream and tried it out when I got home. Within a week, that patch of eczema was gone and it never returned.

As most Aromatherapists know, the powerful healing effects of essential oils had worked their magic and I have used them on myself and my family ever since.

I bought a book about Aromatherapy and a few good quality oils. I was careful to use only tiny amounts and their effects were wonderful. I was keen to try them out more fully once this baby was born, especially on my knee.

During the pregnancy my knee seemed to have improved and was causing me less pain. A consultant explained to me that the hormonal changes during pregnancy allowed for greater elasticity of the muscles and tendons, which may account for the reduction in pain. I wasn't really bothered why it was less painful, I was just grateful that it was.

Six weeks before my due date, I began to experience more severe flashbacks of Callums birth. These had subsided over the past year, I had almost forgotten that I had ever experienced them at all. But now they were back. I often awoke in the middle of the night panic stricken and experiencing the pain and emotional distress of those hours. I decided to consult my GP.

I explained to him what was happening. He listened attentively and seemed to understand that this was a chance for me to have a more positive birth experience this time. He made an appointment for me at the hospital to have a scan so that we would know the approximate size of the baby. I could then make a decision whether to opt for a natural birth or a planned caesarian.

I was around eight months pregnant when I had the scan. I was told that the baby would be around the same birth weight as Callum had been and that there really shouldn't be any reason why I couldn't give birth naturally, but the decision was mine. I spoke with a midwife for a little while and became quite tearful, not really knowing what to do.

I wanted to have a water birth, but this wasn't available in the area either. I so wanted to give birth naturally and not go through a similar experience to the first.

After talking this through with her, she explained that no matter what I decided, no-one would think any less of me. Only I knew deep down what was right for me. For some reason I opted for a planned caesarian. Once the decision was made I felt relieved, but at times I wondered if I had made the right decision. I suppose only time would tell.

My mum came to stay with us and look after Callum whilst I was in hospital so that Tom could be with me during the birth. I was given a spinal anaesthetic, which was the weirdest feeling ever. Trying to curl over with a stomach like a beach ball was no mean feat. I can remember wondering if I would ever feel my legs again. It was bizarre to be wide awake, be able to see your legs and feet and yet have no control over them.

The operation went smoothly, with Tom sitting right beside me throughout. I was nervous but excited and felt quite peculiar with the amount of drugs whizzing around my system. Baby was obviously very comfortable in there as the surgeon had to push down on the top part of my abdomen to 'encourage' baby out and I did wonder if it was ready to see the world.

Then out came Glenn and I was so overwhelmed by seeing

him straight away. He weighed eight pounds four ounces and had shoulders like a prop forward. Within a split second of seeing him, I knew I had made the right decision for a planned caesarian and all the previous angst, worry and self doubt just melted away.

I was able to feed Glenn within an hour and I knew that I was creating the bond very early with Glenn which Callum and I had missed out on at his birth.

After a few days I was transferred from hospital to the cottage hospital close to home. It was much more relaxed and was a lovely end to my stay in medical care. The midwives fawned over Glenn. He was incredibly cute and this gave me ample time to recover.

At home, life became quite hectic and demanding. Callum was in a nursery two mornings a week, which he thoroughly enjoyed and it gave me time to get to know the new soul in our lives.

Callum was two and a half, still a baby himself and he had moments of pure jealousy which soon turned into outrageous tantrums. And yet he could be so loving. I'm sure that he thought Glenn might go back to wherever he came from after a week or so, but when he stayed all the time I think he realised that life was changed forever and he protested. Fairly standard from what I gathered, but hard work.

In early December of 1993, Tom was informed that he would be deployed to the Gulf in January, straight after New Year. I asked if he could defer this, as I was due for a second knee operation in February or March and had the boys to look after. Tom said he couldn't defer the deployment, though didn't explained why. Having been in the RAF myself I knew that under the circumstances it would have been possible to rearrange the date. Perhaps he just didn't want to rock the boat by asking to defer. No matter, he was going and that was that.

I decided that during those three months of his deployment I would stay in Edinburgh with my parents. At the very least I would have company whilst he was away and help with the boys if the operation date was set whilst Tom was away.

Tom and I had a small share in the house, having arranged a small mortgage and extending into the attic space. The long term plan was for Tom to be trained by my Dad how to repair and install showers so that he could step into this job when he left the RAF in a year or so. He had often accompanied my Dad to repair showers and enjoyed the challenge and hands on work, compared to the mundane job he had in the RAF. Things were looking great.

So in February 1994 I spent twenty-four hours in hospital having the second surgery on my left knee. I knew when I woke up that it felt different, though the pain was quite intense after the operation. I was discharged the day after to drive back to Edinburgh and I was so thankful for an automatic car.

The next couple of weeks were extremely challenging with me recovering from the knee surgery as well as night feeding Glenn. However we all got through it and my parents were brilliant helping out.

Whilst Tom was away, I couldn't work out why we were so short of money in the bank. When I checked our account, I could see that Tom was spending quite a bit whilst away on deployment, more than I was on food and nappies for the boys.

I was concerned and asked him about it during our one weekly phone call. He told me it was on "drinks and stuff". I can't say that I believed him. I'm not sure what I thought to be honest. I just knew that something wasn't right.

I chatted to his Mum once about it, explaining he was driving me crazy with this money thing and that life was quite difficult with the children whilst he was away. She seemed supportive at the time, but I was later to discover that this conversation would be twisted and used against me.

Tom returned to the UK in April. Glenn was six months old, Callum had turned three in March. Callum remembered his Dad, but Glenn wasn't so sure. He was only three months old when Tom left and didn't seem keen to interact with his Dad. One day after a few weeks of this, Tom lost his temper with Glenn and threw him onto the settee. Glenn got a fright and began to cry. I was mortified at Toms response. This was his child, his baby and he needed time to get to know his Dad again.

I couldn't comprehend why he would do this, but our relationship had become strained since his return from the Gulf. I was seeing elements to Tom which I didn't like and I wondered if it was simply due to the living arrangements over the past few months.

Tom spent Monday to Friday away at work and the weekends in Edinburgh. He enjoyed helping my Dad on a Saturday repairing showers and we agreed that we should give up the married quarter to save money. I would remain in Edinburgh and start to look for a job. He was due to leave the RAF in a year and we felt happy with these plans for our future.

Occasionally though my mind would drift back to the anger

Tom had shown towards Glenn. I also recalled a day three weeks after Glenn was born. Callum wanted to spend time with his Dad and I suggested they go to the beach which was a five minute walk away. I dressed Callum warmly, as it was early October. He had an all-in-one waterproof suit which I dressed him in with his tiny wellington boots. A cosy hat on his head and he was all ready to go. Off they went and I busied myself with settling Glenn for a nap.

Twenty minutes later I saw Tom walking back, Callum in his arms.

Tom's trousers were soaked to the top of his thighs. Callum was completely soaked inside and out. I met them at the door asking what had happened. Tom became defensive and angry, saying that he had taken his eyes off Callum for an instant and when he turned around, saw Callum rolling about in the surf.

To this day I'm not sure I believed him. Perhaps he was speaking the truth, perhaps it was a genuine moment of distraction.

Whatever happened that day, it was all beginning to play on my mind. Mistrust was setting in. I was trying to make allowances for our living arrangements now, but when I honestly sat down and thought about it, I didn't seem to miss Tom when he was away during the week. He had become quite sullen and wasn't one for speaking about his problems or emotions.

Many months later he told me that, unknown to me, he had applied to be a bone marrow donor but had been rejected. He was furious and distraught beyond words. His own father had died of cancer when Tom was just twelve and it had been a horrendous time for him, his mother and younger brother.

I had known since I met him that he hadn't dealt with much of the issues resulting from that awful childhood experience and it was obviously beginning to come up now. I tried my best to help him, but he seemed unreachable for many weeks. The bone marrow donor application was one way he felt that he could make a difference but it wasn't meant to be. After a few months he seemed to rally and life improved again.

I started a job working shifts. My skills learned in the RAF with small components had helped me get the job as a needle attacher. Basically, I spent my days attaching surgical needles to various types of suture material, whatever was on order. I was good at it and the pay was excellent. I missed my babies during the working day, but it felt good to be contributing to the household again.

Mum was fantastic helping out with the boys, who were in nursery part time and enjoying it tremendously. Glenn was around twenty-eight months old by this time, the bond with his father had improved, though not as close as Tom and Callum were. Callum and Glenn were such very different characters, perhaps even if Tom had been there throughout those early months Glenn might not have bonded so well with him anyway. Who knows.

One afternoon Glenn, Tom and I were outside in the garden. Glenn loved flowers and picked a single flower from one of the flower beds for his Grandma. Tom flew into a rage and promptly kicked Glenn on the backside for picking the flower.

Glenn lost his balance and fell forward onto his forehead. The sound of his head hitting the slabs was awful and he burst into screams. I rushed to pick him up, shouting at Tom, asking why he had done that? There was no need. It was one flower.

Glenn's forehead had started to swell and turn red and I rushed him inside to treat the bruising.

That day, all hell broke loose for me internally. My parents were stunned when I explained what had happened. My Mum tore into Tom when he appeared from the garden. When Glenn went into nursery that week, we had to explain how he had come to have a lump on his head and dark bruising. My heart ached when I recalled Tom's actions. Why had he struck out at Glenn yet again? He was just a baby.

I was in turmoil. There were times I had little respect for Tom. Our ideas about parenting were very different, yet when I tried to discuss things with him, he wasn't interested. Sometimes his responses inferred that he didn't think much of me as a mother to our boys and that I was making a big deal out of silly little things.

When I look back now, I feel this was the end of our relationship. It certainly was for me anyway. I began wondering what it would be like if we split up. This seemed such a cavernous black hole. We had made vows to stand by each other no matter what and I had meant every word. How could I now turn around and revoke them?

Over the following month I tried to speak to Tom. I tried to explain to him that my feelings for him had changed. This was breaking my heart too. I didn't want to fall out of love with him, but I had. Understandably he was upset.

I broached the subject of us perhaps having a trial separation, to try to work things out amicably for the sake of the boys, if nothing else. He didn't want that. He wanted us to stay together and promised he would work on his anger. I wasn't keen but I agreed to give it a few months.

I'm not sure what happened then. Things changed in our relationship and I began to feel very low. I felt useless and worthless. It seemed to creep up on me from behind and I was inside these feelings before I knew what was happening. I was overwhelmed by guilt about the relationship, feeling that I would be depriving the boys of their father if we split up.

I got lower and lower. I didn't want to be near Tom. I certainly didn't want to be intimate with him any more, yet he did. Those feelings I had for him just drifted away. It seemed like my soul had drifted away too. I began to feel numb inside and seemed to be turning all the negativity of the whole world inside myself.

Unknown to me I was in a spiral of negativity and before I knew it I had started to self harm. Small scratches on the inside of my forearm at first. I don't know when it started, nor why. All I know is that the vast emotional pain I was engulfed in was relieved momentarily when I harmed myself. I felt like someone had taken me over. Part of me knew this wasn't a helpful or healthy way to deal with my pain, but I felt driven to continue.

Looking at my behaviour now, I can see it was never going to end well. What was needed was for me to express my feelings to others so that I could get help, but I shut them away. I reduced my food intake, a form of self punishment and I gradually lost weight over the months.

The one thing I did do was contact my friend Bill. I left a message asking him to get in touch, explaining that I felt my marriage was over and I didn't know what to do. He called me the very next day and asked what was happening. Yet again he was a blessing just at the right time.

Emotionally I was a wreck. On the surface I was coping, just. Others could see that there was something wrong. I was beginning to look physically ill. I was signed off work with 'stress'.

The next year is a bit of a blur. I eventually became so depressed and suicidal that I was admitted to hospital for six weeks. I was given anti-depressant medication which seemed to slow everything down in my head and I felt like a zombie.

I met some truly wonderful people whilst I was in hospital. People just like me - ordinary people dealing with all sorts of life traumas. Bill visited often and I always felt comfortable in sharing my thoughts with him. At the very least the hospital stay got me away from Tom. I somehow felt safer whilst I was there.

Looking back, this 'fragmentation' of me was what I now understand as my 'awakening'. An awakening on many levels. An awakening to the fact that life wasn't as I wanted it. An awakening to the non-physical aspects of life.

It wasn't that I hadn't believed in the non-physical, I just hadn't experienced it in my life so far. This awakening was obviously well overdue, but with so much going on I felt overloaded and hence the 'mental breakdown'.

At times in the hospital I was sure that I could see movement around me when no-one was physically there. Mostly this was movement on the floor. I was told by medical staff these were hallucinations, which scared me even more. I was sure I could

see things, presumed there were mice or rats in the hospital and
they were in my room. I was all over the place emotionally.

I had even begun to wonder if I was gay because I didn't want
intimacy with Tom. There were times when intimacy was
refused, sometimes he wouldn't pay any attention and take
what he obviously thought was his right to take. Sometimes
upon refusal of intimacy, his anger could be felt in the darkness
of the room and I would be convinced that he was about to hit
me. He would sometimes leave the room and go to the lounge
to watch television. He never actually hit me. He didn't need
to. I clung to him yet didn't want him, all at the same time.

My mind wasn't my own any more and I couldn't express how
I felt because I didn't have the words. I didn't know how I
felt. It was one of the most scary times in my life. I have often
pictured that period like having a jigsaw puzzle in a box. Take
off the lid of the box and remove all the edge pieces. Then
throw the contents of the box up in the air, let them fall to the
floor and throw away the lid with the picture.

My mind was a scattered jigsaw and I didn't

know how to put it back together again.

No picture, no guide, nothing.

I suppose it was no wonder that I also developed anxiety
attacks. After I came out of hospital I remember looking in my
wardrobe one day and the very thought of picking something
to wear sent me into a complete spin. I couldn't decide. So for
over a year I wore a pair of navy jog pants from my selection

of four identical pairs and any tee-shirt that just came to hand from the drawer. I had other tops for colder weather. Everything else stayed in the wardrobe month after month.

Bill encouraged me to go for some relaxation, perhaps a massage. He felt it might help. My head ached all the time, my teeth gritted constantly. The back of my neck, just at the base of the skull, felt like someone had their fist in it all the time. I thought a massage might be a good idea and he gave me the number of someone he recommended.

I didn't know what to expect. The massage was blissful. I felt nurtured and my body eased. It was the first Aromatherapy massage I had received and I felt much better. Afterwards this wonderful woman told me that I should perhaps take up massage. I looked at her blankly and said I didn't think I could.

She said to me, "Why not? You've got two perfectly good hands, haven't you?"

She was right, I did have two perfectly good hands. What a kick up the backside her words were.

The words got into my head and I began to look for local community classes in massage. I found one and enrolled. It was called 'Aromatherapy for Beginners' and I was extremely nervous that first day. I explained that I hadn't been well and was recovering from a breakdown. Everyone was very pleasant and the moment I started to do a gentle hand massage that first day, I felt like I was 'home'.

Over the weeks we were taught about essential oils, how to make blends of oils and the various properties of some of the most common oils. I bought a book which the tutor recommended and bought some more oils of my own. I began to mix blends for me to practice with on my parents and children, usually a simple hand or foot massage.

I felt 'complete' when I was working this way. I had found something I enjoyed. I felt alive and I felt worthwhile. I looked forward to that weekly class so much. The tutor was excellent and shared her knowledge of essential oils with us freely. I was well and truly 'hooked' on using essential oils. Her enthusiasm about really high quality oils and their potential for healing struck a cord deep within me. This was a path of learning from which there was no going back, only forward to learn more about these wonderful tiny bottles packed full of healing potential.

I became friends with one of the older women in the Aromatherapy class called Rita. Rita told me about a spiritualist church that she and her husband attended each week. They were both retired and what she told me about the church interested me. I felt that there was something else that I needed besides the essential oils and massage. So, very kindly, they collected me one evening and took me along to a gathering. That evening there were many people there, yet I didn't feel any anxiety. I just felt very safe.

After the short service one woman gave messages to people in the audience. When she pointed at me I nearly fell off the seat. She said there was an older man beside her with a hat on. He was saying that he was looking out for me, he was by my side and not to worry. It could only be my maternal or paternal grandfather and I didn't know which.

This was amazing, my first time at the spiritualist church and I had received a message. After this some of the group offered spiritual healing. I had never received this before and wanted to try it. The feeling was very beautiful when the woman placed her hands on my shoulders. I felt so much love and support and softness, like I was on a bed of feathers. I returned several times to the church over the next couple of years.

My parents were very supportive, but Tom openly ridiculed it saying that I was attending 'seances'. Fortunately I wasn't put off by his attitude, knowing that I felt better afterwards and that was the most important thing.

The relationship between Tom and I hadn't improved much. He didn't understand what I was experiencing, because I couldn't explain it. I dreaded him being near me, I didn't even want to be in the same room as him most of the time. It must have been so hard on him too and I truly wish it could have been different for us.

A year had passed since Tom and I had spoken about separation. Our wedding anniversary was approaching and I couldn't believe that I was still stuck in the same place as the year before. I was miserable with nowhere to turn and nowhere to run. The Aromatherapy classes helped, but not enough. I felt so pressured in my unhappy marriage. If I had been thinking clearly, I could have easily just left our home with the boys and started divorce proceedings. It never even entered my head. I felt trapped.

I was attending a psychiatric day unit one day per week, antidepressant medication had been changed several times and nothing felt as if it was going to improve. The drugs I was given seemed to make me feel even more depressed, my brain felt as if it was on fire. I felt I had reached the end of the road.

Early one Sunday morning I drove to the nearest area of sea, connected a hose to my exhaust pipe and led it into the boot, got back in the car and sat with tears streaming down my face. I had parked in a quiet spot yet out of nowhere a man appeared with his young son. He walked past the car and stopped. I was willing him to just keep walking. He didn't. He walked back to the car, tapped on the window and began to talk to me. In a few short words he had me shut off the engine, get out of the car for some air and put the hose back in the boot.

I locked the car and went over to the shore, just watching the sea coming in. He walked away, leaving me to my thoughts. Ten minutes later a police car arrived and parked behind my car. My heart sank. I knew they were looking for me. He had popped into the local police station which (I hadn't realised) was only a few hundred yards away. They were really pleasant, but insisted I go with them to the station. I gave them Tom's number so that he could collect me. Crazy, I know. Why didn't I give them my parents number? I felt a complete fool.

At home, everyone's emotions were running high. Understandably. On the one hand I was unwell and on the other hand I was putting my family through hell. My family insisted that I went to hospital the next day.

I was admitted for a second time, distraught and not wanting to be readmitted. I can recall being checked over by a young Irish doctor. She was softly spoken. She had read my notes from the previous admission. I can't recall saying very much to her. I was overwhelmed with emotional pain, yet unable to access it so that I could speak about what was going on within me. She went out to speak with Tom for a little while and asked him to go home to let me settle into the ward. She returned and started my admission paperwork.

I was in hospital for one week. Tom decided that he wanted
to take the boys to visit his Mum in England whilst I was
in hospital and to get 'his head sorted out' for a few days.
Something didn't feel right and I suggested that he go on
his own. He would have more time to think that way, but he
insisted saying that his Mum hadn't seen the boys for a while
and it would be good for her and them. So I agreed, but I felt a
great sense of unease.

The day before he left I became distressed and one of the
nurses came to talk to me. When I explained my concerns she
said she would call him and speak to him for me. She returned
a little while later to tell me that Tom had assured her he would
return with the boys the following Monday, the day I was due
to be discharged.

My discharge day arrived and as I waited for the paperwork to
be completed a nurse came into the lounge room. She said they
had received a call from my husband. He said for me not to
worry but his car had broken down and he was getting it fixed
and would be home the next day. I felt something was wrong,
but could do little until I was discharged.

Mum arrived to collect me. Within an hour of arriving home
the phone rang. It was Tom. He gave me an ultimatum. Either
I stayed in Scotland and never saw my children again or I left
and joined him in England. He wasn't coming back and he
had the boys. I asked what he thought we would do about our
mortgage payments on the house and the plans he had to take
on the business when Dad retired. He said that he didn't care. If
I stayed in Scotland that was it.

I tried to reason with him, saying he couldn't just take the boys
and not come back. They were my children as well. He told me

he thought I was a useless mother and that they would be better off without me, that I was a nutcase and should be in hospital permanently.

My heart was pounding so loudly that I could barely hear. He hung up the phone and I burst into tears, barely able to stand I was so shocked.

I tried to tell my parents what he had just said. They were shocked but could also see that I was rapidly becoming unhinged. I was shaking uncontrollably and sobbing. I couldn't believe it. Never see my beautiful boys again? I didn't want to live in England. We had a mortgage on the house we shared with my parents. Tom had left in the company car belonging to my Dad. It all felt like some really bad soap on the television, but it was really happening.

Mum and Dad decided the best plan of action was to take me back to the hospital, perhaps they could give me a tranquiliser to calm me. I was in an anxious state. I couldn't breath, my heart was racing and I could barely feel my arms. I was beginning to go into sheer panic. So off we went to the hospital yet again. Mum was in tears as well. I know she was concerned for her grandchildren but also for me. She could see me falling apart at the seams as the minutes went by.

Luckily the nurses on duty were wonderful. They sat us in a side room and one went for tranquiliser medication for me. I'll never forget the male nurse talking to me. My arms by this point were so numb with lack of blood flow due to anxiety that I couldn't move them or feel them.

He knelt beside my chair and quietly said to me, "Yvonne darlin' you've got two choices here. You either give in and let your husband have the children or you fight for them. What do you want to do?"

There was no doubt in my mind. If I gave in, my children would be brought up by a man with more issues than I did and who had shown his violent and angry side more than once. I also knew deep down that if I didn't fight for my sons I might as well have stayed in hospital for the rest of my life.

It was a turning point and I heard myself say, "I want my kids back. I'm not the bad mother he says I am."

We drove home about half an hour later, me much calmer and feeling like a weight had been lifted from my shoulders. The weight of the whole world seemed to have gone. Yes, my children had been taken by their father and I was devastated by that, but at the same time I felt free when I thought of Tom not being around at all.

Mum, being the incredibly intuitive soul that she is, had called our solicitor the previous week and we had an appointment for the very next morning. She hadn't known why, yet the timing couldn't have been better. This was the family solicitor who had known my parents for over thirty years.

She also explained to me what had happened the day I was admitted. Tom had come home and despite disliking her intensely had told her what the young Irish doctor had said to him in the corridor.

Apparently, without me telling her a thing, the irish doctor had said to Tom, "You do realise that you have been a major contributor to this depression and suicide attempt? Your behaviour and actions have driven Yvonne to this."

Mum knew exactly what the doctor was talking about. Tom apparently didn't. He couldn't understand what was going on.

Mum and I discussed if Tom had planned to take the boys all along. I felt he had. When we looked in their rooms, Mum realised that Tom had packed Callum's school uniform. She had packed the boys bags herself and his uniform definitely wasn't in there. Other items were missing too. Perhaps with the truth of our relationship now coming out, he had nowhere to hide either. He had jumped ship instead of staying to sort it out.

I told her what had happened when we had gone to marriage guidance some months previously. The woman was lovely and calmly mediated our conversation. When I got onto the subject of the intimate side of our relationship, Tom became very uncomfortable and after the session was finished refused to go back. I hadn't understood his response at the time, but after Mum explained what the doctor had said to Tom, it all started to make sense. But that issue was for another time. Even though I knew I hadn't been much of a mother to them over this past year, my priority right now was trying to get my boys back home. I had no idea if that was even possible, but we were going to try.

Chapter Two

The next day Mum and I met with our solicitor. He was fantastic and once he realised what the appointment was about he called a specialist solicitor into his office. We spent hours there that first day outlining the situation. It was exhausting. They both felt that I had an excellent chance of getting my children back and put the wheels in motion.

When I attended the day hospital that week, they were shocked at the turn of events. They were also surprised at how well I was coping with it all. There had been no medication increase, yet I was more lucid. I felt more relaxed and less fearful. I was discharged from the day hospital within three weeks.

It was a truly horrendous few weeks. I phoned my children every few days. They didn't understand what was going on. They were six and four. Callum had started a new school and Glenn was in a nursery part time. I had let the school and nursery in Edinburgh know what had happened and statements were required from staff members by our solicitor to build the case.

My private life was dredged up, but if it helped to get the boys back, I knew it was worth it. I was concerned that my past mental health issues would damage any chances I had of having the children returned to my care.

I have no idea how I got through those six weeks, constantly wondering when I would see the boys again. Tom had cleared out our joint bank account, which had included a severence pay from my employer. I had no money at all. The mortgage payment was due and the mortgage lender was less than understanding. All I can say is thank God for my parents. They supported me through everything.

An interim order was granted and Tom had to return the children to me until a full custody hearing was set. He was also ordered to return the company car to my Dad. Tom was furious. He demanded that I give him my old Fiat Panda, threatening to "torch your Dad's car." I decided to appease him and give him the car. It was only a car after all and I didn't want to inflame the situation any further. I filled it with all his belongings and he collected the car when I wasn't at home, as was agreed. At least Dad could sell the company car and recoup some of his money.

A date was set for me to have the boys and despite being ordered to return them to Edinburgh, Tom refused and demanded we meet at a service station and he would hand them over. My sister Julie offered to drive me to collect them.

It was a surreal experience, like something out of a spy movie. We met in a service area on the motorway half way between Edinburgh and Southern England to hand over the children. The handover went reasonably smoothly, the homecoming wonderful. We were so delighted to see them and I felt like I hadn't cuddled them for years.

The boys were traumatised by their experience. Callum in particular. It came out in small ways. He began to throw himself against the walls in his room one day, really distressed. I asked what was wrong. He said that his Dad had told him that God was angry with Mummy. That Mummy didn't love Daddy any more. That the clouds would come down because God was so angry. I got to a point where I couldn't listen to any more. I was incensed that he should fill Callum's head with such rubbish. No wonder he was so confused and upset.

I went out the same day and bought a children's bible with pictures to make it easier for him to understand. I spent time with him explaining that God wasn't about anger. God was all about love. We all have love inside us, so have a part of God inside us.

It took a while, but eventually he saw that it was Daddy's anger and distress that was talking. I tried to explain things simply to him and I had vowed from the moment they came home from their father's that I wouldn't lie to them like he had. Everything would be as open and honest as they could understand at their tender ages.

An advocate was appointed to the case for the full investigation and he visited each member of the family to speak with them to complete his report. He came to the house and spoke to each of the boys individually. They were very nervous, but asked them to be honest about how they felt and answer his questions truthfully and everything would be fine. I was so proud of them when they had finished.

For the past three months I had been working one morning per week as a volunteer at a nursing home assisting with the elderly day care clients. I really enjoyed it and it had helped me to develop more confidence. I often took a few bottles of essential oil blends into the home and offered hand massage to the elderly people during the morning. I was surprised how much they enjoyed it and I would often end up with a queue. Sometimes they would bicker with each other for a session.

I found that my skills in the blending of essential oils improved a lot and produced some truly amazing results. One eighty-nine year old woman had severe arthritic hands. Her hands became so much more mobile after just one hand massage that she was able to use her kitchen taps for the first time in many months. She was delighted and felt more in control of her life.

I was excited by this kind of result and began to realise the potential of both the healing touch and the essential oils. I had been using blends on myself for months now and was beginning to understand which oils worked best for me to help uplift and calm me. It was a wonderful discovery that I could help myself so much.

Eventually the hearing date was set. I was so nervous. It could go either way. Today was the day I would find out if I would be handing the boys over to their father.

I had read the full advocate report. Tom had given dates of events which were wrong. He tried to make out that my mother was a frail and decrepit old woman. Anyone who knew my Mum knew that simply wasn't true. He tried to paint me as some kind of psychotic bunny boiler. Tom claimed that my Mum and I were attending 'seances' yet my Mum had never come with me to any of the spiritualist gatherings. His mother blatantly lied about conversations we had in the past and gave her impression of my mothering skills.

I was genuinely concerned that their side of the story would be believed by the court and I would lose custody of the boys. I hadn't slept for several nights, trying not to worry but I hadn't been too successful.

I sat next to my solicitor, Isla. She had been fabulous throughout the whole case. So supportive. Tom was in court with his solicitor. There seemed to be much to-ing and fro-ing of people. All parties except the parents, solicitors and court staff were asked to leave. I began to feel even more nervous. I didn't know if this was normal.

Isla had been speaking to Tom's solicitor and then the judge. She came over to me and asked me to follow her into a separate room. My legs would barely carry me. All I could think was that she was about to break some horrendous news to me and I was trying to steel myself for it.

She sat me down and said quite simply, "Tom has caved."

I thought, "What does that mean?" My mind thinking that this was some legal term for something.

I asked her what she meant. She said, "He's caved in, he's thrown in the towel. You have full custody of your boys."

I didn't know whether to shout or cry or scream with joy. I had dreamt of this for weeks, prayed it would happen, yet not daring to believe it. We were to share access during school holidays, something I had actively encouraged. We went back into the court, the case was dismissed, all the details were agreed and off we went. Tom looked dejected, but I didn't stop to talk with him. I couldn't bring myself to after all that had happened. I just wanted to get home to tell my parents and my boys the verdict.

When I walked out of the court I was feeling quite heady, almost drunk. My ears were ringing, I could hear the blood pumping through the tiny blood vessels like a drum beating. Surely this couldn't be real. Had I really just been awarded full custody of the boys? It seemed too good to be true and that I would wake up at any moment into reality.

Mum and Dad were delighted. I told the boys that they would be staying with Mummy and that Daddy would have them for a little time during holidays. They were as delighted as I was. Young as they were, they hadn't wanted to hurt either of their parents and I didn't want to have to make them choose. But they chose the parent they felt most comfortable with and despite my depression that parent seemed to be me.

I have always marvelled how they could know that despite me being an emotional vegetable for almost fourteen months, I was fit enough to be there for them both. That I had enough love for them both. It's true that our children have much to teach us if we are prepared to let ourselves be their students.

I got them ready mid afternoon. Tom had arranged with me the day before that he would pick them up after the hearing to spend some time with them before going home to England. We waited and waited. He never appeared. The boys were devastated. They were so upset at him letting them down.

He didn't love them, they said. If he loved them he would have come. It was awful. They were angry and upset and I tried to make excuses for him. I didn't believe that they should hear my feelings on the matter. From day one of him leaving, I felt that the boys should be allowed to make up their own minds about their father. Just because I despised him at the time, didn't mean I had the right to impose my feelings on them. I was so upset for them both after their excitement at the prospect of seeing their Dad. I knew Tom would probably be really upset after the hearing, but a quick phone call would have been better than nothing. After all, this was about the boys, not us.

Weeks rolled by and Tom rang the boys each week. I was happy for him to be in contact. No matter what I felt about him it was important that the boys kept their relationship with him. Holidays were arranged and the boys spent the occasional week or few days with Tom in England.

These were always difficult times for me. I kept myself busy whilst they were away, I had successfully applied for the part-time position as a day care assistant in the nursing home I had volunteered at. I enjoyed the work immensely and I was growing in confidence.

Mum and I redecorated the boys rooms while they were away - I spent a whole week hand painting an eight foot long, four foot high rainbow on Glenn's bedroom wall, with birds and flowers and other little animals peeking out. I was so pleased with it when I had finished it and when Glenn saw it he grinned from ear to ear.

The boys returned from one holiday and at the dinner table Callum blurted out that Glenn had nearly drowned whilst they were visiting their Nana's house with Daddy. I don't know how I stayed so calm at this revelation. I asked him to tell me what happened and he became upset.

He explained that Glenn and he had been in the back garden whilst the adults were indoors. Glenn was four and inquisitive. He had been looking in the garden pond, slipped and gone under the water. Callum was the first one to reach him,

shouting for help. Tom's girlfriend heard him calling and
shouted for Tom to help. Callum had nightmares about it for
weeks. I was shocked. Tom hadn't said a word to me when he
had handed the boys over at the train station. All I ever asked
for was the truth. I shouldn't have to hear this from my son.
Accidents happen.

Another time, Glenn returned with burn holes in his clothes
right through to his vest. He was unmarked thankfully.
Apparently he was standing too close to the fire they had been
having in the garden.

One time on their return, I was told by Glenn that Daddy had
hit him across the head with a piece of wood whilst they were
with him.

Each time my boys told me these things I would question them
very carefully, asking how things happened, if there might
have been an accidental reason for something. They were only
young children and their perspective on things very different to
an adult. I could only trust that they were telling me the truth
and let my solicitor know each time what had happened. I just
asked for them to request that Tom ensure their safety and care
whilst they were with them. Tom's response was that I was
making it all up. He hadn't hit Glenn with a piece of wood; the
boys constantly misbehaved, so got into trouble.

Not long after a communication to my solicitor about the boys
latest visit to their father, Tom declared himself bankrupt. He
was demanding my parents sell their home so that he could get
his half share in the house to pay off his debts. I didn't even
know he had debts that large.

The house was bought and paid for by my parents. Tom and I

had taken out a small mortgage to pay for the loft conversion which had been developed into two bedrooms for the boys and a small bathroom. My parents had worked their whole lives to create a lovely home, a home they deserved and Tom felt it was his right to half of that. Our share in it was only around eight percent of the value of the house and I felt his demands were ridiculous.

Not content with having stolen the company car, which he later returned in exchange for my car and for which I was still paying a small loan, he had cleared out our joint account. Luckily he had been ordered to return my share of that money.

He contributed nothing financially for the boys, saying he couldn't get a job. I had eventually hired a private detective after Callum told us one day that he and Glenn went to Nana's when Daddy went to work. It turned out that Tom had a job working full time and I decided to apply to the Child Support Agency for him to pay something towards the care of the boys.

This was fast turning into a really bad 'B' movie and yet this was our life. For a year we were back and forward to our solicitor. Dealing with the receivers who had taken over Tom's debt was horrendous. The man in charge of the case constantly denied receiving letters or proof of ownership of items in our home. My parents and I were almost demented with the stress of it all. Thankfully I had continued attending the weekly community Aromatherapy classes and these really helped to keep me calm.

Eventually, after a year of this intolerable situation, and after several offers of settlement one of the partners of our solicitors firm decided that enough was enough. The strain on myself and my parents was becoming too much to bear and a more than fair settlement had been offered. Our solicitor gave the receivers forty-eight hours to accept the settlement or he would take them to court. This seemed to do the trick and it was agreed.

The relief was beyond words. I had to cash in the endowment policy on our mortgage and pay this to the receivers and that was us done. It seemed too good to be true, yet still I felt this grossly unfair on my family and myself. Tom had got himself into a financial mess, I still have no idea how, yet he fully expected others to bail him out. The details don't really matter now but at the time I felt he had taken this action just to hurt me and my parents. A malicious response to the whole situation, our relationship breakdown and perhaps even because he had been uncovered, his actions known and on record.

I don't suppose I will never know, as he didn't speak much about his feelings during our relationship, it wasn't likely to happen now. Despite me wishing for an amicable split and to discuss things openly, this was not going to happen and I wouldn't find the emotional resolution I so wanted. Nothing more could be done and I just had to live with it and move on as best I could.

Chapter Three

So here we were in late 1998, finally the court battles and bankruptcy stress over. As our life carried on, I decided that I really wanted to take the Aromatherapy I was learning a stage further. I searched for courses in Edinburgh, comparing what was available. I opted for one and set up a meeting with the principal and tutor of the school, Judith.

I was nervous about the meeting, thinking perhaps she wouldn't accept me as her student. I had written a list of questions I wanted to ask her. I wanted to make certain the course and the tutor were right for me. It turned out that she was. I explained a little of my situation and we chatted for an hour or so. I was able to pay for the course in installments, which suited my circumstances.

I was so excited about this new part of my life, not quite believing that I was about to embark on a diploma course in Aromatherapy. I hadn't studied for many years and knew this was going to be a bit of a challenge. The boys were seven and five, with issues still coming up for them and for me which we were dealing with as we went along.

It was a time of focused intent on the course. I had graduated to a part-time job four mornings a week in the community working with elderly patients, which I enjoyed immensely. I also had another small cleaning job which helped to fund the course.

My parents, yet again, were fantastic and helped out with the boys to allow me to either work or study and were generous with what little money they had by helping pay for the course as well. They could see how much this course was helping with my own healing and the whole family benefited from the massages. Glenn would sneak into my tiny treatment space after I had finished with a case study client and lie on the couch ready for a small massage. It was so funny to see his tiny body only taking up around half the length of the couch and I could never refuse.

I found my relationship with my children improved all the time during this period of learning the massage skills. Despite their attention span only being around fifteen or twenty minutes, those were precious minutes where they relaxed and enjoyed a massage and I was lucky to have the opportunity to massage them with such immense love in my heart. It was a very special experience and one I treasure.

We decided it was time to sell our home and move. We found a bungalow which better suited the needs of the whole family at the time and we enrolled the boys at a primary school locally. I was fortunate to have found a part-time job which didn't include a Wednesday morning. Throughout this year of studying for the diplomas in Anatomy & Physiology and Aromatherapy I still attended the Wednesday morning community education class. It gave me an opportunity to socialise and to practice the skills I was learning on the diploma course.

I remember coming home from one Wednesday class and my Dad was sitting at the dining room table. He was busy and never seemed to take time to truly relax. This concerned my Mum and I. He had taken on so much of the strain since Tom left and had become a father figure to the boys and all he seemed to do was work. As a result he was overworked and at times very grumpy. We got chatting and he suddenly said to me that he had been interested in Reflexology for quite a while.

The next day I collected an enrollment form from the community education department and presented it to my Dad saying, "Put your money where your mouth is."

I knew that if nothing else, the two hours each week spent in the class would allow him time to relax and receive some Reflexology treatment.

Good as his word, he enrolled. He absolutely loved it and was a complete natural. My Dad had always had an enquiring mind and was an avid reader. He seemed to literally absorb all the Reflexology learning and was very enthusiastic, it was wonderful to see him with a sparkle again.

The anatomy and physiology of the body fascinated him and after a year he decided he wanted to take this a step further and attain his Reflexology diploma. How he was going to do this whilst running his own business I had no idea, so we did all we could to support his period of learning and enjoyed being requested as case studies. I had always been close to Dad, but this helped deepen our bond even more. This wasn't to say that we didn't have our differences. We saw life from different perspectives and disagreed at times, just like any other family.

The community education tutor volunteered to be one of my

Aromatherapy case studies. Her input and feed back after each treatment was invaluable and much appreciated. During one of her treatments, she explained that she had 'seen' and spoken with a Native American figure. She described his appearance and said she felt he was some kind of medicine man and was very sure that he was my guide. I was intrigued at this revelation, really wanting to know more. I didn't really understand what she meant by 'guide' until she explained that he was like a guardian angel of sorts, always around guiding me from the spirit world. I wasn't sure I fully understood this either, but I found it comforting and exciting.

In August 1999 I successfully passed both the Anatomy & Physiology diploma and Aromatherapy diploma. I was overjoyed and felt such an enormous sense of achievement. I had spent so many hours studying, often into the early hours of the morning. My bedroom walls has been covered with charts of oil properties and reminders of all sorts of information. It had all been worth the extra effort and the two part-time jobs to get through it.

Mum and Dad had been incredible. They gifted me a magnificent treatment couch which is still going strong over a decade later. My friends in the community class were so pleased for me. They too had helped me succeed and it was so good to be able to share my joy with them. After all the trauma of the past few years I felt things were really beginning to come together and my confidence had been given a huge boost.

Dad and I were asked along to a small health fair at the end of 1999. From our stand I could see across the hall to another stand. A woman was selling prints of her paintings. My eyes kept focusing on one picture in particular, I was drawn to that one and no others. I went over to the stand and started chatting to her. Her name was Mary Connolly and she was a psychic artist. She painted portraits of people who came through to her during meditations or peaceful moments.

Within a few minutes she told me that she felt very strongly that I should write a book. I laughed and asked her, "What on earth would I write about?"

"You and your story, of course," she replied. I wasn't convinced and said, "We'll see."

I picked the picture I wanted, the one that had been catching my eye all afternoon. Apparently no-one had ever been drawn to that particular picture. Mary also gave me a second picture, saying that I would know who to give it to. At the time I really didn't have a clue what she was talking about. How would I know who to give it to? I thanked her profusely, it was an incredibly generous act.

I took this wonderful picture, which was of a Native American Indian medicine man, to my next community education class to show the tutor. When she saw it, she exclaimed, "That's him! That's the man I saw during that massage. This is your guide."

Having this confirmation from her was a great feeling. I still didn't know his name, but I felt very drawn to him and wondered if I would ever see him myself.

Mary was right. A few weeks later I realised exactly who was to have that extra picture she had given me to pass on. When I gave it to a friend and explained how I came to have it, she burst into tears. Without knowing what was happening, I was beginning to tune in to my own intuition.

In January of 2000, I hurt my back at work trying to prevent an elderly man injuring himself when he slipped and fell. At the time it felt like nothing more than a pulled muscle, but by the next morning I was in severe pain. I couldn't bend or flex without pain and there were shooting pains down my legs to the tips of both big toes.

I spent the next few weeks off work, attending physiotherapy and seeing my doctor. They suspected a damaged disc in my lower spine and were even beginning to talk about surgical options. I was horrified and prayed I would find some other way of healing from this injury.

Out of the blue, Belinda called me to tell me about a course she wanted to attend. A friend of hers had organised the course. It was something to do with oils and the spine and Tibetan Reflexology. I wasn't a Reflexologist, so wasn't particularly interested in that, but when I heard her say something about "oils and spine", I knew I had to be there. Mum had also visited her doctor recently and after some tests it was confirmed that she had some arthritis in her upper spine and neck. So if the workshop did nothing for me, perhaps I could help my mum.

The workshop tutor was an American woman called Shellie, who had come to share the Raindrop Technique with people in the UK. I had never heard of it, but was intrigued at what we might learn. This was my first workshop after qualifying as an Aromatherapist, and despite my pain, I was really looking forward to it.

I attended with my friend and a group of other women, all Aromatherapists. I felt so out of place, so newly qualified, but willing to learn.

Shellie explained about the technique and how it came into being. It was a fascinating discovery by a man called Gary Young and had been developed as a result of inspiration from the traditions of the Lakota Indians. This native tribe travelled into Canada to experience the great wonders of the Northern Lights 'Aurora Borealis', as they believed the light from this spectacle assisted great healing to take place. They would draw this light up their spines and allow it to fill their bodies, minds and spirits. Once the border between America and Canada was created, they could no longer travel to carry out this personal healing and so they developed a technique using feathers on the spine to mimic the light and energy flow.

Raindrop Technique is a direct descendant of this practice, using pure, organic, therapeutic grade essential oils of the highest quality, those of Young Living Essential Oils. This is the key to the success of Raindrop, the purity and quality of these wonderful plant extracts. The founder of Young Living, Gary Young, was inspired after speaking to a Lakota Indian named Wallace Black Elk, who explained the tradition of the Lakota people during the Aurora Borealis.

Gary later developed the Raindrop Technique and the ten specific essential oils used during the treatment. Shellie explained that the technique involves dropping neat essential oils along the spine (following a French method of application). Feathering movements with the tips of the fingers, to mimic the feathers used by the Lakota Indians, are used to spread the oil along the spine and to stimulate nervous system activity.

During Raindrop, a vegetable oil can be used if any excess warmth is experienced, effectively diluting the neat oils. In practice, this V6 is seldom required. Following the application of the ten specific essential oils, the 'Vitaflex' technique is used on either side of the spine to enhance the electrical flow along the neural pathways and so to all parts of the body.

After her talk, I will never forget the intake of breath which went around the room when she dropped neat oils directly onto someone's back during the demonstration. I was so intrigued by this, and couldn't see what all the fuss was about. This just felt so right, what were the other women worried about?

After the demonstration, we were asked to divide into groups so we could start to learn the practical aspects of the treatment. I recall thinking that I had to get to a couch and be one of the first people to receive this treatment and I shuffled my way to a couch as quickly as I could.

It was a surreal experience. The oils which were dropped onto my back felt so alive and the various hand movements relaxed my whole back, it was wonderful. Then came the heat at the top of my spine. A heat I hadn't experienced before and which was incredibly intense. Shellie came over at this point, her instinct telling her to check our group.

She asked how I was. Amazingly I felt calm and peaceful and serene, so it was rather a surprise when she explained that the heat was a huge emotional release I was experiencing. She assisted with other oils and V6 vegetable oil was liberally applied to my back, yet the heat continued. If this was releasing via Raindrop Technique, how wonderful to feel so calm with no tears or anguish. I was fascinated by this experience.

Once my treatment was complete, I got up from the couch. My lower back was still agony, no improvement there at all. It was the end of our first day and as I travelled home, I was very disappointed that my back didn't even feel slightly better.

That evening, as I sat in my room, words started to come to me and I felt the need to write a note to Shellie. It took about an hour to complete the note, words just tumbling from my head onto the paper. I wasn't sure exactly why I was writing this note, it just felt important that I did.

The following morning, I got up and as I bent to put on my slippers I realised that I had no pain whatsoever. I was bending without pain for the first time in weeks. I tentatively moved my back from side to side. No pain.

I quickly put my slippers on and rushed downstairs to the kitchen. Mum was there making a cup of tea and I said, "Look, look!" whilst gyrating around the floor.

"I don't have any pain!"

She was delighted and my Dad could barely believe it. "How on earth could this be?" I was thinking to myself. It was truly incredible and miraculous.

I arrived at the hotel for the second day of the workshop and walked straight over to Shellie and told her what had happened. She smiled, a glint of understanding in her eyes. I handed her the note, asking her to read it when she got the chance. She said she would, began to turn away and then she turned back and handed me the note. "I want you to read it out", she said gently.

I should have been panicked, but I wasn't. I read my note to Shellie out loud in front of the group, explaining that my back pain had healed overnight after the Raindrop treatment I had received yesterday. I shared a little of how I had been feeling over the past few years and how I felt something deep within me had somehow just changed after that one treatment.

It was another turning point in my life. From that day on I kept in email contact with Shellie, often contacting her for advice about the technique and the oils. I used the technique from that moment on, with my family, friends and clients. I practised and experimented, loving the technique and the results every time I used it.

I began to build a relationship with these oils gaining a much deeper understanding of them, of the emotions and of myself. I used it to treat my Dad when he fractured a rib, his pain all but disappeared after one treatment and the fracture repaired quickly. The neighbour I treated who had Fibromyalgia. One treatment and she was cycling past my kitchen window the following day and her life has soared to new heights ever since. The woman who had experienced over ten years of back pain and used morphine every day to control the pain. After three months she no longer needed the morphine, her pain having reduced to such a low level. Her outlook on life became much more positive.

These were totally awesome experiences which have only added to my deep belief in the Young Living oils and in the Raindrop Technique. I knew when I received that first treatment and had such an incredible healing experience myself that the potential with these oils and this technique was limitless.

After my experience of the Raindrop Technique during 2000, Dad also decided to further his knowledge of complementary therapies and completed a course in Indian Head Massage and began his personal journey with Reiki energy, taking his first and second degree in Usui Reiki healing. He just loved working with this energy and found it to be of great benefit to him personally and during his treatments on clients.

I have to admit that I was sceptical about energy work. I had no knowledge of it apart from what I had heard from others and of course Dad's experiences. I certainly wasn't drawn to learn this method of healing, content with my path using oils during massage and Raindrop Technique. I did, however, become very interested in Reflexology.

I decided that it was now time to learn a completely new skill, and very grateful that I had already completed the anatomy and physiology portion of the course and would be able to attend for the Reflexology portion only. This made life much simpler and I found that the systems of the body made more sense to me once I began to relate them to the areas on the feet.

I can't say I disbelieved Reflexology, I had always felt wonderful during any sessions I had received, but nothing could prepare me for the insights into the imbalances within mind, body and spirit which I was able to discover during Reflexology sessions.

The healing which occurred with Reflexology was exciting. It was so very different to body massage, yet equally as wonderful. As I learned how to work with the feet, I felt in tune with these wonderful windows to the soul.

Dad and I would discuss our individual experiences of Reflexology, our excitement bubbled over as we marvelled at the healing and the things the feet could show you. We were both in awe of this healing method, how some clients could literally feel areas within their physical body responding to the touch on the corresponding area on their feet. Totally incredible.

Dad and I felt like children on Christmas Eve, and I know

how silly that sounds, but the wonders of the human body interlinked with the effects of Reflexology was like a completely different insight into a new world.

The whole family benefited from our new found skills, the boys loved their mini massages but didn't have the patience to lie around whilst their feet were 'fiddled' with. I learned very quickly from them that I needed to grasp any opportunity and work fast. So I developed my own method of working on both feet at the same time, one hand on each foot. A skill I have been very thankful for over the years.

Dad attended a workshop about the Universal Technique of foot Reflexology given by Chris Stormer a few months later. He loved the technique that Chris shared, but was more than a little unnerved by her forthright and unusual take on life.

I can fully understand his confusion after I attended one of her seminars. However, her words made me think. They made me question myself and my beliefs. I have attended quite a few of her seminars over the years and each time I resonated more and more with her insights and began to look at the way I was leading my life through my thoughts.

Chris' Universal Technique (or Rei-flexology) coupled with Language of the Feet uses feather like touch on the feet, sometimes no touch at all. The healing which occurs is so incredibly powerful and deep. It is a wonderful method of Reflexology and is carried out on both feet at the same time. Through learning this technique, my inner self was beginning to come out to play.

I had grown close to Judith, the tutor of the complementary therapy school where I trained, and we became good friends.

Out of the blue she asked me to help her run her business whilst she was abroad on holiday or away teaching. I was delighted to be able to do this for her.

It wasn't difficult work, responding to phone enquiries about courses and sending out information packs to prospective students. As a prior student I was able to share my experience of being on one of Judith's courses and answer questions about their content. I really enjoyed this part-time role and it gave me much more confidence and experience.

A few months later, Judith asked me to fill in for her. She had a ten week complementary therapy course which involved teaching adult students a variety of therapies over the ten weeks. A sort of taster of what these therapies involved. Judith asked me to teach Aromatherapy for the three week slot on a Tuesday evening, as she wouldn't be available. I agreed, but was very nervous.

When the evening came, I didn't want to go I was so nervous. I had put together some simple information and made up four bottles of blended oils for the students to use in class. I planned to teach them how to carry out a simple hand massage, a foot massage and a face massage over those weeks.

I can remember my stomach doing back flips as I stood at the front of the class with around ten women looking at me. "What am I doing up here?" I asked myself. "I must be mad!"

Judith had given me one piece of advice before teaching that first class. She told me to remember that I wasn't 'teaching' I was simply 'sharing information'. So despite my nerves, I survived the evening and we had fun using the blends for the hand massage.

From what I could tell, the students had enjoyed their first experience of Aromatherapy and so had I. The following two weeks weren't quite as nerve wracking and I found that I actually enjoyed sharing my knowledge with these lovely people.

And so began my teaching role. I was asked to tutor Aromatherapy classes at the high school each term, Judith not being available on these evenings. She lived in the Highlands during the week and only came to Edinburgh to teach her complementary therapy school students at weekends.

If anyone had ever told me a few years previously that I would be standing in front of complete strangers 'sharing information' about essential oils and massage, I would have told them they were nuts. Me stand in front of a class and teach? No way.........

But those classes were an incredible teacher to me as well. I learnt such a lot from the various people who came, sometimes they came term after term. Mostly they were there for the social aspect, but they put their hearts and souls into the massages, some of them even going on to take diplomas in Massage and Aromatherapy.

This experience was also very humbling for me. I began to realise the effect one small pebble has when it is dropped into the pond. I was affecting these people's lives, the lives of their families. People were healing from long term ailments, their friends and family health had improved. All from me showing them a little about massage and sharing my knowledge of the wonders of essential oils. We became like a small family, I enjoyed heading to my evening job once a week to share some relaxed space with such lovely souls.

I have to say that I am forever grateful to Judith for that shove to stand in front of a class. I know I was thrown in at the deep end, which has happened so often in my life. She perhaps saw potential in me which I was completely unaware of.

Chapter Four

As the boys grew, their emotional and spiritual well-being became more important to me. I watched as they worked through their feelings about their parents divorce, often feeling immense guilt over the whole thing.

I would often catch myself thinking, "Perhaps if I had only tried to love him a little more, things would have been fine." But I knew deep inside that this was not the case. Our relationship had ended because it was meant to. We weren't right together any more, and by staying together much more damage would have been done to us and our two boys.

The boys expressed much anger and many tears. Glenn started to be bullied, mainly name calling and threatening behaviour from another boy in his year. He was desperately unhappy and he told me he just wanted to die. I knew it was time for me to find someone who could help him.

I tried many avenues, but was told that neither of my boys were 'serious enough cases' for the counselling help on offer. After several days telephoning charities and other organisations, with little progress, I decided that I would contact a friend to ask if she knew of any private counsellors who worked with children.

I had no idea how I would afford private counselling but I wasn't prepared to sit back and do nothing.

Glenn was eight at the time and in my mind I was looking for someone with a gentleness and compassion who would be able to help him.

In the most roundabout way I found Lily, a beautiful woman with sons of her own, flowing blonde hair and the most wonderful twinkle in her eye. I made an appointment with her after giving her a brief explanation of what Glenn was experiencing.

She was amazing with him. She came up with some wonderful ideas for Glenn to leave his 'baggage' behind with her and after six weeks, he was much happier and at ease.

Callum then decided that he wanted to speak to Lily about his feelings, I think reassured by Glenn's experience. He saw Lily less often and was able to work through his anger towards his father and his feelings that somehow he was to blame for our break up.

At times during these sessions, my heart broke listening to their words. They were so young and yet had experienced such immense hurt. I learned a lot from their process and the way Lily helped them turn their negative emotions into a more positive outlook and an uplifting experience.

I learned to detach myself from their words too. This was their experience and not mine and it was good for me to realise that I wasn't alone in this. Someone else could help them, it didn't always have to be me fixing things.

As I watched my sons healing and becoming happier, I knew that it was time for me to begin to heal myself. I asked Lily tentatively if she would be willing to take me on as a client once Callum had finished his sessions. To my surprise, and relief, she said she would be delighted to work with me.

I'm not sure why I thought she wouldn't. I think looking back I felt I didn't deserve such help. I knew that to help my sons grow and develop into happy young men I must attend to my issues and heal deep parts of myself. I had seen how the counselling had helped them and, to be honest, I wanted to feel happy inside again. I didn't want to feel occasional bits of happiness. I didn't want to be in survival mode each day. Not any more. It was time to move on.

I can remember wondering what I was going to say to Lily. In one respect I wasn't even sure what I wanted to heal inside of me. I still felt very disconnected from myself and I began the sessions not fully appreciating the enormity of the undertaking. At times I felt sheer panic and wanted to run away. The room felt too claustrophobic to stay in.

I slowly began to realise that this was my inner defense mechanism. It was how I had survived during the abusive period of my marriage. I had run away in my head. The more we talked, the more I learned about myself. I learned how I dealt with my feelings. I learned about the way I thought about myself and my life.

It was quite a revelation to discover that I had loathed my very being for a long time. I thought very little of myself and my thought patterns were very self destructive. Lily helped me to see this and gradually, little by little, this changed. I became calmer and a little more accepting of myself. That felt good, really good. I knew we had a way to go, but it was a great start to my new life.

During this time, Dad discovered that he had Type II Diabetes. It came as a bit of a shock to us all and knocked the wind out of his sails a little. But he was a determined man and set about changing his diet so that he wouldn't have to take tablets or graduate to daily injections. He lost some weight, stabilised his blood sugar levels and began to feel really good physically. He had more energy and felt young again.

I was delighted for him, pleased that he had this new lease of life. He was still self employed and repairing showers at seventy. Most people thought he was in his early sixtys, he was such a young looking man with an energetic outlook on life.

Towards the end of 2002, Callum decided he wanted to stay with his father for a while. He wanted to get to know him better and after the counselling sessions with Lily he felt that he needed this time to improve his relationship with his father.

Part of me was devastated, not wanting him to go. Yet part of me knew that this was something he had to do. He had to work this out for himself, no matter what happened. At age eleven he was in his last year of Primary School and hadn't seen much of his father for years.

Tom agreed for Callum to stay with him and his partner and enrolled him in the local school. Arrangements were made and before I knew it Callum and I were on a flight. I handed Callum over to his father at the airport, it was a peculiar experience.

I mentally imagined that Tom and I were still in a loving relationship. It was the only way I could deal with this situation. After all the hurt he had inflicted on me and the boys, I was about to walk away and leave Callum with him.

When they left the airport I was sure my heart would tear in two. I cried all the way home on the flight, not quite sure how things would turn out. I could only hope for the best outcome for Callum, that he improved his relationship with his father. But I wanted him to come back home too. I couldn't imagine life if he decided he wanted to stay with his father permanently.

The next few weeks were very strange. It was only five weeks to Christmas and I really wasn't in the mood for celebrating. I was seeing Lily weekly, my whole life seemed in turmoil and out of control.

I had to be strong, Glenn was still at home and needed his mum, yet my heart was breaking inside. I missed Callum so much. He called once a week and I got the feeling he wasn't that happy, but he said things were going okay.

Christmas was 'survived' that year. We made sure Glenn had a good time, but our hearts weren't in it. A few days after Christmas, I got a call to say that Tom was sending Callum home. He was proving to be a handful, apparently his behaviour wasn't very good and Tom thought it best if he returned home.

I was elated that he was coming home, but devastated that this was the scenario. He was being sent home. He hadn't made his own decision. Perhaps I was naive, but I had hoped Callum would improve his relationship with his father but decide after a short while that he still wanted to stay with me. I couldn't imagine how Callum must be feeling.

He came home just before New Year, emotionally distraught and angry. Angry at his father for the outcome and angry at himself for going to stay with his father in the first place. It was obvious that he was bitterly disappointed at the outcome of his visit. Perhaps he was also embarrassed. It didn't help that Glenn shunned him on his return. Glenn had felt abandoned by Callum and thought that he had been a traitor by going to stay with his father.

"How could he go and stay with someone who hurt us so much?" he asked me.

Again, I was so thankful for Lily. She helped me and my family put Callum back together again within a few weeks of his return and helped him to understand that it wasn't anyone's fault that the visit hadn't worked out the way he had planned and hoped for. Gradually his anger subsided and he realised that his decision to go to stay with his father was an extremely courageous one. He had no idea what that stay would be like, but had still gone. I was immensely proud of him, but very glad he was home.

My counselling sessions with Lily became less frequent and great progress was being made in my healing process, though I came to a point in the counselling where I felt stuck. I felt I wanted to tell Lily something, but was unable to find words to express whatever it was. I didn't seem to know. This was a little strange to me and I couldn't figure out what was going on.

A few months after Callum returned, I had an appointment with Lily. I had it in my head that I was going to stop seeing her, yet deep down I wanted to continue the sessions.

Within fifteen minutes of being in her room, I found myself

saying words which I didn't know were there. I almost blurted it out and then sat back in amazement at what I had just said. I had described a scene to Lily about an abusive part of my relationship with Tom and yet doubted what I had just said.

Lily was very patient and understanding, explaining that doubting yourself and the information which had remained hidden for so long was all part of the process. This revelation was deeply shocking to me. Where had this been hiding in my head? How could I not have realised? Why didn't I do something about it? Why hadn't I just left my husband instead of staying and experiencing this?

My head was spinning with questions. What proof did I have that any of this information was real? Perhaps I was making it all up?

Over the next few days I began to experience flash backs. I also began to experience the fear I had felt. This felt so silly to me. Tom wasn't living anywhere near me and I had no reason to feel frightened. I was a very different person now and I knew he couldn't hurt me any more. Yet the anxiety still came, like waves of sheer panic.

"Where was all this coming from?" I kept asking myself.

I contacted Bill. He was the only person around at the time of my breakdown who might be able to shed some light on what I was experiencing.

We met for lunch and chatted. I told him everything that I was experiencing and asked if I had ever said anything to him. Bill was open and honest and told me that he was in no doubt that I had experienced the abuse I described. He had witnessed my

behaviour on many occasions and some of the things I had said
to him then had left him in no doubt.

I thanked him for his honesty. It was a relief to know that I
wasn't mad; that I hadn't made all this up. But then it made it
all so much more real. Up to that point I could pretend that it
wasn't real. Now I was at a point where I couldn't kid myself
any more. It was time to face the reality and I had no clue how
I was meant to get past this.

I took a little time off work, I couldn't deal with my job as
well as all the emotional turmoil I was feeling. I needed time
and I was fortunate to have such an understanding boss. This
eased the pressure I felt. Slowly Lily and I worked through the
emotions which were bursting through. It wasn't pleasant, but
I knew it must be done. I had to move past this so that I could
feel whole again.

Things went well and after a few weeks I felt almost ready
to return to work. I felt stronger and less weighted down by
the vast amounts of baggage I had been carrying around for
years. My anxiety had all but disappeared and my head wasn't
spinning as it had been. Life was improving all round and I felt
much happier.

I wrote this poem to describe that experience -

Survived!

Shadows all around
Past hurts not quite healed
Future hurts - too afraid to live
Petrified of feeling
Feeling means hurting
Pain - excruciating!
Overwhelming
Consuming
Suffocating.

Breath!

My God, there is air
I'm not dying
I can keep breathing
I'm still here
I didn't shatter into tiny pieces
Like I thought I would
Presumed I would
Feared I would.

Survived!

Around this time one of our cats, a beautiful but timid little soul called Cassi, had been for her annual check up at the vet. Two weeks after this visit to the vet she developed a limp and seemed to be a little lethargic. We thought she had perhaps twisted her leg somehow and took her back to the vet for investigation. He found a lump on her shoulder and decided to carry out some blood tests.

The following day we were stunned when he called to tell us that she had bone cancer which was quite advanced and there was nothing that could be done for her. We couldn't believe that she had appeared to be so healthy until a few days ago. Even our vet was surprised that a lump could appear so quickly, as he had checked her thoroughly during her annual visit.

She was euthanized later that day and we were heartbroken. She was such a lovely cat with the most beautiful eyes, which looked like she had applied mascara. She had brought us such pleasure over the years and at the time we had no clue of the significance of her passing.

A few months later, Dad began to experience severe pain in his back. He had been having niggles on and off for some time and thought he had perhaps twisted his spine whilst repairing a shower. Nothing seemed to ease the pain and his back wasn't improving.

My Dad had a very high pain threshold, he never complained when he was ill and had an amazing capacity to heal. I had seen him have a really heavy cold and go to bed very early and wake up the next day completely cold free. So this lingering pain he was experiencing was unusual.

Mum and I had been out shopping and returned home to find

him in a chair, grey faced. He had collapsed at one of his jobs and come home. He was very hot and in a great deal of pain. I knew this wasn't a back injury, this needed proper investigation. We visited the doctor several times over the next two weeks, some blood tests were done but no diagnosis was forthcoming.

Eventually his pain became so bad that he was admitted to hospital for some tests and in late July he was diagnosed with pancreatic cancer with a secondary tumour in the liver. I don't think I will ever forget that day in the hospital, the look on my Mum's face. The devastation I felt inside was indescribable.

Dad wasn't surprised. I think he knew deep down it was something fairly serious and had somehow figured it out. But Mum and I hadn't anticipated this at all. Treatment options were offered, though prognosis was poor.

Dad opted to have chemotherapy in an attempt to shrink the cancer. However, it was made very clear that this was only going to extend his life for a short period, the cancer was advanced.

I called Julie and Martin to let them know what had been said at the consultation. Then I called a few other family members who were waiting for news, each one shocked and upset by the news. I remember feeling numb, yet panicked all at the same time.

What kept spinning through my mind was how I could break this news to my boys. This was a task I didn't relish and knew that no matter how gently I managed to tell them, they were still going to be devastated. They had looked upon my Dad as a surrogate since their father left.

It was one of those surreal, bizarre days that we have all had at some point in our lives. Mum, Dad and I stopped off for a cup of tea on the way home. It was difficult to know what to feel or think or say. Everyone around us was carrying on like everything was normal and inside I was screaming. I wanted to run. I wanted to stand in the middle of the car park and shout and scream. I wanted to turn back time and start again. I couldn't. I was feeling such pain inside that I thought I would stop breathing. Somehow I got through the next few hours until the boys got home from school.

They both knew that their Grandad had been feeling very unwell, but they were still young, Callum was twelve and Glenn nine. I kept thinking that they shouldn't have to be experiencing this. Not after what they had already been through in their short lives. None of us deserved this.

I sat them down in their bedroom and explained where we had been that morning and that Grandad was very, very ill and had cancer. They asked if he would get better from it and I explained that he wouldn't. The expression on their little faces as it dawned on them that he was going to die. We just cried and hugged for a long time. I didn't know what else to do. There was nothing I could do except hold them and be with them through this. Yet it didn't seem enough.

That day I spent some time in my room alone. I was restless but didn't really feel like doing anything. I got my dowsing crystal out. I was learning to use it to test which essential oils to use during treatments and to assist me to trust my intuition. I asked if Dad was going to get better from this cancer. The crystal rotated in a 'no' direction. I threw it across the room and it disappeared behind my drawer unit. I didn't want that answer. I wanted to know that he was going to experience

a miracle. I wanted to know that he was going to get well. I
wanted hope, but there didn't seem to be any.

Somehow we got through the next couple of weeks, waiting
for appointments for Dad to start his treatment. By the time
the appointment came through for his chemotherapy his blood
sugar levels were elevated. The doctors wanted to have this
under control before giving the chemotherapy.

We went home and spent the next few days balancing his blood
sugar levels by adjusting his food intake. That was successful,
but Dad was beginning to turn yellow and when we returned
to the hospital he was sent for a scan. This showed that his bile
duct was blocked due to the size of the tumour.

It was then decided that he should be admitted for a procedure
to insert a stent (a small tube which held the duct open) into
the bile duct which would alleviate the jaundice and the
chemotherapy treatment could go ahead.

Dad was frightened. I had never seen him like this. We talked a
lot during those days. He shared with us that he was frightened
to die because he didn't know what was on the other side. He
wanted to meet up with his mother, yet was frightened about
what might greet him.

He told us that every year on his birthday, the day she had died,
he wept for her. He had missed her so much since her sudden
death on his eighteenth birthday. All his demons from that time
came back to him now and again I called on Lily. She was
fabulous. Time was at a premium and what she was able to do
for my Dad was give him more peace of mind.

Dad had also asked a Reiki friend, Ian, to do some healing

work surrounding his future and this seemed to help a lot too.
At the time I wasn't really sure what this meant, but if it helped
his peace of mind, that was good enough for me.

So Dad went into hospital for the procedure to fit the stent.
He wanted Mum and I to have some fun with the boys, so we
opted to go to the beach. The hospital had my mobile number
in case of any problems and we planned to be away for only
a couple of hours. It was a lovely day in early August and the
boys were having so much fun on the beach.

After an hour on the beach we received a call, we needed to
return to the hospital, Dad wasn't well. We bundled the boys
back into the car and rushed back. Mum visited Dad and I took
the boys home.

Dad had experienced a really traumatic time in the procedure
room. They had tried three times to insert the stent, but the bile
duct was too narrow. We hadn't realized that this procedure
was done with just a local anaesthetic. Bless his heart, when
they were about to attempt this procedure a fourth time he
refused, offering to stick the tube up the surgeons backside.

Mum told me afterwards what it was like when she went in
to see him. He was so pale and small in the bed and when he
came round from the morphine he had been given, he was
convinced that Mum had saved him from a prisoner of war
camp where they had been experimenting on him. He was
delirious and in such pain. I saw him later that evening, and
was shocked at the sudden decline in him. He was a little more
lucid by then, but he seemed to be so different. Broken.

Dad came home to us the next day. We were grateful, we just
wanted him home to be nurtured and loved in his own safe

space. It became very obvious that he didn't have long. His
weight loss was dramatic and he was struggling to shower or
move around without assistance. Even with both me and Mum
there with him full time, it became such a struggle for us to
look after him. He wasn't sleeping at night, in so much pain
and neither of us was getting any sleep.

So one morning, after a particularly bad night I called our
doctor. He had been brilliant, calling in if he was passing by
and he arrived within an hour to check Dad over. He asked us
what we felt about some respite care for Dad. He suggested a
short admission to give us a breathing space, especially with
the boys needing me too. He also felt that in a hospice, Dad's
medication could be balanced with his Diabetes. It wasn't
something we particularly wanted to do, but we felt that it
might be the best option for the whole family.

Later that day Dad was admitted to the Marie Curie Hospice
in Edinburgh. It was a long day, with discussions about
medication he was taking, how he had been physically,
mentally and emotionally.

The staff were relaxed and caring and I instantly knew that Dad
would be okay here. It was hard to leave him there though. He
was so poorly that neither Mum nor I wanted to go. But we
needed sleep and my boys needed me.

The Morphine and other medication Dad had been taking was
stopped completely and replaced with Paracetamol and his
pain levels monitored. Within twenty-four hours he was like a
different man. He was lucid and smiling and eating again.

Mum and I could barely believe our eyes when we saw him
the next day. How could this be possible? When we spoke with

the medical staff, it became apparent that Dad had experienced toxic dementia. His body was overloaded with drugs (Morphine in particular) and because his liver function was affected by the cancer, it couldn't handle the levels of Morphine in his system. I was intrigued that his only medication was Paracetamol and his pain was reduced and manageable.

We were relieved that this had obviously been the right decision. We had both left the day before feeling guilty at leaving him there, that somehow we had failed him by not being able to cope at home. Dad was 'back' and we could laugh and joke with him.

He asked me to give him a small treatment, a Reflexology or foot massage. This became my daily routine when I visited. He would joke with the nurses that he had his own personal therapist. There were other volunteer therapists who visited the hospice, but Dad refused anyone other than me. It made me laugh that he waited for me to come in and one of the first things he did was to point at his feet and smile.

I felt this was the least I could do for him, wishing I could do so much more. Wishing I could take this all away for him. Sometimes I felt so useless, here I was able to turn other people's lives around, yet couldn't do that for my own father.

Yet I know he felt wonderful after each session. So much so that at night, when he perhaps couldn't sleep or was feeling restless, he would wander around the hospice, giving Indian Head Massages and Reiki to visitors and staff and any patients who were in need.

I recall one of the senior nurses speaking to Mum and I one day, concerned that he would use up his energy by doing this.

We just laughed. It was what he loved to do and if it made him happy and feel useful, it was a blessing. We explained that he also would be receiving healing energy when the Reiki energy flowed through him to the recipient. To stop him giving this gift to others, would be like limiting his air. So the nurses were happy to let him carry on, monitoring him to ensure he wasn't expending too much energy and resting when he needed to.

His friend Ian visited regularly and whatever healing he had been able to do on Dad's future had given great peace of mind. Everything was sorted, peace was waiting.

Bill was also a regular visitor and unknown to me at the time, Dad had asked Bill to conduct the service once he had passed away.

As the days went by I began to feel changes in Dad's feet. Slight changes at first. I wasn't quite sure what I was feeling. By mid September he was very frail and mostly bedridden. I continued to massage and work on his feet daily. I can only describe his feet as 'emptying'. They felt colder each day, yet were warm to the touch. I knew deep down this meant that he didn't have long.

One day Mum asked him if he would like her to stay beside him in the hospice that night. He smiled a huge smile and nodded and within an hour was deep in a coma. The nurses moved him to a single room with a small guest bed. I brought in a CD player that evening and played gentle soothing music for him.

On Saturday morning, I spent some time with him, working his feet and talking to him. Sunday was Glenn's tenth birthday and I can remember sitting beside his bed and saying, "Dad, you've got two options here. It's today or you're going to have to wait till Monday. Don't you dare die on Glenn's birthday."

I suppose it was a strange thing to do, but I meant it. I really didn't want this to be happening - not now. I was making a huge effort to ensure Glenn's birthday would still be celebrated. Please let it be today or Monday - never would be even better.

Ian visited that day and Mum told me afterwards what happened. Dad had requested weeks previously that no-one give him or send him Reiki healing. I think he felt that the healing might give him more time, but that it would therefore also prolong his pain. Often people who are desperately ill will rally for several days after receiving Reiki and then decline once the energy has been 'used up'.

During this visit, Ian decided for some reason to do a little Reiki on Dad. He moved around the bed, placing his hands gently on various areas. Lastly, he placed his hand about three or four inches above my Dad's head and seconds later Ian's hand flew against the wall with great force. Mum and two other visitors were in the room at the time and witnessed this.

Dad had asked that no Reiki be given and by placing his hand above my Dad's head, perhaps Ian was stopping or stemming the natural flow and clear passage for Dad to leave by. I'm not sure, but it was certainly my Dad's way of saying "enough!"

Mum stayed at the hospice that night as well. She was exhausted, but it was totally right that she be with him. The following day, we celebrated Glenn's birthday. He opened his gifts at home then I took the boys into the hospice for a little while. Glenn wanted to thank his Grandad for the birthday present he had given him.

After their brief visit, a friend took the boys for a couple of hours. I was planning to have a birthday meal and some fun later in the day and Glenn had invited a friend to the house for the small celebration.

In the early afternoon of September 21, I was working Dad's feet and felt a sudden change. I rushed for a nurse as Mum stayed with Dad.

It was time, he was leaving and nothing was going to stop that. I held onto his feet as he gently passed. I'm sure I held my breath, willing him to breathe again. I felt his feet emptying and know the very moment he left and the music which was playing.

The nurse told us afterwards that in all her twenty years as a Marie Curie nurse she had never experienced such a gentle passing.

It was a weird day. I was so upset, yet angry. How could he do this? How could he die on my sons birthday? It was such a mess. It was so unfair.

I called my sister, Julie to let her know that Dad had just passed away. She and Martin were on their way to the hospice. The nurses were wonderful, preparing the room for people to say goodbye to Dad. A rose was placed on the pillow beside his head. I was overtaken with the urge to complete the treatment I had been in the middle of doing.

"I must be mad," I thought. "He's already gone, so what difference will it make now?"

I had only completed one foot. In Reflexology, when only one foot is completed the client can feel very lopsided until the other is completed and balance is achieved. So this was my driving force. Knowing full well that my father's spirit had left his body, I still felt compelled to return to the room on my own and complete the session.

The nurse said it was perfectly fine for me to do that and Mum was happy for me to do it. So I went into the room and gently finished working his other foot, the tears streaming down my face. It was like a last farewell and an honouring of a deeply loved father and teacher.

That evening, the family gathered, all except Glenn. He had chosen to go to his friends' house for a few hours. He was very quiet and I truly felt for him.

Bill arrived to support us; my cousin was there with her husband; Julie and Martin; Callum, Mum and me. We sat around the dining table and gradually the tears turned to hysterical laughter as we regaled tails of Dad's antics over the years.

He had a very quick and mischievous sense of humour, so once we got started the room was filled with raucous laughter. Tears of joy ran down cheeks and ribs began to ache with laughing so much. A fitting family farewell.

Chapter Five

Two days after Dad passed away, I was back teaching the evening classes. Dad had asked me if I would take over his Reflexology class, which I had promised I would. I explained to the staff what had happened and that I would be tutoring both Aromatherapy and Reflexology.

The staff and students were shocked and surprised that I was choosing to teach that evening, just a couple of days after losing Dad. I knew in my heart that this was something I must do. The bottom had fallen out of my world over the past few months and I had to get back into teaching complementary therapies. Part of me felt that none of it really mattered, yet I was pulled to return and teach.

It proved to be absolutely right, my mind needed to focus on something completely away from family life and funeral arrangements and grief. Teaching students about essential oils, massage and reflex points diverted my brain for two hours. It was an enjoyable respite.

Two weeks after this first class, one of the students confided in me that she had seen my father standing beside me as I taught that evening, a yellow light around me. I had no idea she could see auras and spirits. His presence didn't surprise me one bit, perhaps he was even checking up on me to make sure I was teaching the Reflexology the right way.

Later that week, I was shopping with Glenn. He desperately needed some new school trousers. As I selected sizes for him from the rails in the shop, he piped up behind me, "Mum."

"Yes, sweetheart?" I said

"I think I know why Grandad died on my birthday."

There were other women nearby and I heard their intake of breath as they overheard what Glenn had said. I can remember thinking, "Oh my God, what is he going to come out with?"

There was utter silence around us, everyone close by had stopped. It was a static moment in time.

"Do you darling? Why is that then?" I replied to him.

"Well, I think that when Grandad died, all his best bits went into me."

My heart lurched. I could feel the emotion around me, the other shoppers sighs as they overheard his answer. Tears began to well up in my eyes.

"I think you are probably right, Glenn," I said.

When I got home later I told Mum what he had said. Glenn has always had some rather profound things to say from a very early age. He had often stunned us all with some of the things he shared and this was no exception. Mum and I hugged and shed some tears, but knew that somehow Glenn had processed his Grandad passing away on his birthday. It gave me hope, real hope that everything would be okay.

Mum and I had a busy week there was much to arrange for the funeral service. She decided to buy a beautiful silk flower display of roses for my cousin, who had been a great support for us. We placed this display into my treatment room for safe keeping. A couple of days later, Mum called me into the room. She asked me to smell the flowers. I sniffed them closely and could smell a rose aroma. I looked at her. How was that possible? These were artificial flowers. Mum asked me if I had perhaps sprinkled them with Rose essential oil. I hadn't. No-one had. Yet these flowers smelled of rose, most distinctly. In fact, the aroma of Rose in the room was very obvious. My bottle of Rose oil was safely shut away in a wooden oil storage box inside a drawer.

This was the first of some very strange events after Dad's passing. Whilst I was on the phone to my cousin one evening, she stopped talking and shouted for her husband to come and see what was happening. She was in her bedroom on the upper floor of their house. There was moisture on the outside of the window. Someone or something was drawing or writing in the moisture.

I heard her husband say, "What is that?"

He rubbed his hand on the inside of the window, convinced it was something on the inside. The writing continued. My cousin copied it down onto a piece of paper before it disappeared. When we looked at it later, we couldn't decipher it. Some were symbol type images which we searched the internet for, but nothing resembled them. We felt this was from Dad somehow, but we had no idea what it meant.

One other evening I was getting ready for bed. Everyone else was in bed asleep. It was a warm evening and my window was open slightly, my room facing out into our garden. I could smell smoke. Instantly I went around the whole house checking for this smell. There was nothing. I went out into the garden perhaps someone was burning garden rubbish late at night. There was no burning smell outside.

"I must have imagined it," I thought to myself.

When I returned to my room and sat on the bed ready to slip under the duvet, the smoke smell was there again. I sat quietly and was very still. The smell remained for many minutes then just disappeared. I was left wondering why these strange things were happening.

After we lost Dad I found that all the anxiety and stress surrounding my poor relationship with Tom had gone. I felt stronger, yet didn't know why. Somehow it just didn't seem to matter any more. I had no idea when that had happened. I have to say that I was very grateful. There was enough to keep my mind busy without that as well, because two weeks after Dad passed, we lost Tuffi, our Red Burmese cat.

He was gorgeous and had spent many hours sitting with Dad in those last days before he was admitted to the hospice. Tuffi died of liver disease, though he wasn't very old.

We were stunned and began to wonder when this would all stop. When would we be finished with all this loss? It just seemed harder to bear as Tuffi had really been Dad's cat. It was like a last piece of him was gone too.

We still had three cats, Kooki and Ruben who were half brothers and Abi, a lovely female cat who Glenn and Dad had picked after we lost Cassi. All I can say is, thank goodness for these small creatures. By not doing much of anything other than being themselves, they helped us all through this difficult time.

I had also begun to have great difficulty sleeping. There was a period where I just couldn't shut my mind off. Words and thoughts tumbled around and around, driving me to distraction. One night in particular I was still awake at 2am. I opened my window fully and stood looking out at the garden in the moonlight breathing in the cool air. Words began to surge forward and I heard 'write' in my head over and over.

I sat down on my bed and began to write. It turned into a poem, the words appearing on the page without much thought from me, or so it seemed. I came to learn that each time I had difficulty sleeping and words came jumbling into my head, I had to sit down and write it out.

Afterwards I always found that I went straight to sleep. As if my mind was finally purged of the words which were so desperate to be released and formed on a page. I had never written poetry before. I wasn't too bothered whether these poems were any good, just happy to be rid of the words onto paper so that I could sleep. Most of these poems were about Dad or an expression of the emotions I was feeling. Some were sad, some were happy. I suppose it was simply one way that I could express myself at the time.

Poem for Dad

You're going now,
I can sense it.
No longer the pain to feel.
Begging you - pleading
Don't go! - Don't leave me!
Don't leave US.
Yet knowing you must.

Wishing you peace; tranquillity.
For you had none.
Your soul in turmoil endlessly.
Sorrow for all you suffered.
Wanting the suffering to end.
But not.
Loving you.
But not.
Please stay!
You can't.
You must!

Take care of him, this special soul.
He deserves the best.
No evil in this soul.
Only love.
Unconditional love.
True, honest love.
And I hate you for that.

They've called you because of that.
But I love you for that.
~ Always ~

Yvonne Jevons - 2003

I missed Dad so much. I kept expecting him to walk through the door after his work, we all did. So one day I decided that I wanted to see a psychic. I hadn't been to one before and I was rather nervous. What if I saw someone who was a complete fraud? The thought kept knawing away at me but my opportunity came one day when I saw an advertisement for a health fair in town. I made my plans and went along one Saturday afternoon.

I had told no-one about this, perhaps in case I was disappointed. I'm not sure. I walked around the stands, trying to pick someone I felt was right for me. I spent ages, unsure if I was even doing the right thing. I stood at the doorway for a while, looking at the whole room.

I felt drawn to one woman in particular. She was a very unassuming soul. I knew I had to go to someone and I headed her way. As I sat down my heart was thumping so hard, I was very nervous.

Her name was Lynn. She was lovely and asked to hold my hands for a moment to connect. Within a few seconds she released my hands and began to talk. She connected with my Dad straight away and told me things about the day he passed away that no-one but me and Mum knew. A real confirmation that it was him coming through.

Tears were streaming down my face as he sent his love. He was happy and everything was okay when he passed over. Everything was sorted out and his mother had been waiting for him. I was so overwhelmed. I was happy for him, at last he had the peace in his heart and was reunited with her again. Lynn told me not to worry about the boys either, they were going to be fine. Just give it time.

I thanked her, took her business card and went outside. I was taken aback and yet delighted. I had hoped to connect with Dad, but hadn't expected to. From what I understood it really depended on who wants to come through with a message.

I told Mum when I returned home where I had been and what Lynn had said. It was an emotional day for us as we chatted about Dad and what had come through in the reading.

From that reading and from some information which Ian, Dad's friend, had shared with us, I began to wonder about my Dad's illness and the trauma in his life. I sat down one evening and began to piece together all the ailments Dad had experienced throughout his life, one physical symptom at a time. Mum was really helpful and able to give me more detail about his life than I had known.

I had been using the book, The Body Mind Workbook by Debbie Shapiro for some time, both on my own body 'symptoms' as well as clients. This book and others like it, outline the body/mind theory. This is a way of understanding what the body is trying to tell us. That there is something going on at an emotional level deep within us and that this then manifests in the body as illnesses or pain. It's the body's way of getting our attention that something needs to be addressed.

I began to get a clear picture of common issues running through my Dad's life. During this bit of detective work I became very aware of Dad's energy around me. I felt he was telling me to share this information, to tell people to begin to listen to their bodies so that they can understand how their emotions greatly affect the physical well-being.

This led on to Mum and I discussing the death of his mother.

Mum was able to tell me details I hadn't known. Details of the accident when she was killed and that she had just received the all clear of cancer. Suddenly, Mum and I looked at each other.

I blurted it out first. "He killed her. Dad's father, George, killed his wife. He pushed her in front of the car."

We just looked at each other in complete silence. This surely couldn't be right. Yet deep inside I felt that it was and I had goosebumps all over. It all made sense in that moment. I just sort of knew.

It was my Dad, Eric, and his twin sisters eighteenth birthday and there had been a small celebration at home. Eric, his mother, father and aunt had walked to the bus stop nearby and waited for the bus to arrive. His aunt boarded the bus and as the three of them waited to cross the road on the way home, a car approached.

The next moment Eric's mother seemed to fall or trip into the road and was hit by the car. She was killed instantly, her face very damaged. Apparently, this was how Dad remembered her and this was what had scared him so much about passing over. What if she looked like that? What if he couldn't find her because he couldn't remember her face before the accident?

Eric's father never pursued the case for prosecution, despite the driver being drunk behind the wheel. Eric's mother had asked him a few years before her death if he thought his father was having an affair. Eric replied that he didn't know. His father did marry very soon after her death and it turned out that he had been seeing this woman for a while.

Mum and I thought that perhaps once it was clear that Eric's mum had recovered from cancer, his father felt trapped. When she was hit by the car, she was holding onto George's arm and the force of the impact ripped the sleeve right out of his jacket. My Dad saw it. I think he saw what really happened, that it was no accident.

This was huge information to process. I wasn't exactly sure how I felt. How should I feel knowing this? At times I felt really angry, yet had nowhere to direct it. All we had was a really, really strong instinct that this information was correct, there was nothing written anywhere and none of the people who were actually there at the accident were still alive. All we had was instinct. My head buzzed for days, sometimes I felt sick at the very thought of what had taken place that day.

I spoke with a friend about it and realised that I couldn't really do much with the information. It was all very much in the past and it was time to somehow move on. I decided to visit Lynn again. She confirmed much of my findings. I was relieved that I wasn't going mad. But I also wished it wasn't true.

What came through to Lynn after this confirmation was that Dad was desperate for me to share his story to help others and also to help release all that pain from our family history.

At first I didn't really know what he meant. I didn't know how to share this information. But gradually it became clear. I was to share this with students in some of my workshops, particularly those interested in body mind theory and Reflexology students.

These Reflexologists have direct access to all organs and systems through the reflexes on the feet and have a prime opportunity to help their clients become more in tune with their bodies by understanding this body/mind correlation.

I share my notes with you now. I hope they help you understand a little more:-

Seventy year old male

- diet controlled diabetes for two to three years
- abdominal pain in the past with no medical cause found
- crushed knees as a young man
- kidney stones (fifteen to twenty years ago)
- overweight in abdominal area for years
- pancreatic cancer with liver metastases

Breakdown of 'symptoms':

Diabetes – pancreas – can represent the sweetness in our life (this can be too much or not enough); being able to integrate love into our life.

Abdominal pain / indigestion – fear; dread; anxiety; the stomach can be emotionally linked to food, love and the mother and nurturing.

Knees – fear; perhaps inflexibility and an inner resistance.

Kidney stones – can be 'lumps' of undissolved anger or unshed tears; old issues which haven't been released.

Overweight – fear; protection; insecurity. Being overweight in the stomach area can represent anger at being denied nourishment/nurturing.

Cancer – deep hurt or longstanding resentment; a deep secret or grief which eats away; possibly carrying hatreds which are all of deeply personal issues.

Outline of life events:
- His mother killed by a drunk driver on his eighteenth birthday. He witnessed this.

- He wasn't allowed to grieve properly by his father who also stopped him from playing music in the house.

- Eric adored his mother and each year on his birthday he still cried for her.

As you can see from this brief outline, there are distinct pointers and commonalities which can be tied into the significant life events which my father had experienced. These life events and the fact that he found it incredibly difficult to speak about the death of his mother in particular had a very real impact upon his physical health.

Never before had I understood as clearly how loudly the body can shout for help when it wants to be heard. Dad asked me to share this information in this format to groups I taught. To help them understand that our thoughts do effect our bodies. Without us changing our thoughts and dealing with our 'stuff' we cannot improve our physical health.

Chapter Six

Despite the grief of losing Dad, the revelations after his death
and the strange little events since his passing, life had taken
a different turn somehow. After he passed away I thought it
would never be possible to be happy again. The pain inside
was so intense it took my breath away. Mum and I had learned
to appreciate the smallest things during Dad's illness and
somehow each day I found joy in the little things in life.

My perspective on life had changed. Life is too short to get all
knotted up with things which really don't matter that much.
What did matter was my immediate family, our happiness and
expressing love and appreciation for each other. Sometimes I
felt like it wasn't really me experiencing this parental loss. It
felt like someone else's life.

We had lost another of our cats earlier in the year and we had
been devastated. She was very young and had wandered onto
the main road. Things surely couldn't get much worse. Every
little set back seemed to be so magnified during this time.
Understandable, I suppose. Each hiccup or event felt like finger
nails drawn down a chalkboard, really grating on our raw
nerves.

Mum and I discussed whether we should perhaps get another kitten. We knew how much delight and fun these animals brought into our lives, yet we were concerned about any more impact on our already raw emotions if we lost yet another one. We decided to go ahead. This time we would get two kittens, as Ruben and Kooki were a bit older and the kittens would keep each other company and play together.

So entered Alli and Poppet into our family. Each of the boys picked their kitten. The first night they were home with us, each kitten slept beside the boys. Callum and Alli formed a bond and Glenn and Poppet were inseparable. When I checked in on them later that night, the boys were sound asleep, and the kittens tiny furry bodies were curled up beside them. Matches made in heaven.

These additions to our family were just perfect. Not that our other cats were forgotten. Each cat had its own special personality and the ones we had lost were missed dreadfully. But animals have an incredible ability to help people heal after devastating life events.

Months rolled by and I spoke with Lynn a few times. She was so helpful, giving me a greater insight into my intuition as it developed, as well as helping to guide me on my spiritual path, though I didn't know it at the time. I was just getting through my life day by day, finding as much happiness within it as possible with no thought to a 'divine purpose' or path. I am certain however, those wheels were well and truly already in motion and nudging me onwards.

Around July 2004, I was driven to learn Reiki. I wasn't just drawn. I knew I had to do this, to learn Reiki. I didn't know very much about it and had never felt any great interest in it.

Yet here I was with an absolute yearning to complete First Degree Reiki.

During a chat with Lynn, Dad 'popped in' to say hello. He asked her to tell me that by doing the Reiki it would lead to much greater peace for me inside and a greater satisfaction in my work. I knew a Reiki Teacher who I trusted and so I booked myself a space on a weekend workshop.

I can remember turning up on the first day wondering what I was doing, how I had arrived at this point. Everyone else seemed to know what they were doing, I felt clueless, despite things being explained throughout the two days.

My first attunement was surprising. I didn't know what to expect. I felt tingles and saw many colours as I sat quietly with my eyes closed. Suddenly my Dad's face, clear as day and almost in 3-D, appeared right in front of me. I was overwhelmed with emotion and love engulfed my entire body and beyond. Tears of joy leaked from under my eyelids and slid down my cheeks. I had never experienced this feeling before. It was beautiful.

We were shown hand positions and practiced this on each other. Yet after the workshop, I didn't feel much different. I'm not sure what I expected I would feel like, but I didn't feel any energy in my hands like the others, nor did I experience any heat or cold or sense the recipients energy beneath my hands.

"Maybe the attunements hadn't worked," I thought to myself.

Yet I knew they had. Recipients could feel the energy from my hands, but I felt nothing. I found this quite peculiar. I felt a bit cheated. I wanted to experience the energy like other people.

Perhaps because I didn't feel or sense the energy, I didn't use it much on myself or others.

The Reiki energy brought some emotions to the surface. There seemed to be such a lot going on everywhere which reminded me of where I used to be eight years previously. I felt sure that this was so that I could rejoice in my achievement of being alive, as well as acknowledge the work I had done for myself personally and professionally.

Mum went to see Lynn for a reading soon after my Reiki course. During the reading Dad apologised to Mum for not going to the doctor earlier when he had symptoms. We were not to blame ourselves. When Mum told me what he'd said this set my tears off because there was still an element of blame or guilt hanging around. I felt I should have been able to help him more.

He also said for me not to worry about the boys, they have a bright future. It was so very obvious he was looking over us, which was comforting for us all. This year on his birthday, we burnt birthday cards with little messages of love for him. No-one was tearful. We simply stood quietly whilst they burned and then we all went indoors and carried on with our day. It was more a small remembrance ceremony to mark the day.

I was still working part-time and Mum looked after the boys till I got home. Since Dad died we hadn't been to any Chi Kung classes for a while. I had enjoyed these classes very much and Mum and I both felt it was time for us to return to them. Evenings were awkward, I didn't have extra money for babysitters as well as pay for the exercise class but I missed it a lot. I found great peace during the class, finding the moves calming and yet powerful somehow. I discovered a class which was held on a weekday morning and we enrolled. It was fabulous to be back exercising and building up our inner strength again.

Over those weeks of Chi Kung, I began to feel energy pulsing in my hands. Before when working with the 'ball of energy' during a Chi Kung exercise I didn't really feel anything. Now I began to feel my hands radiating. It was such an incredible feeling that I ended up with tears flowing down my face, I felt so happy and alive.

I hadn't felt this energy before and wondered if this was the Reiki energy showing itself to me. It gradually became stronger and stronger over that year. I was so pleased as my senses developed and I found myself going deeper into my soul as each month went by. It was a wonderful feeling to be more aware and able to enjoy when these moments of complete contentment enveloped me.

I began to have an insight into the way Dad led his life after taking his Reiki training. I had more understanding of some of the things he said or did. I was trying to bring the Reiki way of life into my heart and I was beginning to use it each day.

I felt that I was much less reactive to situations now than a year ago. I was able to step back from situations a bit more easily and not allow myself to become embroiled in things which had no bearing on me and that I could do nothing about anyway. It felt such a good thing to be able to do, as it meant I wasn't using my energy in a way which hurt me or others.

There were still days that I wished it didn't hurt so much, missing Dad. I knew this was relative to how much I loved him, but I really wished it was less painful.

Mum and I attended one Chi Kung class where we were working on our energy centres (chakras) and everything was going well, until we began to focus on our heart energy centre. The moment I held my hands over this area, I felt like I was hit in my stomach by such an enormous feeling of loss and sadness that I could hardly breathe.

It took me by surprise initially and tears were rolling down my face whilst doing the exercise. Thankfully, I was able to breathe through the emotional pain and attain peace through the breathing. So within a few minutes, I had regained my composure. It was difficult to accept that Dad wasn't coming back and very hard to imagine life without him around. This felt a bit weird after a year of coping reasonably well. Maybe I had tried too hard to 'cope' and the emotions had to find a way out somehow.

As I healed through doing Chi Kung, using Reiki and seeing Lily occasionally I realised how awful my depression must have been for everyone involved. For the first time in a while, I wasn't comfortable with my 'breakdown' being the only thing I could do at the time. This led to some confusion again. Certainly my low mood was nowhere near the level it had been before but I felt like my soul had been separated again, after getting it reasonably whole. I really wasn't sure why, it didn't seem to make sense to me, but it was how I felt.

One morning, I had a strange experience as I woke up. I awoke from a very deep sleep with an image in my head of Dad. I was very close to his face and he was trying to say something, but I couldn't quite hear him. Then his lips formed 'I love you' and he was gone in an instant. My body was then hit with an enormous pain and emptiness, as I realised it was a dream and he wasn't there.

This brought up more feelings of my personal journey. Sometimes during my sessions with Lily, I felt so suffocated that I wanted to run outside into the garden to breathe fresh air. Despite me telling myself to get a grip, that I wasn't going to die, I realise now that Lily was right. She had said on many occasions that, in essence, those reactions were life and death. I had thought that was a bit melodramatic. But I was beginning to understand more fully what she meant. If I had allowed those feelings to truly take hold of me again, and without her immense support throughout, I may not have survived mentally or emotionally.

With that realisation comes responsibility – having to acknowledge that without a huge amount of inner strength, I would not have survived. That strength came from within me, supported by others. But it lay and lies within me. That was a very difficult concept, as I had always believed myself to be weak and without merit. Only fleetingly could I accept that I may just be a good person and worth more than life had thrown my way. Worth more than a subject of distorted power games.

I knew it was important to carry on with the work I was doing. To keep opening my heart, no matter how scared I was. I knew it was the only way I would ever accept myself and perhaps, who knows, even begin to love myself. This was a refreshing change to what I had felt about myself for most of my life. A really wonderful step to truly healing the wounds within and releasing the emotions which bound me to those wounds.

Though scary, it was also a little exciting. I had seen glimmers of the potential in my life, even without my Dad. I had felt periods of great calm and serenity within, so knew that even more was possible. I had such incredible support from people around me and from Chris and Shellie. Each time I faltered and couldn't see my way out of negative spirals, they were there at the other end of my emails guiding me back to my self.

The Woman Within

This woman that I am within
So unsure of who she really is
Four decades I have behind me,
Who knows how many to come.
Once was whole, or so I thought.
No longer mine, fragments drawn back together,
A jigsaw with unknown picture.
No need for eyesight on this journey,
Obscuring what truly lies beneath.
A steady hand rests upon my shoulder
Guiding, supporting - always with me.
Even in the darkest places
This angel holds the light before me,
So I may see the pathway which I must follow
To feel that wholeness in my heart
To free my phoenix from its ashes.
I love you deeply
- my friend, my Angel.

8 December 2003

Chapter Seven

Early in 2005, Mum and I finally admitted that we didn't have the financial means to carry on living in our home. We had struggled on for many months, but without Dad's income from his business, finances were extremely tight. I can recall getting angry with him, as he must have felt invincible and hadn't any life insurance arranged, though our bank had also contributed to this by failing to arrange life insurance on the mortgage properly.

But there was nothing else we could do and so we began to house hunt. We were determined that the boys were to have as little disruption to their lives, so it was really important that they stay at the schools they were already attending. At least this would provide stability for them.

We found a house suitable for our needs. It wasn't what we really wanted. We really wanted to stay where we were. We loved our home, but bills were harder and harder to pay and there was no other way out. We moved house in April of that year, having cleared out vast amounts of belongings and items which hadn't been used for a while.

I suppose when I look back, this was a cleansing period for all of us, though at the time it was tough going. Mum found this move really upsetting and I worked so hard at keeping positive for everyone, yet inside I had no clue how this was all going to turn out. I just knew that it was right for us. It was a way out of our financial predicament and at least we would still have a comfortable home. There was even space for a very small treatment room, so at least I could continue to do the work I loved.

Our male cat Kooki, decided very quickly that he really didn't much like the new house. Ruben, Alli and Poppet seemed to like it just fine, but Kooki was very grumpy. Within six weeks of us moving he disappeared. We looked everywhere locally and I spent many nights wandering around near our previous house calling out to him in the vain hope that he would turn up.

We even spoke to Lynn to see if she had any idea where he might be located and if he was okay. She felt strongly that he was still very much alive and she was shown that he had moved in with an older couple somewhere.

Weeks went by and there was no sign of him and we resigned ourselves that he wasn't coming back. He was such a strong character and we missed him not being around. We were also truly dumbfounded that another cat had left. I knew enough to realise that he was needed more by someone else than by us and that was why he hadn't returned. But it didn't stop this loss from hurting.

Ruben, his half brother, slowly began to come out of his shell. He had always been quite a timid cat. Kooki had been 'in charge' of the cats and without his presence now, Ruben was clearly beginning to shine.

We settled in really well in our new home. The neighbours seemed pleasant enough and the house felt light and cheerful with a few decorative additions and changes. The boys were reasonably happy, still close enough to school to be able to walk each day.

I was beginning to really tune in with some of my clients during treatment sessions. I had found a few times that I sensed someone else was doing healing work at their feet whilst I was massaging their back or doing Reiki at their head. This was a strange phenomenon for me, but it didn't feel scary in any way. It felt quite reassuring. The presence I felt in the room was very loving and nurturing.

Sometimes I also experienced a picture popping into my head or a word or thought would pop in which made no sense to me at all. As this started to happen, I spoke to other colleagues and it seemed that sometimes this was information coming through for the person I was treating. I was excited and a little awestruck that this should be happening.

I also began to have a recurring dream. It came to me for a few nights and I awoke from it each time in a sheer panic. I dreamt the boys were both hit by a car, but they were fine after it hit them. I found it weird at the time. A few days later, they both bought themselves remote control cars with pocket money they had saved and I put it down to that.

I had pushed one part of the dream completely aside, because I couldn't make sense of it and it wasn't that clear. Anyway, when the boys were hit in this dream, afterwards I had a very hazy image of a frog which had been run over and one of its eyes had been badly damaged. It was an unpleasant vision and I had to work really hard to push that image away.

Months later, on a beautiful summer night, Callums kitten Alli was struck by a car. The car didn't stop and left her in the road. Luckily some local children knew who she belonged to and came to tell us. Mum was distraught, almost wailing.

I remember thinking, "Another one bites the dust." I felt very numb.

As I held her tiny body, I felt like I was transported back in time. I had seen this before. I had actually seen this. I had seen the frog being killed, the damage to its eye and here we were with exactly the same injury to Alli. I hadn't understood the dream. Not that I could have prevented this from happening. I didn't know what to think or feel.

Callum was heartbroken. We all were. Another lovely little soul gone. I didn't really react, too numb with the realisation that my dream was about this. The details were too coincidental not to be linked.

I was beginning to think that our lives could be made into a black comedy film. It would be hysterically funny if it weren't for the fact that this was really happening. Surely life just couldn't keep going this way?

My 'old' brain was telling me, "see what happens when you get to enjoy yourself? Something bloody awful comes straight in there to bring you back down." And yet my heart was telling me it was okay. Alli was needed for something else or she was only meant to be with us a short time for some reason. But it still hurt.

A few days afterwards, I asked angelic beings if Alli was okay. I got a hazy image, not even that. More like an impression of

someone. It gradually became clearer. There was Dad with all
the cats we had lost sitting around his feet. I could just make
out what I thought was Alli. I knew she was okay and didn't
suffer with the swiftness of the accident, which was also a
blessing. I don't know how I knew. I just did.

At the end of August I did a home visit to a new client, Carole.
She had booked me to give her a Raindrop treatment. She was
a lovely woman, who admitted to me that she worried a lot and
couldn't seem to lose weight or improve her energy levels since
she had a brain tumour six years previously. She suffered a
constant headache, which she described as feeling like they had
stitched her head up too tight when they removed the tumour.

Around eight oils were chosen using my dowsing crystal. It
was quite an array of unusual blends compared to what I had
used before. I seldom had a client who didn't absorb the oils
very quickly. I had never seen it quite so obvious before. I put
three oils on her back, feathered them in and the oil stayed on
the surface of the skin. This can be because the body is 'toxic'.
Perhaps that the liver is overloaded and cannot handle any
more in the body to process or it can also be an indication that
the person is processing huge amounts of emotional issues.

I thought, "Oh no, I've still got more oils to go here, maybe I'll
have to skip some."

Then suddenly the skin just took the whole lot. They absorbed
instantly. I did a slow and gentle massage of her back and went
on after that to do a little Reiki. I say Reiki, but I don't know
what it was. I removed some hooks which I had been shown
how to do at an evening workshop a few weeks previously and
was also pulling stuff down and out of her feet. She said she
felt like electricity was running through her when I was doing

it, which I could also feel running through me. The energy was
very strong and I became really hot as I worked. Then I felt
drawn to her head and ended up pulling something like a cord,
though I couldn't see it, I just felt I needed to do it.

The whole thing was so bizarre. I felt so strongly that the
whole energy healing 'thing' was out of my hands. My hands
were being guided to do what was needed with me being a
fairly clueless participant. It was a strange feeling. I couldn't
feel someone taking my hands nor did I hear someone saying,
"Right this is the next thing you need to do." Maybe that's what
I was expecting. I had heard other people's explaining that
they hear and see things as they work and had presumed my
experience would be similar, forgetting that everyone channels
energy differently.

I was so excited about this latest treatment and she felt
completely wonderful afterwards. I couldn't believe how
powerful it was, for me as well as for Carole. She had booked
to see me a few weeks later and I was looking forward to seeing
her again to see what happened with her after the treatment.

Carole arrived for her Raindrop treatment looking so much
more alive and relaxed. She is very special and as I worked
with her I could sense the energies around me. I sensed they
were either angels or other light beings who were helping and
guiding me so beautifully. I felt huge tingles throughout my
whole body and felt so charged up when I worked on her. It
was fabulous.

I felt I needed to work at her head, so moved to that end of
the couch and was standing looking down her covered body. I
started working again and became aware that I was working on
her angel wings and smoothing out the feathers and making the

shape of them in the air behind her. At this point she expressed how she felt, like she was on fire with electricity. I asked if this felt alright and she asked that I continue as the sensations were wonderful. My arms were almost trembling with energy. I then smoothed her aura and held my hands over her back for a while.

At the end of the session I placed my hands together and bowed a huge thank you to whoever was assisting. I still had my eyes closed and I became aware that I could make someone out at the other end of the couch. I could see that someone was bowing back. They were dressed in a white type of robe made of a delicate cloth with a gold trim on it. They bowed and then stood upright. I could see it was my Dad. I was dumbstruck.

I was then aware of more people around him, smaller and they also bowed. He was ushering them gently away, the treatment was complete. They too were dressed in white robes and when they turned to go, I realised they were our cats, walking on their back legs. They then seemed to merge into human form, although I couldn't see their faces. I was almost jumping up and down with excitement.

After the treatment I also thanked Carole for giving me the opportunity to work on her, it was such a privilege. She was amazed at me saying this, I think, but it was true. She was very open, which allowed me to do so much more. When I explained that I had been working on her angel wings she was so excited and couldn't wait to tell her friend.

After she had gone, I went back into my treatment room and sat there for a while and thought, "Wasn't that such a great experience and special gift?" Especially as it was Dad's birthday that day. I couldn't feel sad, I was too excited.

I emailed Shellie late that night. I explained what had happened during the session that evening and she emailed me back the following day. She was overjoyed for me that I was beginning to have these visions and experiences. Her advice was to go with it, just as I was doing.

I was just beginning to realise that I have been blessed with the gift of being a channel to help heal others and couldn't deny it's existence or run away from it. This was a part of me; of who I am. This profound experience got me thinking and I wasn't sure if I was perhaps losing my mind or if these visions and feelings were real. I spoke to my Mum about them and she didn't bat an eyelid, accepting what I was telling her because she felt the truth of my words.

Later that month, Chris Stormer was presenting a workshop in Edinburgh. I couldn't get the time off work to attend the full five days of the workshop, but was able to go on the weekend. Mum was happy to look after the boys for me.

In the weeks leading up to the workshop, Ruben had somehow managed to find frogs in the garden next door. We would occasionally find a frog hopping around the house or sitting on the vacuum cleaner, with not a mark on them. It was such a strange thing.

The morning of the workshop, I was woken at 5am with a weird noise in my room. I put the light on and there was Ruben chasing a frog around my carpet. This was getting beyond a joke and it took me quite a while to capture the frog and release it outside. I didn't bother trying to get back to sleep, instead watching a beautiful September sunrise.

I arrived early at the venue, positive I could feel a presence in the car beside me. I went inside and Chris greeted me with a huge hug and informed me that Dad was already there. It didn't surprise me one bit. I found it comforting that he was so evidently around. During the workshop, Chris' insights into how the body speaks to you were fascinating.

We did one particular exercise in pairs. I was working with a woman I didn't know and we were tasked with scanning the other person whilst they stood or sat quietly with their eyes closed. By scanning, I mean either looking at the person with your eyes open or closed and sensing or seeing what may be around them. Sometimes this can be a feeling or a word in a particular area of the body or energy field.

I hadn't done this before and was a little nervous. But it was great fun and taught us to trust our intuition more. The woman I was working with saw two things in particular. She saw a panda face at my abdomen and flippers on my feet. We couldn't figure this one out and called Chris over to help us out.

We chatted for a few moments and then Chris asked how I felt about pandas. I love pandas and she then asked if I had viewed life in the past as very black and white, almost strict thinking. I started to laugh and agreed with this. It was one of my traits that I was learning to soften. Then we got to the flippers. Chris burst out laughing and turned to me, eyes gleaming.

"The dolphins are calling you, Yvonne. They want you to come swim with them on one of my soul safaris in South Africa."

"Oh", I thought.

I can recall seeing dolphins during a treatment in one of Chris workshops. Occasionally I saw other sea creatures during meditations or treatment sessions of Reflexology or massage. This was something much more real. I had wanted to swim with dolphins for some time, without really knowing why. I mulled this over during the rest of the day.

I also spoke with Chris about our cats, how we had lost so many in such a short space of time and on top of losing Dad how painful this was for us all. She reminded me that our animals are here to help us heal and grow. When their job is done, whatever that may be, they leave either by just going to a new owner or by leaving physically. She also explained that it was a sign that we as a family were evolving very rapidly. Things were changing very quickly, hence the change of cat energies too. Each cat had taken on or shown us something which reflected things going on in the family.

At that moment the penny dropped about Cassi and Tuffi in particular. They had each developed an ailment which Dad later became ill with. Cassi had cancer. Tuffi died of a liver problem in the organ where Dad's cancer had spread to. As for the others, well my head was spinning with this information, let alone think about the other small creatures. I told Chris about Ruben and how he had been bringing frogs into the house over this past couple of weeks, around five in total. Chris looked me in the eye and asked, "Do you like frogs?"

"Yes", I replied.

"What do frogs do?" she asked.

I thought about it and said, "Swim about, jump, eat insect type things and make more frogs."

"Leap of faith", said Chris. "That's what I am being told. Take the leap of faith."

By this she meant the soul safari. I would so love to have gone on one, but not alone. My Mum and the boys would have to be with me. There would be no point otherwise, I felt that. But surely this was just a wild dream? Me in South Africa? Surely not.............I didn't mention much to Mum that evening when I got home. I had brain ache.

Once the boys were tucked up in bed and Mum had gone to sleep, I decided to go outside for a while. It was a lovely warm night and I often sat outside at night in the peacefulness for a little while before going to bed. Tonight was different. My head was full of possibilities. I sat outside for a short while and then decided I really needed some sleep for tomorrow's workshop day so went to bed.

I was still awake and unable to sleep two hours later. I got up again and went out into the garden. I sat on the back step, my brain still working overtime with the information I had been given that day. I became aware of a presence beside me on my right. I looked down and there, sitting perfectly still beside my right foot, was a frog. I began to laugh quietly in the night, it was the very early hours of the morning and there I was sitting on my back step with a real frog beside my foot, telling me once more to take that leap of faith.

In that moment I began to see the bigger picture and I knew I had to take action of some kind.

All of these experiences were not coincidental. I realised that a greater influence was at work, our move to this new home, though not ideal for our physical needs, had enabled a little financial freedom. It had freed up enough money for me to have the opportunity to take my family to South Africa on a Soul Safari. A special healing and awakening adventure for us all.

The next day at the workshop, I spoke with Chris and told her about the frog. We laughed at the image I described from the previous night. It was becoming clearer to me what my next step was and she gave me the contact details of the person organising the Soul Safari in October. Chris wasn't even sure if there were any spaces left and I promised I would email Nelia that night when I got home.

This second day of the workshop seemed to disappear very quickly. It was a day of relaxation and foot knowledge shared by Chris and I had a wonderful experience during a treatment session. I was very relaxed during this treatment, though completely aware of the room occupants and noises. Within moments of the treatment starting I became aware that I seemed to be flying. I was high up in a beautiful clear blue sky and could see the ocean below me sparkling in the sunlight. I felt so free and light and could feel the air passing over my wings. I was an eagle, with long brown wings outstretched as I glided around the sky. I saw what I thought was a submarine below me, but as I focused more on the object I could see it was a huge whale, gliding through the water.

I turned slightly in the sky and began to feel myself flying downwards, graceful but very fast and I plunged straight down into the water. I held my breath, thinking I would surely drown but the moment I entered the water I had become a dolphin. I felt the movement of my body, the flick of my tail as I dived deeper and deeper towards the ocean bed.

As I concentrated on what I was seeing, I felt another change in my form. This time a turtle, my legs pushing slowly but powerfully. The scenes were incredible, full of vivid colour. Colours I couldn't describe and nothing like I had seen with human eyes. There seemed to be a structure of some kind on the ocean bed, I could see mermaids and fish all around this structure. Light coloured pillars reaching up out of the sand. The light from the sun providing rays through the water, yet I knew we were too deep for light to penetrate. Then instantly I was high in the sky, an eagle once again. The ocean was below me and I could see the whale slowly gliding though the waves.

I wanted to see more, feel more. I was engulfed in such a radiance of love and well-being that is difficult to describe. Not euphoric, but a deep contentment right in the centre of me. Nothing I had experienced quite this deeply before. I was moved and in awe of what I had seen. The treatment was drawing to a close. I felt it had been only a few minutes, but nearly an hour had passed. I shared my experience with the group. It was a profound experience for me.

"A real connection to Mother Earth," someone said.

That evening I emailed Nelia asking if there were still spaces available on the Soul Safari in October and waited for her reply. The following day, her response was in my inbox. There were four spaces left and did I want to book them?
I felt like I had gone mad. Who was I to be thinking of spending money on a trip like this?

People like me just didn't do those kinds of things..........but who were 'people like me'? I wanted to go. I wanted to take my family for a well deserved break and if we could also receive some healing from the experience, that was even better. I hadn't discussed this with anyone, other than Chris. Mum didn't have a clue what was in my mind.

I had asked her that morning, "Would you fancy going to South Africa if you had the opportunity?"

She had replied, "That sounds nice. Yes, if it was possible." I didn't explain further and she still didn't know what I was planning. I replied to Nelia's email and asked her to book the four places for myself, my mum and my two sons. When I hit the 'send' button, my heart was in my mouth. It felt like a crazy stunt, yet it felt so right. That day I found some time to explain to Mum what I was planning and asked her if she was up for it. She was tearful, stunned at this revelation. To my relief, she agreed that she was very much up for it.

And so began the planning of the trip. It was all very last minute, just a couple of months till the Safari. For days I hunted the internet for flights, working out dates for the best deals and connections. Several times I tried to book flights, but the transaction wouldn't process. I began to think we were destined not to go. But the instant I changed the dates of the flights to incorporate a few more days before and after the Soul Safari week, the booking and transaction processed first time.

It seemed like the whole thing was becoming more bizarre, but the universe knew what it was doing and I had to let go and allow this to develop, without me trying to control it. That was a challenge in itself, letting go the control. 'A work in progress' would be an excellent phrase to describe that particular aspect of my character.........

Chapter Eight

So, my decision made to go to South Africa, I was urged by something inside me to receive a Second Degree Reiki attunement before going. I spoke with my friend and colleague, Ann, asking her advice. I didn't necessarily want to do a full Reiki day or receive a certificate, but I felt it was important for my experience in South Africa that I receive an attunement. I didn't really know why. Whatever the reason, I felt sure this was what was needed and Ann agreed to attune me.

So the day after Glenn's twelfth birthday, I received my Reiki attunement from Ann. It was really amazing, my left arm at one point was actually quivering with energy flow and there were several images which came through to me.

The first image was of a young woman, Indian in origin I think, with an ankle bracelet of bells, dressed in a full ankle length skirt. She was almost gypsy like in appearance. She was running up a flight of stone steps towards a huge stone carved Buddha. She kept looking around, as if she was being chased but I wasn't aware of feeling any fear, as it gradually became apparent that she was me.

The second image was of a young oriental boy, perhaps around fourteen years of age, dressed in orange robes and with a shaven head. He was laughing and talking to someone on his right who I couldn't see.

I felt a little tired afterwards and later in the day felt totally exhausted. I also began to feel very cold. This was normal for me after treatment sessions and would seem to be normal after attunements too. I had come to learn that feeling this cold meant that there was some very deep inner healing taking place. I was delighted I had received this attunement. It felt right and all part of my preparation.

Our adventure had begun the moment I had bought the tickets and paid for the Soul Safari and on a cold morning in October 2005 we got up very early, showered and left for the airport. We had a lovely flight to Amsterdam and from there on to Johannesburg.

The boys were excited. They knew we were going to be swimming with wild dolphins and seeing all manner of amazing wildlife. Despite being an educational experience this certainly had all the hallmarks of an exciting holiday.

We arrived at Johannesburg airport and were greeted by a young man who was driving us to our bed and breakfast accommodation. This took a little longer than anticipated and so when we arrived at our destination the streets were dark and we hoped that we would have access to our rooms this late.

We were greeted by the owner Christine and her small white fluffy dog. Christine was originally from Scotland and had moved to South Africa with her husband, Ian, a number of years ago. She was welcoming and pleasant and showed us to our rooms. We settled in with a cup of tea before going straight to sleep. It had been a long day of travelling and I was glad that I had been guided to fly a few days earlier so that we could rest before the Safari week started.

The following day, I awoke early to the sound of birds outside and decided to go for an early swim in their pool. It was freezing, but it felt so refreshing to be in the water. It didn't feel real. We were actually in South Africa. I thought this would never happen.

Christine was delightful, taking us to local shops and attractions. This was totally unexpected, and we felt like we were staying with family, not in a B&B. In the evenings Christine and Ian opened their newly created outdoor bar area and we spent many happy hours chatting and laughing. This was a long way from our usual evening activities at home. I felt really alive and relaxed.

The weather in these early days was warm and sunny, just coming into spring time in South Africa and it was a lovely gentle transition from the cold weather of October in Scotland.

Our first day of the 'Soul Safari' was a visit to Constitution Hill. We were greeted by our guide for the day, a gentle man called Obi. He guided us around the prison and the Constitution Court chamber. We were shown the area where they now educate children about the history of apartheid, a vibrant fun area with lots for the children to do.

In the court chamber, Obi explained a little about the furnishings and construction and what these meant. Some of the walls were really rough, others very smooth. This represents the roughness of South Africa in the beginning and the smoothness representing the desire for smoothness

and refinement of the running of the country. The carpets
represented the Atlantic and Indian oceans around South
Africa.

We visited the prisoners area, small cold cells and I stood
in one alone for a few minutes before the rest of the group
arrived. I could feel the immense sadness and pain, I thought
this was mine at first but the walls were impregnated with the
sorrow and hardship of the people who had been imprisoned
there.

It was the most magnificent day, the sun was shining and much
as this visit to Constitution Hill was a little hard on the heart
and soul, it was extremely rewarding and we left with hope in
our hearts.

As we descended the steps into the car park, my dear friend
Shellie appeared. She hadn't let me know she was coming and
it was fantastic to see her. She had injured her foot right before
the journey to South Africa and she was sporting a plaster on
one foot and was on crutches. I was delighted and over the
moon to see her. What a wonderful reunion.

Our next port of call was Soweto Township. This was a real
eye opener for the whole group. We visited a small building
which served as a drama centre for the local people. We were
seated in the courtyard in the sunshine and were then treated
to a show. It was nothing like I have seen before, we were in
the middle of it, not seated apart. It was wonderful, extremely
entertaining and the main characters were dressed in traditional
costumes and interacted with us the whole time. I had sore
sides from laughing so much.

After this a horse drawn carriage arrived and we were given

a tour around Soweto, seeing some fairly desperate sights.
School had just finished and the children were walking home.
Despite the corrugated iron homes, these children wore pristine
white school shirts and were full of life, waving and laughing
as we rode by.

We had our tour and entered the local community centre, where
we were served lunch whilst the actors from the show stood
and chatted to us. I met a beautiful woman that day called
Sabelo. Her name means 'sharing'. Despite the language
barrier (her English being around one million times better than
my non-existent South African) we managed to converse quite
well.

It was no coincidence I happened to sit next to her. She
explained that she had lost the love of her life to AIDS just
the year before. She now looked after his two sons from his
previous marriage on her own and was just getting her life back
together again. My heart ached for her and I realised we were
not so different. I shared some of my story with her.

She explained that the community looked after each other.
Some days a family may not have enough food and the others
will share their food, whatever they have, so that others didn't
go without.

The boys were chatting too, quite shy at all the attention. One
man had drunk a little too much and was asking the boys if
they attended school at home. He explained to them, very
slowly and leaning precariously to one side, that here in South
Africa, you had to pay for education and he couldn't afford
to send his child to school. This made him very sad. He told
Callum time after time that he must study, he must get his
education, for learning was the future of the world. Slurred

words, but heartfelt sentiment.

These people had very little material items, yet were inwardly more content than most western people I had met in my life. We felt really welcome and there was so much laughter and warmth that day.

It came time for us to leave and dozens of people appeared. It felt like a continuation of the wonderful show we experienced earlier. They were singing so beautifully and there were people on stilts and young children dancing.

That evening we packed our bags ready for the following day. It was to be a 5am start travelling in a small coach all the way to Southern Mozambique. Christine and Ian opened the outdoor bar yet again and we spent a laughter-filled evening with them, their two daughters, Shellie and her partner. I discovered the most delicious drink, which was smooth and warmed the very depth of my belly. The bottle was covered with imitation leopard skin and I nicknamed it 'wee hairy thing' as I couldn't remember the name of the drink when I ordered.

This description sent us all into raucous laughter that evening, though we were barely drunk at all. Drunk on the excitement and atmosphere, and meeting my dear friend after such a long time. It had been two years since we had seen each other and this was a great opportunity to connect again.

The following morning we were up, showered and ready for the arrival of the coach. It was a long journey, interspersed with singing, food stops and comfort breaks. We were travelling to the Farazela Border Post at Kosi Bay. I had all sorts of magical ideas of what this border post might look like and when we finally arrived in the late afternoon it was an ordinary little building surrounded by miles of shrubbery and not a lot else.

We produced passports and visas and shortly afterwards the
4x4 vehicles arrived to transfer us to our accommodation.
The boys elected to go in the open top truck and travelled the
extremely rough track for the few miles to camp. It was an
exhilarating experience for them.

There wasn't room in the truck for everyone. Mum and
I chose the slightly more sedate and less bumpy 4x4 car,
along with Shellie. As we arrived, we were directed to our
accommodation, tented rooms on wooden stilts and wooden
walkways between. It was wonderful.

We immediately changed into swimming gear for our snorkel
test, which was to ensure that everyone was competent enough
to complete the swim with the dolphins the following day.
The water in the pool was really cold but it was good to be in
water and feel the weightlessness of my body after such a long
journey.

Glenn had elected to share my tent and Callum was in a
tent beside his Grandma, slightly further along the wooden
walkway. I had never stayed in tented accommodation quite
like this. There were wooden steps up to the room itself, which
had a small balcony. Inside there was a very large double bed
shrouded with mosquito netting and an en-suite bathroom with
toilet, washbasin and shower.

Glenn was fascinated. "It's a tent but not a tent," he said, his
eyes sparkling with excitement.

That first night we met Kurki, a wonderful woman who did all
the cooking for the guests. The dining and the lounging area

was set on a massive wooden platform overlooking the jungle. The Indian Ocean was just a few moments away and we could smell the salt in the air and hear the roar of the waves. By now it was dark, and I was longing to be closer to this ocean that I could hear and smell and I wanted to sink my feet deep into the sand.

The meal was wonderful and welcomed by my tired and hungry body. We all spent a little time in the lounging area that evening before retiring to bed. As I lay in bed that night, Glenn sound asleep and snoring gently, I could faintly hear the ocean. It was almost singing to me and I had already decided that I wanted to be up early to go for a walk along the beach before our dolphin swim.

I woke as the dawn broke. It was around 5.30am. I had slept really well. Glenn was still asleep. I quickly put on some clothes and quietly left the room and headed down to the beach. As I walked along the wooden planks of the walkway, the sound of the ocean got louder and louder.

As I walked between two huge sand hills on either side of me I was met by the most beautiful sight. The waves of the Indian Ocean were rolling in and crashing onto the sand. The sound was reverberating around my whole body. I looked around and all I could see, stretching for miles to either side of me was golden sand and sea. The sun was breaking through some early morning cloud and I walked down to the waters edge. The water was quite warm on my feet and I longed to go in.

I turned and went back to my room. Glenn met me as I opened the door. He had woken up and wondered where I was. I put on my bathing suit and he accompanied me back to the beach and waited while I took a short swim. The power of the water was immense and I was laughing out loud as I rolled and tumbled around in the surf.

It was a wonderfully invigorating start to the day. Glenn and I returned to our room, showered and got ready for the day. We ate a simple but filling breakfast and an hour later we headed along the beach with our masks, snorkels and flippers. My stomach was churning with excitement. I had no idea what to expect and the walk along the beach to the launch site was delightful in the morning sun.

At the site we were given instructions about the launch of the boat, how we would be sailing over a reef to get to the open ocean. I looked at the waves which were rolling in and wondered how we would ever maneouvre our way past them. We launched the boat with the whole group pushing it into the water off the shore. There were foot straps on the floor of the boat to slide your feet into and rope around the sides of the boat to hold onto. Once we were all secure and our gear safely strapped in, we set off. It was one of the most exhilarating rides I have experienced. We bounced our way through the waves and our Captain soon navigated us through the reef with experienced handling of the throttle and wheel.

We travelled at a fast pace along the length of the beach. Courtney, Nelia and the Captain searched for signs of dolphins. Suddenly fins appeared to one side of the boat. It was a pod of dolphins with two calves swimming alongside us. They swam beside us for a short while, the calves clearly visible beside the adult dolphins. We were told to prepare ourselves as we would be entering the water shortly.

My heart was pounding in my chest. A quick image from a scary shark film from my childhood, accompanied by the music, popped into my head and I dismissed it quickly. If there was something in the ocean ready to eat me, I don't suppose there was much I could do about it.

We were soon over the side, into the water and I could hear my heart pounding in my ears. This was part excitement, part sheer terror. I breathed through my snorkel deeply, slowing my breathing, and calming my heart rate. As I began to calm, I could hear the dolphin chatter through the water. My eyes filled with tears of joy at the sound. I hadn't spotted any dolphins yet, but I could hear them. That in itself was incredible.

I popped my head out of the water and looked around. Nelia was waving to me frantically and pointing, indicating for me to put my head down again. I did so and right at that moment three dolphins swam directly below me. I was ecstatic. I wanted to dive deep to see them more clearly, but in an instant they were gone again.

I looked up again and we were being called back to the boat. One by one we were collected and as I am rather short, this was a less than graceful scramble into the boat. Mum was sitting in the boat, tears running down her face. She had elected to stay in the boat and as we all entered the water, the dolphin calves had swum right past and had rolled right in front of her so she could see their bellies.

Apparently she instantly vomited over the side of the boat. This was unusual for Mum, as she never got seasick. My own stomach was flipping back and forth and I felt deeply nauseous. Within minutes I too was vomiting over the side of the boat, unable to stop myself. Not the result I had expected after my first dolphin encounter, but apparently this can be quite normal after such a deep connection to these incredible souls.

Part of me was mortified that I was being sick in front of all these people, yet I couldn't stop myself and just had to let it go. Within a few moments I had composed myself and we were back racing across the water, the dolphins had disappeared again.

In the distance, Nelia had spotted something else. It was a whale. I couldn't believe our luck. As we got closer we could see where the whale had surfaced, it's 'footprint' clearly visible on the surface of the water, like a very large, round pancake. We followed the whale for a little while, its back and fin appearing above the surface as it travelled at great speed through the water. Then, it too was gone.

We had been out in the boat for quite some time and we headed back to the launch site, skipping over the reef and beached the boat on the sand. I realized I could barely move my legs as we exited the boat. I felt wobbly and unsteady and again extremely nauseous. Nauseous but happy, if that's possible.

I could see Chris walking up the beach with Callum. That was the wonderful thing about the group, everyone was looking after each other. He was shivering all over after his experience and I discovered later that he had several dolphins swimming around him during his time in the water. They had been coming towards him at great speed, then veering around him, playing.

I began to understand the power of these creatures. Just being close to them, swimming in their space, we had been deeply affected by their high energy. We hadn't been close enough to touch any of them, yet their presence had triggered emotional healing. The healing we needed after these past years of heartache and pain. Others in the group were crying, their emotions unable to be tethered. This was good, it was the release which they needed to heal and move on.

We trekked back along the beach at a much slower pace this time. I couldn't move quickly, my body felt exhausted. Glenn had also had a wonderful experience in the water and was chatting to the other young boy in the group, Michael. He had come along with his mother and I was glad the boys had someone of a similar age to spend time with during this safari experience.

When we got back to our room, we showered and got dressed. I felt quite awful, queasy and wobbly all over. Callum was still quite shivery, though he wasn't cold. We all gathered in the lounge area and had a snack before having a rest period prior to the afternoon foot exercise.

I lay on my bed for a while, my head was spinning a little. However, I felt much better after a rest and we joined the group for a discussion, led by Chris. This was a really interesting gathering and we were tasked to draw a foot for the following day. We could pick whether it was to be a right or left foot, or both and draw it as an animal or whatever came to mind. Just allow ourselves to be guided and draw from our hearts and intuition.

We had a short break then, left the lounge area whilst it was set up for the next session and returned a little while later. The whole deck area was to be used with each of us lying in a circle with our heads on the inside of the circle and feet pointing outwards. We each made ourselves comfortable on pillows and cushions and covered ourselves with light blankets. We were about to experience a sound journey, facilitated by Nelia, Courtney and Carlos, a young man from Peru who was a crystal healer. The crystals he had with him were beautiful and he was an interesting man, with a gentle nature.

Nelia, Courtney and Carlos sat in the centre of the circle. There was a multitude of instruments laid around them. I understood this was to be some form of meditation, but I wasn't prepared for the profound experience I was about to have. I was settled beside Glenn on a comfortable cushion from the sofa, covered with a light blanket. We were asked to close our eyes and begin to breath slowly and deeply. The roar of the ocean was all around us in the silence and lying on the wooden decking I could feel the vibration of the waves pounding onto the beach.

Gentle soothing sounds began to play, all manner of instruments and the beautiful sounds of singing. My body was deeply relaxed, the sounds flowed into and around us and within minutes I began to see images playing in front of me. It was like watching a movie on a big screen, there was so much to take in and so fast.

I saw a Native American Indian and knew this to be my guide. I was told that he was my husband in a previous existence. I felt such overwhelming love inside me and he told me that he will return to love me unconditionally again. Tears began to well up in my eyes. Slowly they began to run down my face and into my ears as I lay there. I mopped them up with a sleeve. They weren't tears of sadness, but of immense joy and love.

Then I saw my Dad. He was dancing around a fire in a clearing, silly dancing the way only he did. He was celebrating and so happy. He told me that the knot that keeps appearing in the chain of my dowsing crystal (which it seemed to have done a lot recently) is because I am always in knots. He said that he has taken it for a little while so that I can start connecting on my own without relying on the crystal for answers to my questions. I had misplaced this crystal a couple of days before and hadn't yet found it.

The image changed again and I saw the most magnificent white unicorn with my guide on it's back. He beckoned to me and I climbed onto the back of the wonderful creature. I began to see this scene from a little further away and I realised that the woman on the back of the unicorn was also a Native American Indian. The woman was me. I was a Native American Indian. At that point we flew on the unicorn - above trees and water whilst all sorts of scenery unfolded beneath us.

Another scene began and this time I saw an Indian wedding. It seemed to be my wedding to my beloved. I could see my Dad there, dancing again and the love which enfolded me was almost too big for my body to hold.

As the sound journey came to a close, the tears were flowing down my face. What I had just seen was incredible. I hadn't seen anything like it before. I had no clue what it all meant, yet at the same time, I did know.

After the meditation, Carlos came to each person with a handful of quartz crystals. We each picked one from his hands and I gazed into mine. It felt really special. It felt like that whole sound journey experience was inside the crystal and I held it in my hand for hours afterwards.

That night we gathered around an open fire and Courtney showed us some simple drumming techniques on a Djembe. We sat for a long time drumming and having fun and in the darkness we could hear other drums from another camp somewhere nearby. I thoroughly enjoyed this, never having been much of a musician.

After an excellent sound sleep, we rose early the next morning for a second dolphin launch. There was no dolphin swim that day, we spent a long time looking but only saw dolphins in the distance.

I was finding the boat ride very nauseating. I had never been much of a sailor, and it was great as long as we were moving, but once the boat stopped and wallowed with the swell my stomach began to object. I felt very, very rough after this launch and lay on my bed for a while in the late morning.

An idea of what to draw for my foot picture came to me and I quickly drew it before I forgot. It was simple, yet I felt very connected to it. It was a simple outline of a foot in pink, there were no toes and I wrote the number '1' in the centre. From my perspective meaning 'at one' with myself, no separation.

I lay down again and drifted along on my thoughts. Suddenly I knew that Mum and I weren't to do the third and final launch tomorrow. I asked myself why, asking for guidance both from myself and any angelic presence who would like to help. I thought that perhaps my stomach was being spared the swells of the ocean. But there was much more to it. Instantly I realized this was the first step of letting the boys go. Letting them go in the sense of allowing them to spread their wings for themselves, in a group where we trusted them to be safe. A time for them to be who they were without their Mum or Grandma in their way.

I felt emotional at this thought, but knew it was time. It was a big step for me, after all that had happened, yet I felt comfortable with it. I suspected it would be easier for them than it would be for me.

We had some free time that day. I decided to take my small pocket kite down onto the beach for a while to fly it. It was a simple kite with no spars, the material pockets just filled up with air and it was easy and enjoyable to fly. It was exhilarating to fly my kite so close to such an incredible ocean. In my head, I was flying right up with the kite, soaring all over the sky. I was on my own on the beach, the sun was shining and warm on my skin. I could feel the freedom of the flight, my hands sensitive to the moves the kite needed to make in the wind high above me.

Suddenly I felt hands touch mine, yet when I quickly glanced down, there was nothing there. I relaxed again and felt the same feeling. I closed my eyes for an instant, breathed really slowly and deeply and instantly felt my Dad's presence behind me. I could feel his hands on mine, we were flying the kite together. I smiled and laughed openly. Again, grateful for this connection to him.

I paddled in the ocean after this, just enjoying some time to myself before joining Mum on a short trip to a local market. I found the most delightful hand carved left foot, made from a dark wood. It was around six inches long with a scooped out area where the ankle would have joined to the foot. It was a small trinket holder and I knew some of my crystals at home would fit nicely into it. I also splashed out and bought a brightly coloured wrap for myself as a reminder of our wonderful experience here.

Late that afternoon we sat in the lounge area as a group and shared our foot pictures one by one. We each described what our picture meant to us and then the members of the group commented on what they saw or felt about the picture.

It was an enlightening experience to hear other people's views on what was drawn and I was stunned at some of the insights my boys gave about the pictures they saw. They seemed to see straight through the drawings to the core of what was going on for the person who had drawn them, in a natural and easy way. I felt so proud of them, watching them opening their hearts to share their wisdom.

After our evening meal we adjourned to the open fire and drummed again for a while. It was light hearted and such fun. I spoke to Nelia about my decision not to go on the launch the following day. I explained my reasons why and she agreed I was doing the right thing. She assured me that the boys would be well looked after.

Glenn and I stayed by the fire once everyone had left. He wanted to sit awhile on our own, just watching the flames and glowing wood in the darkness of the night. Suddenly Glenn noticed a shape in the fire. One of the slender logs had burnt through and seemed to have formed the shape of a dolphin. We laughed at this poignant sight.

When we left the fire and returned to our room, it was very quiet. Glenn went into the bathroom to brush his teeth before bed as I knelt on the floor of the room sorting some clothes in my bag for the following day. I felt a change in the room, the presence of a large energy is the only way I can describe it.

I didn't say anything yet Glenn immediately returned to the room, feeling alarmed by the presence he had also felt. Glenn had told me weeks earlier that he sometimes saw a figure at his bedroom door which unnerved him a little. It was a dark figure which said nothing and only appeared when it was dark. I had told him that I felt it wasn't there to harm him and that we would work out between us why it was there and if it should be elsewhere.

This was the same figure he had seen at his bedroom door. He felt frightened and unsure. I asked him to ask the figure to leave, that we would deal with this another day. It was late and we had another early start in the morning. Suddenly the presence was gone. I said that we would talk to Shellie the next day to ask her advice and this made Glenn feel more secure.

We rose early the next day. I had slept really well and felt good about my decision not to go out on the launch that day. Carlos was at the launch site with all his crystals laid out on a table in the rest area. Mum and he got chatting and she ended up receiving her very own crystal workshop from him. She was fascinated at his knowledge and they shared a common bond through these magnificent crystals.

I helped to launch the boat and watched as it set off to sea, my heart aching as it sped off. I felt quite emotional and though in that instant I wished I was beside my boys, I knew it was the right choice to stay behind on shore.

It was a glorious day, really warm and I enjoyed the time waiting for the return of the boat. I left Mum with Carlos and sat on the upstairs decking next to the bar, soaking up the sun and enjoying the peace of this place. When the boat returned, the boys were delighted that they had seen more dolphins. Mum and I had seen whales following the boat again too. There had been no swim in the water, but they had a fantastic time regardless.

Later that morning, after a lovely breakfast, I had the opportunity to speak to Shellie about the figure who kept appearing to Glenn and tell her that we had a visit from it the previous night. I didn't feel that it was a threat in any way, but valued her insight into what it might be and why it was coming to him.

Glenn, meanwhile, was drawing a picture of this figure and when he showed it to Shellie she immediately felt that this was some kind of spirit guide. She explained to Glenn not to feel frightened. She advised him that the next time this figure appeared, to ask it (out loud or silently to himself) why it is here. If he doesn't get an answer or response, then he could ask that Archangel Michael assists the spirit to leave and go into the light.

Glenn was happy with this, these were things he could do and he felt much more comfortable. He also realized that no-one was laughing at him. This was real, not fantasy. He is a sensitive soul, like so many, who can feel the presence of spirits when they are around. This is perfectly normal for millions of people, most just don't openly talk about it much.

We packed our bags that day and left for Pongola Game Reserve. It wasn't too far away and the weather deteriorated as we drove. It was overcast and chilly when we arrived. We were shown our sleeping quarters, comfortable wooden lodge rooms overlooking the lake and reserve. It was lovely.

Soon after we arrived we were taken on a boat ride on the lake. There were hippos and rhinos everywhere and we managed to get very close to the hippos which were basking in the water with their snouts just visible.

That evening we dined well, the food was excellent and the boys discovered there was a very large television in an area off the dining room.

The following morning, very early, we went on a small game walk with two rangers guiding us. The boys were fascinated by the bugs they found and the rangers enthusiastically explained what their purpose was in the chain of life in the bush. We ate a hearty breakfast on our return to the lodge and had a little free time before setting off in two 4x4 vehicles.

We saw a multitude of animals, including a giraffe who stopped right in front of us for about half an hour. It wouldn't move and we stayed quietly in the vehicles just watching it and the other animals nearby until it decided it was time to move on. The sun was setting as we neared the lodge, the sky a wonderful bright pink.

After this game drive a poem came into my head. A poem about the sound journey we had experienced. I wrote it down, copied it out and gave the copy to Nelia to share with Courtney and Carlos, as they had each inspired the words. The experience of the sound journey had affected me deeply and I somehow knew that I had changed inside because of it.

Sound Journey

Drums and singing
All different sounds
Gentle and subtle
Vibrating my soul.

Beautiful singing
Touching my core
Wistful and delicate
Making tears flow.

My journey is long
Through many lifetimes
Magical and glorious
More tears flow!

Indians dancing –
A marriage I see;
My guide was my husband –
Many years ago.

On a white winged unicorn
With love we ride.
Radiance, brilliance emanates all around
Such beauty and grace - my heart soars.

Many messages he has
For me to pass on.
To trust and to honour
That these are true.

A message for me
(I can't quite believe)
Once was my husband
And vows to be so again....

The journey is over
I feel great beauty inside.
My heart is so full
I feel truly blessed.
Thanks to the sounds
Heaven has sent.

Inspired by Carlos, Nelia and Courtney –
Mozambique Oct 2005

I was quite surprised with myself. I hadn't shared any of my poetry with anyone and felt quite shy at handing this over to Nelia. I thought that she might think it was rubbish. However once she read it, her face lit up and she gave me a big hug and she promised to share it with Courtney and Carlos when she met them the following week.

As we ate our evening meal that night, we were gifted the sight of a thunder and lightening storm in the distance. I say gifted, because the lightening was pink, not white or blue-white. I hadn't seen such a beautiful sight as this pink light flashed across the sky and down to the earth. It lasted for around thirty minutes and I was enthralled with the shapes and patterns this storm was making in the sky.

During our stay at the game reserve, Shellie expressed her desire to come to the UK to teach the Raindrop Technique and asked if I would organize a venue and advertise it for her. I was really taken aback and didn't feel at all confident about it. However, I agreed and we arranged a few dates for 2006, and I said I would look into venues when I returned home to the UK.

Part of me was excited, I would be assisting Shellie with these workshops and was eager to learn more from her. The other smaller part didn't truly believe that I was capable of organizing this for her, but I was determined to help her teach more people and share this wonderful technique and her other knowledge with as many people as possible.

I awoke early the following morning and sat out on the verandah, sipping coffee and listening to the wildlife as it began to stir in the early morning sun. We breakfasted and left the game reserve, heading back to Johannesburg for the last stop of our journey, the Lanseria Lion Park. It was a long journey and by the time we arrived at the Lion Park I was over tired and grumpy.

Our accommodation was basic and very different to the welcome we had received in Mozambique and the Pongola Game Reserve. I think it would have been okay if we all hadn't been so tired, but our nerves had become a little frayed. It had been an intense week, emotions had risen to the surface to be healed and some people were feeling very raw.

We went to bed very early that night, our tented accommodation was right in the central compound of the Lion Park. As I lay on the camp bed, I heard the lions roaring really loudly all around. They felt so close, almost inside the tent.

For some reason I began to laugh, very quietly, to myself. I had no idea why. I really wanted to cry but as the lions roared, my body was shaking with the laughter which was welling up inside me. I eventually drifted off to sleep, so exhausted that I was glad it was to be our last day tomorrow.

I was awake early again the next morning in time to watch the most beautiful sunrise. When we arrived the previous evening it had been dark so we couldn't see anything outside the wooden fencing of the compound. It turned out there were animals all around us, birds, an ostrich and some impala, grazing on the grass nearby.

As I headed to the shower block for a shower, I realized that a small giraffe had got into our compound. It was absolutely beautiful. Apparently her name was Purdey and she had a knack of being able to get into the compound through the main gateway.

Shellies partner Alan spent a long time enticing Purdey out of the compound, he tried using a banana and other bits of fruit, but she wasn't interested. He grabbed a slice of bread from the table and held it out under her nose. Her eyes lit up and she began to stick out her tongue to take the bread.

The group members who were awake were rolling about with laughter, of all the things she could be enticed with she fancied a slice of white bread. Alan received a round of applause when Purdey finally stepped through the compound gateway and he shut it behind her and locked it again. It was a fun way to greet the morning and lifted my spirits no end.

After breakfast we met our facilitator for the day, a young woman called Gail. Her eyes were incredible. Vibrant pools of colour which drew you deep inside. She had been doing project work with the white lions for a long time, working with children with all sorts of physical and emotional difficulties. When these children connected with the white lions, their ailments and emotional difficulties improved. They were healing just by being close to these lions.

As she explained more about her work, I was fascinated by her story. She had been around lions all of her life and her passion and love for them was obvious. I was so excited that we had this opportunity to visit them.

She chatted for a little while, asking us if we had particular things about our lives or within us which we wanted to heal or move past with the help of these lions. This question had been posed to us the day before and for the life of me I hadn't come up with anything concrete. I had begun to have a niggling ache at the base of my skull, nothing too painful, but I was aware that the area felt strange.

She went around the group, one by one, listening to what people were requesting to be addressed. I was honest and openly admitted that I hadn't come up with anything in particular. I said that I felt I had done enough personal work to enable me to be open to whatever was to heal or happen for me.

Gail looked at me and said she could see that I had done a great deal of personal work, I presumed she could perhaps see my aura or somehow just knew. She explained that she could see my dolphin guide. He had his snout nestled into the nape of my neck, at the base of my skull. Apparently she could see it quite clearly.

I was astonished. I didn't even know I had a dolphin guide. Suddenly I realized that the feeling I had at the base of my skull was this dolphin. The same feeling I had experienced years ago during my 'depression' though less intense now than it had been then.

Slowly, my brain put some pieces together and I understood that although this strange feeling had been very uncomfortable at the time, my dolphin guide was assisting me somehow during that time of my life. With this realization, tears welled up in my eyes. I looked at Mum and her eyes were also brimming with tears.

We departed not long after this in a large truck with seats in the back and wire mesh around the sides. It was a glorious day and getting hotter as each hour passed. The lions were beautiful. There were quite a few cubs with the female lions and they were basking in the sun and rolling in the dust. Our last meeting was with a male white lion.

When I saw him I had to catch my breath. He was magnificent. Proud, yet playful. Gail had said to us earlier that if we wanted a really good picture of the lions, we were to ask them in our heads. I looked at the lion and asked him if he would pose for some pictures for me so that I could capture his magnificence. At that moment he turned and stared.

It was as if he was looking straight into my soul. I felt like I had been punched in the centre of my chest and solar plexus, I could hardly breathe. Tears began to roll down my face. I wasn't sad. I was filled with the most intensely huge love. I felt I couldn't hold any more of this love, it felt so enormous. I turned to my Mum and she too was affected, with tears rolling down her face.

We couldn't speak, we were so overwhelmed. This was an experience I hadn't expected at all. I took several photographs of this beautiful creature, one of which I still have as a screen saver on my computer. Every time I look at it, I am filled with love and remember our connection that day.

We spent a couple of hours journeying around the lion park. We were given the opportunity to walk around and see the other animals. One of these opportunities was to go into an enclosure with two baby white lions. Only four people were allowed in at any time, so that these babies weren't overwhelmed.

When it came to my turn to enter the enclosure I was bubbling inside with excitement. I slowly sat beside one of the lions, who promptly laid his head on my shoe and looked up at me. I put my hand down to stroke him and he nuzzled at my hand.

Then, ever so gently, he took my little finger between his teeth. There was no pressure to his bite at all and he held my gaze.

Each time I tried to pull away, he wouldn't let go. We sat like this for many minutes and I felt so blessed for this meeting. Eventually he opened his mouth a little and released my hand. There was the smallest indentation in my finger, nothing more. He could have quite easily bitten much harder and done some real damage, but that hadn't been his intent at all. I felt that meeting with the baby lion was very special. I could have scooped him up in my arms and taken him home, he was so gorgeous.

After this I joined Glenn. He was on a large wooden platform area looking at the giraffes. He wanted to feed one, so we bought some food at the shop and returned to the platform. One of the giraffes came over as it saw the bag and Glenn offered it some food. The giraffes tongue stretched out for the food and it nearly wound around Glenn's arm it was so long. We laughed loudly as the giraffes tongue licked up and down his arm looking for more.

After the trip around the park, we returned to the accommodation to collect our bags. Gail asked us how we had enjoyed our time there and we all agreed that it had been an incredible experience. She asked us if anyone knew what a lion's roar represented. I recalled the previous night when the lion roared and I couldn't help laughing.

I volunteered the response, "Laughter?" and she said, "Yes, that's what it is."

We were asked to lie down on the ground, one person at a time. The first person lay down and the next person then lay with their head on the previous person's abdomen. We set ourselves out like this till we were all laid out in a wiggly line. The first person was asked to laugh and as she did so, her abdomen bobbed up and down. The persons head on her abdomen bobbed up and down, which made that person laugh, which made her abdomen bob up and down, then the next person's head bobbed up and down, which made them laugh and so on until the whole line was laughing............

It was an extremely amusing experience and a great way to end the trip. A reminder to take life less seriously and enjoy every moment. That lesson I certainly understood.

Life is too short. Every moment is precious. Wasting precious time on emotions which are damaging you inside can be much better spent on healing old wounds and hurts and moving on into a happier, more contented space inside.

I felt that I had somehow managed to release old parts of me which weren't very beneficial to me any more. Parts which I had held onto for a very long time and which were preventing me from being a stronger and happier person inside. I felt happy.

Chapter Nine

We returned to the UK refreshed and recharged. The students at my evening classes saw a huge difference in me after the trip to South Africa. I didn't appreciate how different I was, though I felt more peaceful.

Once we returned it was many weeks before Glenn asked me to help him 'talk' to his guide. He hadn't seen him since we had been in South Africa and he felt he needed to find out a few things about who the guide was and what he was here to do.

We sat quietly, Glenn closed his eyes and we asked if the guide would come forward. Nothing happened. We waited and waited, but we felt nothing in the room. We weren't sure why, but it seemed like Glenn's guide had gone.

Suddenly I had an idea and I closed his bedroom curtains so that the room was darker. Within minutes Glenn could feel his guide's presence. Glenn wasn't too sure about using the dowsing crystal, so I held it between my finger and thumb and tested out which was the 'yes' rotation and which was the 'no' rotation. Glenn asked questions and the dowsing crystal would rotate one direction or the other to give us the answer. This can be a very laborious task, as you can only receive a 'yes', 'no' or 'maybe' reply, so questions need to worded carefully.

After quite a while, we had built up a picture of what this guide was here to do. He came to Glenn only when it was dark. Apparently as a young boy, he had been afraid of the dark, just as Glenn had been. He came to Glenn in the darkness to help Glenn get over his fear. He was also here to assist Glenn and protect him and all Glenn needed to do was ask for him and he would be right there beside him. We even managed to figure out the guide's name eventually.

Glenn was delighted with the information we had been able to piece together and was much more settled after this. I was happy that I had been able to help him and let him see that this type of contact was normal. It was still quite new to me and I was literally stumbling my way around. I knew that my sons were helping me to trust in these experiences simply by them having them in their lives. I had no choice but to go with the flow and we were supporting each other through this learning.

I had become more interested in clairvoyance and crystals and was much more open to trying new things and listening to new ideas. My friend Ann wanted to go to a Health Fair in town and asked me to go with her. On the programme there was a variety of talks and I felt drawn to going along to the talk which was being given by a crystal healer. I was becoming more interested in the healing properties of crystals and had used some during sessions on clients, so felt that this talk would prove valuable.

Ann and I went to the health fair on Saturday 1 April with the full intention of attending the crystal talk. However, I met Elma there. She had been one of my Dad's colleagues during the Reflexology course. I knew her slightly and liked her very much. After speaking to Elma for a few minutes, I was drawn to go to her talk instead. Her talk was to be about Native American drumming, some rather special scents and dragons.

Elma's husband had died some years ago, they hadn't been married that long. After he died, she had spent time travelling and was in America horse riding when she fell and broke her back. She was fortunate to have a medical team appraise her very quickly and a titanium plate was used to help repair the damage.

During her recovery she got to know a Native American Indian who welcomed her into his group and where she felt very much at home amongst them. They showed Elma how to drum during the time she spent with them. She was deeply honoured and humbled by their actions and kindness during her recovery.

Her talk was certainly very interesting. There were around twenty-five people in the small room. Elma guided us through a short meditation to introduce us to dragon energy. During this meditation, instead of the pink fluffy dragon she was guiding in, I saw a red one. I thought it was purely my imagination. After the meditation she asked if anyone wanted to take part in a little demonstration.

During this demonstration, she would bring in dragon energy and allow the participant to connect with this dragon energy under her guidance. I was intrigued but sceptical. I trusted Elma, of that there was no doubt, yet I wasn't sure about this.

My arm suddenly seemed to rise up from my side and before I knew it, my hand was up as a 'volunteer'. I can remember looking at my arm as if it didn't belong to me and wondering what on earth it was doing in the air. Elma was delighted that she would be working with someone she knew and I found myself being 'selected' to take part.

At first I felt very silly standing in front of the audience.
My friend Ann was in the audience and I focused on Elma
and trusted all would be well. She asked me to select an
essence, which I did. It was pale pink and had a divine aroma.
Apparently, this would bring in a pink, fluffy dragon and I
couldn't wait to see.

So there I stood, in front of a room full of strangers, whilst
Elma guided me to take deep breaths, close my eyes and invite
the dragon in. At first I wasn't sure what I could see. Then, still
with my eyes closed, I saw a small form appear from the top
left corner of the room, flying in very gracefully. Not a pink,
fluffy dragon that I had been promised but the red one who had
briefly appeared to me minutes before. Elma guided him beside
me and then asked if I could see him.

"Oh yes!" I said. "I can see him – I can FEEL him!" His energy
was very distinctive and strong.

She asked if I felt comfortable with the idea for his energy to
merge with mine. I wasn't sure about this. What did that mean
exactly? Again, though, I trusted and agreed.

I didn't feel hugely different as he merged with me, nothing I
could even begin to describe, just different. She asked me to
'look' behind me to see if could see his tail. Indeed I could. I
had a tail. It was vibrant red with golden coloured triangular
lumps down its length and a golden spear shaped tip.

Oh, wow! I could feel the most incredible and immense love
fill me, my body tingling. My eyes were filling with tears of
absolute joy and gratitude. This was an amazing experience.

After a few moments, Elma asked me to open my eyes very gently and describe what I could see, if anything.

I opened my eyes slowly, thinking wildly, "Oh, what am I going to see?!"

As I opened my eyes, I realised I was seeing almost through an opaque film. It was a little like how a fly sees, with multitudes of images, but not quite the same. It was bizarre. Gradually this gave way to 'normal' eyesight and I could see my friend sitting in the back row, her eyes wide. I was then directed to close my eyes and let him go. I was reluctant, I was enjoying this but I let him go and watched him fly up towards the corner of the room and he was gone.

As I took my seat beside Ann, she quickly whispered to me that she had seen my red snout. I couldn't believe it. Thank goodness she was there. Ann was able to see auras and energy with her eyes open and after such a strange experience I was beginning to think I must have been dreaming.

When I spoke to Elma later, she explained that she thought the red of the dragon was to do with some anger I was possibly holding on to. "Fair enough", I thought. I could understand that. However, I was soon to discover that his red was nothing to do with anger, but about his power and strength. It was such an awesome experience and at that stage I had no clue what was going to happen within just a few short weeks.

On occasions I had been very fortunate to have had a unicorn come in to work with me whilst treating a client. I was able to see its magnificent white form very clearly and watch as it directed the pure unicorn energy to a client to aid healing. Until that time I hadn't seen a dragon and didn't know very much about them at all.

Twice over the following weeks I was aware that Red Dragon (as I now called him) was around. I wasn't sure what he was doing or perhaps asking me to do, but I sensed that he was assisting with the healing I was doing. My world had been turned upside down since connecting with this red dragon. All sorts of doubts had emerged, doubts about my own sanity at times, let alone anything else, yet I wasn't in the least bit frightened.

Not long after having Red Dragon come into my life I visited a friend. Her dog, Mavis, had fallen ill. I worked on Mavis with an essential oil blend called Joy. She wouldn't allow me to work on her paws, as I had planned to do a little Reflexology. I rubbed a single drop of Joy oil on my hands, I stroked and gently massaged her back, opened my heart to her and told her everything would be fine.

Where these words came from I'm not sure and what would be fine, I had no idea, the words just flowing from my mouth without having come from my brain, as so often happened these days. She left the room fifteen minutes later. Her owner called me that evening to say that Mavis had started convulsing three hours later, was rushed to the vet, who had diagnosed diabetes. Her blood glucose levels were extremely high. She was given insulin and allowed home with an appointment for the following day.

Mavis was back and forward to the vet for days, having seizures and her blood sugar levels were unstable. Mavis would come to her owner each time she was about to have a seizure and receive all the love in the world whilst convulsing. I wasn't convinced Mavis had diabetes. I had been constantly drawn to her head area when I was with her. Sadly, it was discovered that Mavis had a brain tumour and she passed away a few days later.

I was devastated at the news, her owner bereft, but thanking me for helping. She felt that without me working with Mavis, her diagnosis would have been more prolonged, as would her pain. Until I worked on Mavis her symptoms had been confusing and there was no conclusive diagnosis. I cried at the news and felt a little guilty that I had perhaps accelerated her demise, yet knowing I had been there to work with her.

I had a class to teach that night and knew my youngest son would also be devastated by her death, as he had had a very special bond with Mavis from their very first meeting. So I headed home at the end of my working afternoon, dreading the prospect of seeing him. He was very quiet when I broke the news about Mavis and clearly upset.

I headed off to my evening class as usual, my mind still numb. It was a fabulous class that night. We worked in silence and very slowly. Everyone was clearly giving from their hearts. I was offered a treatment myself from a lovely woman on the course. Her treatment was very gentle and soothing, superb to receive. I really needed it after the events of the day.

Nearing the end of it, Red Dragon appeared with Mavis. There was so little time and I thought she was there because I had been thinking about her all day. In my head, I asked if she could come back later that night when I had more time to spend with her. Off she went and I wasn't even sure if she would come back. It was a little unnerving, but I felt strongly that she had come back for a reason.

At home later that night, I sat down in my room to meditate for a few minutes. But it felt wrong that I do it there. It wasn't right. So I went into the garden with a big candle, which I lit and placed on the step in front of the garden seat. Within moments of sitting down, in came Red Dragon with Mavis suspended in the air beneath his wing, nothing attaching her to him, just there.

She offered me her front paws to work, which I did and then she offered me her back paws. My eyes were closed in the darkness. I felt that I was to speed up as there wasn't much time, though I didn't know why. I felt a bit silly, my hands working on 'invisible' paws - an 'invisible' dog - but I carried on, knowing somehow that it was vitally important.

When I was finished, Mavis laid her head on my lap for me to lay my hands on her head. I could really feel the slight weight from her head on my knee. It was then that I started to tremble. At first I thought it was the cool night air, but I could hear Red Dragon tell me to 'hold on', he would show me what to do.

The energy flowing through me was intense. I have no idea how long I sat there. It felt like hours, yet was possibly only a few minutes. Then she was all done, session complete. I blessed her for coming back.

With my eyes still closed I then realised that there in front of me was a small queue of cats we had previously owned and who had all passed away. After Mavis there was Solo, a cat we had cherished in our family and who died around ten years ago. I was guided to work on his liver and kidney area. Abi then followed on and lastly there was dear Kassi. She needed her shoulder area worked. I could also make out a black cat in the background, but it didn't come forward.

By this time my whole body was trembling with the immensity of the energy flowing through me. This was what Red Dragon was speaking to me about. No wonder he had said to 'hold on'.

It was totally mind blowing, I could barely take it all in.

They left as quickly as they had arrived, all the little creatures just hanging in the air beneath the wings of my red dragon guide. It was like he was nurturing them there and carrying them home after their healing.

I was left wondering, was this a dream? Was I hallucinating? Had it really just happened? There were so many questions, so many thoughts in my mind. I could barely think straight.

The next morning I told my Mum and my sons what had happened the previous evening. There was no disbelief, just acceptance that it had happened exactly as I explained it. During that day I decided to have a reading done. I needed confirmation of what had happened last night and hoped that some sense could be made of it all.

When I saw Lynn, my friend and psychic, the confirmation came through, but so did much, much more.

I was told that, "Red Dragon is here to assist you help others to ascend. Not death necessarily, but ascend here on earth from one vibration to another and also for those already on the other side to ascend to their next level. You were chosen to work with him. Few have the strength to work with him because of his immense power. He will be bringing in more animals for you."

I was astounded. What I had seen was exactly as Lynn was

describing to me. I was exhausted after the healing session with Red Dragon and her reading. It was so much to take in. So much for me to accept. So much for me to believe. Yet there seemed little doubt.

I had been chosen by this red dragon to help. I wondered if I pretended not to see him, pretended everything was the same as it had been before our connection I could perhaps return to some kind of 'normality'.

Lynn laughed when I said this to her. She explained that I was here to do special things. Each one of us is, in our own way. I had chosen to do this work long before I arrived as a human and that it was part of my divine purpose here.

My mind was reeling, I thanked her for her time. I had a lot to process. After the years of self doubt, this was a lot to take in and a lot for me to be able to accept. Yet these kinds of messages were coming to me more often.

A few days later, I was travelling in the lift at my workplace when suddenly I felt a presence in the lift with me. This wasn't unusual. The building was very old and many elderly people had died in the hospital wards over the years.

I closed my eyes and could see a small pink pig. I laughed out loud, thankfully on my own in the lift. I explained that it was a very short journey to the floor I needed to get off at and that this 'healing' would need to be very quick. I sensed an acknowledgement and filled myself with pure love for the little pig.

In an instant it was gone. The doors of the lift opened and as I walked to my office I wondered why a pig of all things would come to me in the lift at work.

Mum and I had a good laugh about it later when I told her and I never did find out about that pig....................

Chapter Ten

So life continued on. The boys were settled in school and doing really well. Mum was enjoying her home and arranging the garden, filling it with new plants and creating a comfortable space for us to be in.

I had an occasional client and was still enjoying my teaching immensely. I worked with Red Dragon more often and found that when he was assisting me during treatment sessions, my body was much more able to handle the energy passing through me. I was becoming used to this level of energy and for that I was very grateful. In the early stages of working and connecting with him I was physically exhausted afterwards, but not now. He was a part of my life.

As we learned how to work with each other he changed colour. At first he came to me one evening still red in colour but with black spots all over him. At first I thought he must be ill but when I checked in with him he explained that he was changing. He was mirroring my change.

He was gradually turning into a black dragon, a deep violet black. He shimmered when I looked at him and it took a while for me to realise that we were developing together, supporting each other as we grew together spiritually.

During this period of my life I kept most of my 'spirit' experiences to myself. I spoke about them to only a few people. People I knew who understood and didn't look at me as if I was mad. They too had experiences with 'spirit' and it was so good to be able to talk freely.

After Glenn and I had connected with his guide and discovered his name I was inspired to do the same to find out my guide's name. I had just referred to him for so long as my Indian guide and felt it was time that I knew his name.

Using the dowsing crystal had worked really well for Glenn, so I decided to use it to try to figure out my guide's name. So I sat down one day in my treatment room with some gentle music playing and meditated for a little while. I then began to ask questions.

I asked if it was time for me to know my guide's name and received a 'yes'. I asked what the first letter of his name was 'F' came to me.

"Okay," I thought. "That's a good start."

So from there I began to go through the alphabet for the next letter. The first word was 'Flies'.

"That's not terribly inspiring", I thought. I wrote it down on the pad beside me and asked if there was more, "Yes". And so it continued. The next word was 'with'.

I thought that was a bizarre second name and couldn't think what this could be. So I closed my eyes and asked for some guidance. Perhaps an image or the rest of the name. Or perhaps I was wrong and hadn't asked correctly, but this felt correct.

Suddenly I saw my guide flying on the unicorn and it suddenly struck me. I asked if his name was 'Flies with Unicorn'? "No". I was a little bemused. I had just been shown this and yet that wasn't his name. What else could I ask? Then it began to dawn on me that the unicorn is a horse, so asked if his other name was 'horse'?

"No".

This was becoming silly and I began to feel like I was being ridiculed. I took a deep breath and I checked again that his name began with 'Flies with'.

"Yes".

So I relaxed again and closed my eyes. Suddenly the word 'pony' sprung into my head and I asked if this was the other part of his name?

"Yes".

Wow, could this be it? Could this be his name? So I asked again, "Is my guide's name Flies with Pony?"

A resounding "Yes".

The dowsing crystal was circling wildly in fact, almost like it was shouting at me "of course that's his name!!!"

I was elated. Finally I had a name. At first it didn't seem that impressive to me but of course this was the English translation of a Native American Indian word. Goodness knows what that might be. Even if I did find out, I was doubtful I would be able to pronounce it anyway, so I was more than content with 'Flies with Pony'.

I shared this with Mum and she thought it was lovely. I had his framed picture hanging on my treatment room wall and apparently she often 'chatted' to him when she was in the room, so she was also delighted that she could address him using his name.

Since then this has sometimes been shortened to 'FP'. After finding out his name, I felt much closer to him in a way. I felt that with each step like this I was becoming a little more complete somehow, although that feeling didn't make much sense to me at the time.

Shellie contacted me that year and visited from America to train people in the Raindrop Technique, Tibetan Reflexology, Pet Reflexology and Chakra healing. I helped her organise the workshops and I was blessed to be learning so much from a very gifted woman.

After the workshops were all complete, she explained to me that she wanted me to start teaching the Raindrop Technique and Tibetan Reflexology. She felt that I was more than capable. She had observed me during these workshops when I was assisting others and answering questions when she was busy with another student.

I hadn't expected this. Teaching the community education classes was one thing. This was quite another. Yet she had great confidence in me, more than I had in myself. I finally agreed. I loved the techniques and my enthusiasm made it easier for me to share with others.

I organised a few small workshops. The first one was so nerve wracking. Yet it felt great. A strange thing happened after the workshop was over. I was packing all the equipment into my car and had returned to the room I had hired to collect the last few items. As I walked out into the car park, the sole of my right shoe, which had been fine, flew off and landed in front of me.

I stopped and stared at the sole. I knew what this meant instantly. It was my right foot, indicating the past. My past 'soul' had left. A part of the old 'me' was gone. I burst out laughing. What an interesting thing to have happened.

I emailed Chris and Shellie later that night and told them what had happened. When they replied, I could almost hear the peels of laughter coming out of the emails. They too knew what this meant and were rejoicing at this huge step forward for me.

The smaller house we had moved into had provided the chance for us to get back on our feet financially, but with two growing boys and a plan in my mind to begin offering small workshops from my own space, I knew it was time to look for a slightly larger home.

Trying to organise venue space was becoming a challenge and the thought of having a space at home large enough to have a small group of 5 or 6 people for a workshop was very appealing. I wouldn't have any outlay if a workshop didn't run and I felt very enthusiastic at the prospect of not having to lug around vast quantities of equipment. The house just wasn't right for us any more.

So I began to look around at property in the local area. I was mindful that I wanted as little disruption as possible for the boys, so a house within their school area was important.

At this stage, I had no idea how I would afford a bigger house. It all seemed such a crazy idea, yet felt right. This strange optimistic drive was appearing in my life again and a deep sense that everything would somehow work out.

I had sleepless nights, convinced I was either losing the plot or just plain stupid. I had seen a house and decided to view it. It didn't look anything special, yet I was drawn to it. So I took Mum along one Sunday afternoon. It was an interesting house, it seemed smaller on the outside than it was on the inside. There were enough rooms for everyone, plus a treatment room big enough to use as a small training room.

Upon entering this room, the top of my head (my crown chakra) started to buzz and my ears began to ring. I didn't hear a word the woman was saying to us, I couldn't quite grasp what was happening.

I spoke with Lynn about what I had experienced whilst viewing the house and she said that my guides were almost shouting at her that we needed to do this. This house was definitely for us and that the buzzing on the top of my head was my crown chakra opening very wide connecting to Source, a sign that this place was very special for us.

She suggested that I ask Dad to look after this house and protect it till we got the mortgage arranged. I did just that and asked all my guides, including my dragon, to protect the house so that if it was meant to be, it would be ours.

I had finally been given the name of 'Red Dragon' after

much searching. His name was Dominic. I don't know what I expected it to be, perhaps something a little more exotic or grand, but Dominic suited him well enough.

When I checked in one evening, I could see Dominic lying on the roof of the house. He was lying on his front along the roofline. I was in hysterics. Somehow I conjured up the courage and took the leap of faith, secured a mortgage and made an offer on the house.

Within a few days my offer was accepted. I couldn't believe it. I was excited and petrified, all at the same time. When I got the news that I had been successful, I rang Lynn. She told me that Dad had already paid her a visit that morning and told her we had got the house. She knew even before I had received the news myself from my solicitor. This kind of thing never ceased to amaze me.

So in September 2007, the day after what would have been Mum and Dad's wedding anniversary, we moved into our new home. The boys hadn't even viewed the house, trusting us enough that it would be great. When they arrived at their new home from school that day, I was delighted to see their faces light up as they looked around.

In my heart I knew I had made the right decision. Not long after this move, Shellie asked me to arrange some venues for her to come to Edinburgh to offer some workshops. This time she was offering Reiki workshops, as well as a very fast type of energy which had been gifted to her through some form of direct initiation. I didn't really understand the details of what she was talking about, but was more than happy to arrange venues to facilitate these workshops.

She also explained that she was now using her real name, Kiannaa instead of the nickname I had known her by. It was strange to be calling her by another name, but she had grown spiritually and she felt it was more appropriate to use that name instead of Shellie.

There was much interest in what she was offering and I was really excited at the prospect of her coming again so soon. She had already explained to me that she was going to attune me to Third Degree Reiki (Master), which I was over the moon about, though had slight reservations without knowing what my reservations were.

Kiannaa set aside some time to attune me to Reiki Master degree. I was a little nervous beforehand and realized that I had doubts. I was doubting that I deserved this next step. I spent a few minutes in the garden alone, searching my heart why I had these doubts. Gradually I felt ready.

"I do deserve this gift", I said to myself. I think that I was perhaps more excited than nervous. The excitement of knowing there were great changes ahead.

I returned to the room, sat down and closed my eyes. At first, as Kiannaa worked, I could see beautiful purples playing in front of my eyes. I felt filled with a great love - for myself, the planet, humankind and the universe.

I became aware that my guides were there in front of me, along with those who have helped me along the way – 'Flies with Pony'; my dolphin guide; Dominic (who tells me that he is no longer black - he is any colour I wish him to be. I wondered when that had happened, he'd kept it very quiet); the Oriental boy I had seen in a previous Reiki attunement, older than he was when I last saw him (from this vision I am told that I am growing and evolving. As I grow spiritually, he also ages); the white lion from South Africa and of course Dad.

By this time I was unaware of what Kiannaa was doing around me, I was so focused on these images. The next moment I felt the right side of my head become very large. This wasn't a vision, it was a sensation, a physical feeling. Then my right ear, still attached to my head, felt like it moved very quickly across the room and back again. It was a very peculiar feeling.

My dolphin guide left the group and flew off to my right and behind me. He placed his snout into the base of my skull, I could feel the physical moment of connection. Suddenly he began to rotate. This was new.

Next I saw Native American Indians and others around the fire dancing, celebrating. I saw myself standing in the fire, but couldn't feel any heat. As I raised my arms to each side, I could see the most beautiful feathers underneath. Flames burst from the feathers and I was propelled upwards. I was flying.

The attunement was so beautiful that I was lost for words afterwards.

That night I barely slept, I could feel energy coursing throughout my whole body and I felt so happy inside. The following morning I was up very early, helping Kiannaa gather all the handout material ready for the first day. We packed the car and set off for the workshop venue.

Before we even began to attune the students at the start of the day, I could sense all their guides and angels gathering. When I closed my eyes and focused on the room I became aware that there were so many non-physical Angelic beings that they couldn't all fit in the room. I could see them hovering outside the windows waiting to help and guide us all. It was a wonderful feeling knowing they had gathered for the start of this special course.

During a treatment I received on the first day, I was very deeply relaxed, really far away. I could see a winged horse which turned to fire and then saw the most amazing coloured skies. It felt so peaceful that I didn't want to come back from wherever I was.

On the second day all the students were learning how to do a distant healing on someone. They all had their distant healing 'subjects' arranged for a set time and everyone sat down and focused on their task. During this time I felt beautiful energy in the room as everyone worked silently.

When I finished my distant healing I focused my attention on the room. The energy was incredible in its magnitude and love. With my eyes closed I could see columns of light emanating from the top of each of the students heads. It was an incredible sight.

The last day, our fourth day of intense long days of energy work, was a special day where we would be attuned to the energy Kiannaa had been gifted. I didn't think I could possibly buzz any more. My palms were burning hot with energy, not painful but hot and with a 'full' feeling. They weren't hot to the touch but I could feel the energy surging through them.

When I looked at my palms with my eyes closed I could see white light shining through them. I felt like a small child as I gazed at them in wonderment.

During the attunement, I had the most incredible experience. This is what I wrote afterwards:

"I am flying, almost floating up a tube of some kind. It is circular with different coloured lights shining through it. Rainbow colours. The material the tube is made from seems vaguely familiar and looks identical to Moldavite crystal, only a see-through white instead of green.

I come to a chamber, round and lit with gentle lighting. White light shines through the walls and there are seats, like in an ancient amphitheatre. I am aware people are all around on the seats, but just light, I can't see any physical form.

A bright multi-coloured robe is placed on my shoulders. It is flowing and feels wonderful, all the way down to my feet. People are celebrating and I am given a goblet to drink from. As I watch this unfolding before my eyes, I wonder if this is a ceremony. That's what it feels like.

I don't want to come back from this place, it is strange but also seems familiar."

A few days later Kiannaa was teaching a 'Language of the Feet' workshop to a group. I was looking forward to it. I had attended a few of Chris Stormers workshops and knew that Kiannaa had been taught by Chris, but she had added other aspects of her own too.

Kiannaa asked me to sit down in one of the reclining Reflexology chairs so that people could look at my feet. She wanted the students to use their instinct whilst looking at my feet and see what they came up with.

Someone asked, "What's that?" pointing at one of my feet.

Kiannaa replied, "It's her Star, the planet where she's from. She's a Star person."

I was stunned. No matter how hard I tried I couldn't twist my foot around enough to see what they were talking about.

I asked Kiannaa later how long she had known. With a smile and twinkle in her eye she replied, "Ever since I first saw your feet at the Raindrop workshop in 2000, sweetheart."

It was an interesting few days. There seemed to have been so much 'weird' information coming into my life and I was just trying to come to terms with it, yet not really knowing what to do with it all. I was glad Kiannaa was there, I could talk to her about anything. I decided that I just needed some time to allow this information to settle within me and perhaps I would then gradually feel calmer inside when I thought about it.

On the back of my right hand I had a small ganglion. I'd had it for years without it causing me any discomfort at all. Yet since the Reiki workshop it had been really painful. I was in constant pain and had difficulty gripping things with my thumb and forefinger, at times even holding things in my right hand was too much.

Kiannaa thought this may have been an injury in a previous existence, though I was unsure. Despite all this work we had done, the small ganglion was still bothersome and the feeling in my forefinger and thumb was poor.

Kiannaa suggested that I sat down quietly, focus on my hand and ask it what it was trying to tell me. I hadn't thought of doing this. So later that night, as I applied oils to my hand before going to bed, I asked what my hand was trying to tell me. I closed my eyes and instantly I was shown Christ on the cross.

I know I wasn't Jesus, that didn't feel right. Perhaps I had been crucified?

'Yes', came the answer.

Oh my goodness. I got a strong feeling that I was there when he was killed.............perhaps I was one of his followers? I decided to talk to Mum and Kiannaa about it the next morning. I explained to them what I had experienced the previous night.

Tears flowed down Kiannaa's face and she said that she knew we had met and worked together before. We chatted for a while and I admitted to her that I was a little thrown with this kind of information. It felt like it was happening to someone else, yet when I thought about it I felt the goosebumps throughout my body. These are my 'truth bumps', an indication to me that truth is being spoken or thought about.

As I got ready for bed that night I was compelled to ask again if there was more to this. I wanted to know why I also had pain in my right shoulder blade area, for many months, which just didn't seem to want to go away. I closed my eyes as I asked these questions in my head.

I was shown a man, a soldier, coming towards me. I was trying to get off a cross, I think to try to save Jesus, but this wasn't clear. The soldier then stabbed me with a sword. Suddenly I could see the face of the soldier. It was my ex husband, Tom.

In that moment our relationship made sense. We had obviously been together in other lifetimes. I was a little overwhelmed, yet part of me understood that the hurt and heartache we had experienced in this life went much further back.

I had a glimmer of understanding that we must have loved each other so very much as souls to have agreed to hurt each other so much. It takes the great love of the soul to be willing to come here and experience great pain inflicted by the other to learn something that you have each agreed to take part in. Yet this notion seemed too incredible to be correct. Perhaps I wasn't quite ready to accept it yet.

I received an email from Kiannaa after she returned home. In it she explained that she was 'honoured' to be working with me again. I didn't understand it at first. She explained that I gave my life for Jesus, that my love for him was so great.

"So yes," she said in her email, "I am honoured to be working with you again."

This was all so much to take in. I felt so small and insignificant in the grand scheme of things. But this information would seem to be true. People were coming into my life who also had connections with that time. I kept being told by my guides and other people I barely knew that it was in readiness for work I would be doing in the future, soul and etheric work. I didn't really understand.

I began to think I didn't know who I was any more. It all felt so conflicting yet correct. My friend Amy had been a treasure. She listened to my ramblings and confirmed what I was either being shown or feeling, as she also experienced the full body goose 'truth' bumps.

During this period, I found that I was much more comfortable outdoors, connecting with nature and in fresh air. My mind was busy. I was processing a myriad of thoughts, skirting on the periphery of some very intense thinking. I found that if I thought about these things for too long, my brain literally ached. I was doubting my thinking process, doubting my thoughts and not quite sure what to believe or what to feel.

I did a little meditation, only ten or fifteen minutes at a time and occasionally would experience a 'conversation' in my mind. I had been pondering the recent developments and thinking about the doubts I was having when I heard, "We know you have many doubts, that you are wondering what you can or cannot believe in what you are shown or told."

I agreed. "I am no more special than anyone else," I said.

The reply came to me, "That may be so, but you bring with you great gifts from many lifetimes."

I wondered to myself what these might be and how I was to use them if this were true. I felt deep inside that 2008 would bring forth this knowledge or would bring people into my life to show me what these gifts were and how I was to use them.

I felt the new energy Kiannaa had brought through had a big part to play. I had been working with this energy for a while and was often asked to help people remotely, like a distant healing. I would literally spend just a few seconds THINKING it and it would seem that it had worked. I was a little confused and didn't believe this was possible quite so fast and with such incredible results.

"Great healings are going to take place if you just let them,"

I heard in my head. Was this just my wishful thinking? I
certainly wasn't Jesus, nor did I have his healing gift.

Then I hear, "You are wrong. You weren't Jesus, but you too
have his healing gift."

How was that possible? I didn't recall any of the 'disciples'
healing others. "Yvonne, but they did. You were part of a group
who did just that."

I asked, "Was I an apprentice?"

The answer came, "Yes and no."

"What do you mean, yes and no?" I asked

"He was teaching you how to use your gifts - they are already
there waiting."

I wasn't quite sure what that meant but recalled earlier in the
year that I had asked if it was my destiny to move or emigrate
away from Scotland. I was told that my 'work' was here in
Scotland. I remember being so disappointed. Much as I loved
Scotland, I had begun to desire a life in a more temperate
climate. I was beginning to feel that this 'work' simply
involved me sharing my knowledge and experience with others
about essential oils and energy work and perhaps I could do
that anywhere.

Perhaps many of the people that I was to work with were in
Scotland and maybe that would help to bring through great
healing energy; evolved energy. Energy to aid the planet to heal
and to aid her ascension - but also to aid her survival. I didn't
know what that all meant, but it felt very important.

Chapter Eleven

In early January 2008, after making a last minute decision to attend a Sekhem training course I drove to Aberdeenshire. I had trained some people in Raindrop Technique a few months previously and spoken at great length to a woman there about Sekhem. I had decided that this was my next step and felt comfortable with the trainer. I was excited to be learning a different energy healing technique and knew very little about it.

The workshop opened with us connecting as a group. We stood in a circle which created a beautiful energy flowing from and through each other - we were one. I saw light emanating from each persons heart, the light beams then joining in the centre of the circle and moving upwards in one massive beam of light. It was a wonderful start to the workshop and a really lovely way to connect the group for the work to come.

Vicki invited us to pick a card from those laid out on the table. I picked the Prince of Wands. This card indicated a move and change in life, with a reminder that change is essential to growth. I was reminded that we have the strength and elasticity to roll with the changes we experience.

I was then drawn to pick an Angel card which was "Hello

from Heaven". Some of the message read:- "Your loved ones in Heaven are doing fine - feel their loving blessing. In your quiet moments, you can feel their presence. These really are true visions, and I ask you to trust your intuition. Archangel Azrael is known as 'The Angel of Death', since his primary role is to help people cross over to Heaven at the time of their physical death. Far from being a morbid role, Azrael surrounds the newly crossed-over soul with loving light to make the experience uplifting and comforting."

Both of these cards were poignant. I knew that I was changing and needed to grow again and that part of my role was to help people ascend - in both human life (getting to know their true self better) and in transitioning to spirit form upon death.

Vicki then asked me to go through to her treatment space for my first Sekhem initiation. I was excited and yet still wondering why I was here. I felt that this was meant to be, but still didn't truly understand why. My experiences during that Sekhem initiation were fast and incredible. There was so much to absorb, it would take me days to piece together what I was shown. Each day adding to my knowledge and showing me how to use the energy and information received.

At the start of the initiation there were many colours, playing in front of my closed eyes in waves, swirls and curtains. Mostly purple and orange, really beautiful to watch and very familiar.

The images played out like a movie on a screen and I watched in awe........I saw myself back in the light chamber again - it was a continuation of the attunement ceremony I was shown in November last year. I was given the goblet again and was asked to physically put the goblet to my lips and 'drink' from it. I did this and held the goblet out to be taken from my hands, feeling rather foolish but going with the flow.

My crown chakra was buzzing and I flew up another light tunnel incredibly fast. Immediately from there I saw small craft flying - they appeared from out of the side of a hill or rock. The dust and rocks were falling as they blasted out and into the air. This felt rather strange in amongst this beautiful feeling but I had a sense they had perhaps emerged from their resting place, though I don't know why I would think that.

In the next instant I was inside one of the small craft flying it. I was told over and over to hold the energy and follow the flow of these visions/experiences. The white unicorn appeared, Flies with Pony on its back. I joined him on the back of the unicorn and we flew through the very stars of the universe.

I saw a huge figure, light emanating from every cell, the light so bright it was electrifying. I saw a smaller figure, perhaps a small child, who was kneeling at his left side. I became aware that I was the other figure already kneeling to his right. He placed a hand gently on my head then instantly the image was gone. I began to see tubular water energy moving gracefully around in front of me. This vision had also appeared to me during another initiation, it was familiar, beautiful and mesmerising to watch.

More colours appeared pulsing with life. Not colours you saw on Earth. They were almost 3-D they were so alive. Suddenly there were too many images of people for me to be able to see them properly. The word 'Resolution', 'a joining' popped into my head. I saw Earth from space and beams of light start to emanate from various locations on Earth, as well as one or two other planets. I was told these are all the places I had been in my lifetimes. The beams all joined above the Earth into one giant beam of light and form into a huge quartz crystal pillar. I was in this beam of light - inside the crystal pillar. This was a particularly powerful image and my body felt like it was buzzing all over with electricity.

I felt a great amount of love around and inside me and had a sense that it was now "my time" - that I was to step up and do the work I had agreed to do. I was still unsure what this might be. I saw a three dimensional diamond shaped crystal rotating slowly in front of me. Then pale pink lightening flashes against a purple background appeared, followed by images of trees so clear that they looked like photographs.

I became aware that Vicki had left the room to allow me space to complete my initiation. This was when a burst of bright, white energy entered my body. I felt goose bumps all over, and I was filled and then filled again, as wave after wave of energy enveloped my body.

I stood up, arms outstretched to either side of me allowing the energy a direct channel for it to flow freely, soaking it into my cells. I drew this energy around me and become aware that each one of my guides or helpers on my journey were there in the room waiting. Just as we started the day in a human circle, we formed a circle - a circle of one human and several light beings.

I took the hand of the guides on either side of me and I began to quiver all over, the energy in the circle was immense and beautiful. After a few moments the energies from our hearts flew into the centre of the circle and created an energy ball - pulsing, alive, pure. Within seconds this formed a massive crystalline column of light shooting above us and out into the universe. Tears trickled slowly down my face. They were tears of joy and love. This love was becoming bigger and deeper each time I connected with it.

"It is such an honour to be gifted this beautiful experience," I thought to myself. "Thank you so much."

I left the room, reluctantly. I was in silent awe. I had a lot to think about, to process and understand. I felt this had been a massive connection of some kind for me. I recalled the trip to South Africa with Chris - the foot I drew. No toes - all ONE. Was this what I asked for 3 years ago and everything over those following months had combined to fulfill my request? I was sure of it. I knew it. I had no idea where this would take me but I knew it felt right. No matter what, it was right to be there then. It was the first day after a new moon and it was a wonderful start to this New Year.

On the second day of the workshop we meditated as a group. I saw Earth again. I was flying. As I flew I was making beams of golden light round and round the Earth, faster and faster. The energy bands became gyroscopic and they moved around and around of their own accord - maintaining the energy, invincible and impenetrable.

We were asked by Vicki to remotely or etherically visit Linda's house. Linda was one of the group and she had been experiencing a denseness in her home. I was unsure what to do to help and asked for guidance. I was shown the Earth again with the energy bands and gyroscopic energy. I realised then that I was to do the same thing around Linda's house. I started running the energy round and round, faster and faster until the gyroscope appeared. Light was emanating everywhere from the house. After a few moments I was guided to rotate the house (etherically) through 180 degrees to align its energies better.

How I did this I had no clue but I saw the house rotate and it felt so much better, calmer.

After the meditation I shared my experience. Some had felt this energy as a wind blowing and Linda had a vision where all the windows blew out of her house and she felt that all the denseness inside had gone. I was stunned that people had experienced what I was doing.

During a healing session that day I worked with a woman called Alison. I lay down on the treatment couch and as she connected with me I felt energy flowing down my legs. During this session I kept hearing in my head that I needed more nurturing. That I couldn't do this journey alone and needed to focus on what I desired and that this was all preparation for what was to come. I was told again, as Lynn had said to me early last year, that my work was global, not local. I was to work to rid myself of financial issues, to create the funds to do the work. I knew that my fear still held me back in this area.

When I opened my eyes after the session was complete, I couldn't stop the tears. I was racked with emotion but I wasn't sure what I was really feeling. Vicki asked me what was happening and from nowhere I heard myself saying, "I feel I don't deserve this gift." I was so shocked and stunned at the words I was hearing coming out of my own mouth. Where had that come from?

Afterwards I felt exhausted and drained and I retired early to bed to give my body and mind time to adjust.

The following day I felt wonderful. We learned some new healing techniques during that day. It was fascinating and most enjoyable. When it came to my treatment session, I lay down and Vicki came over to the couch, held my hand, and uttered 'Sa Sekhem Sahu'. She placed each of my arms across my chest.

My eyes were closed and in that moment I could feel myself flying feet first into another place completely. The speed was incredible. I heard in my head that once the treatment started I was to focus on a golden energy ball, keep all thoughts focused on the light no matter what. I would be shown what to do.

The energy was beautiful. I focused on the energy ball which I could sense beneath my feet. I was shown the diamond three dimensional shape again. I placed a golden energy ball at each point and the diamond slowly rotated. I was inside this diamond shape and I felt like I was inside a protective cocoon. I could 'see' my left thigh clearly. The tissue beneath the skin was bubbling, growing. The withered tissue was reforming to become strong.

After this session I felt elated, magnificent and invincible. I felt that I could do anything, I had been shown that anything is possible. I knew this to be true but now I felt it. I picked an angel card at the end of this third day - our final day. The card was 'Divine Order'.

"How significant," I thought.

Vicki closed the day with a gentle and uplifting meditation. The new moon hung above the hills outside Vickis home. It was a lovely way to end the three days of wonder and transition.

My drive home was a stream of constant revelations. It was very dark by the time I left and the road in front of me seemed to lead me towards the Moon in the sky, till the road just seemed to disappear and it felt like I was really driving on the Moon and not on Earth. The journey was full of personal realisations and connections as I drove.

I recalled the evening when Kiannaa was adjusting her presentation for the Reiki workshop and she had called me through to see what had happened on the screen of her computer. She had decided to change or adjust the background for this presentation and at the bottom left of each slide was a small blue ball. On this one particular page as she was working, a small golden energy ball had begun to move around the little blue ball. We were both stunned and it did not appear on any other slide. We had no idea how it had formed nor why it was there.

It was what I had been shown throughout the past few days. As I drove, I was told that this energy was with me every moment and cannot be turned 'off'. It was flowing all the time and that I work with it constantly. The journey, despite being a little over three hours, felt like around ten minutes in actual time. I wasn't in the least tired.

On my arrival at home, the electric locking system of my van began to work on its own. When I locked the van, the locking mechanism locked and then unlocked several times. As I tried to unlock it again to check it, it unlocked the doors and promptly locked them again. I left it to its own devices, sure that it was a glitch and all would be well in the morning. However, the following morning I had an interesting task trying to 'beat' the self-locking to enter the van.

I decided to take the van to the garage where I had taken it for the past two years for servicing and repair. Whilst I was there, I became aware of many paintings around the waiting area.

One in particular drew me to look closer to discover they were paintings of the Stones at Callanish. One was of the 'language' the stones speak. I was totally dumbstruck.

I asked the receptionist how long the paintings had been there. She replied, "Since September."

I had been in that waiting area twice since September and hadn't seen them. It began to dawn on me that this was why the van was 'playing up'. I had to be there to see those paintings. As I sat on the couch staring across the room at one painting in particular called 'Meanings Lost in Time', my body became charged.

I can remember thinking, "So this is what they look like when high vibration energy flows through them." Though I didn't really know what I was thinking, what that really meant.

I then heard, "The energy is the key to unlocking the information inside the stones everywhere. The resonance and vibration which this energy exudes as the energy builds in speed and frequency allows the stones to speak their truth. The diamond 'cocoon' is the chamber which you place yourself in to enable your pure being to channel the energy and protect you. It allows only golden light in or out; only love in or out. No other energy is able to taint this sacred space. Light is the key and the diamond 'cocoon' and the energy together will enable access to information and other energy which will be required soon."

I really wasn't sure what this was all about, but didn't doubt the information at all, which was most unlike me of late. I was trusting this kind of information more since the workshop with Vicki and just allowing it to enter. I had learned that when the time was right, I would just know what to do, no matter how crazy or silly that might seem. I was excited and thrilled to be a part of whatever this journey was and was enjoying working with some of the most beautiful souls I had ever met.

After the Sekhem course I found myself questioning guides and light beings even more. My connection seemed to have become stronger, more clear. I was enjoying using this new energy with clients and on myself and I felt that new doors were opening. Doors which held infinite possibilities for my life.

The course had given me a new perspective and I was keen to find out more. The only way to do that was by looking inwards at my 'self'. I knew that answers didn't lie anywhere else but in my very soul.

Because I had experienced some pain in my back during the course, I decided to ask one evening what my back pain was trying to tell me - one word came through 'POWER'.

"Power of what?" I asked.

"Your power. Use your power. Do not run from it nor hide from it."

I was a little unsure what that meant, though I was aware that I was able to channel a great deal of energy for clients during healing sessions. I wondered if this was what had been meant.

I asked, "Is there something else it is trying to tell me?"

The word 'LOVE' appeared before my eyes in capital letters.

"Love myself?" I asked.

"Yes. But also to love your power and use it with love."

I was beginning to understand a little more. I was then shown the Sekhem symbol of the heart with the infinity symbol. The heart represents 'love' and the infinity representing 'power' and infinite within that power. Together, used as intended, they balance the power with compassion; wisdom; empathy and pure love from the Divine. This creates great strength - within oneself and a compassionate strength of the energy.

I mulled over this insight for some days, toying with it and letting it settle within me. One week in particular I found that during treatment sessions with clients unicorns were coming to me to assist the healing process. Flies with Pony, my guide, rides a Unicorn so of course they had been around me for years.

I had looked up various websites and discovered that Unicorns bring through the purity and compassion of the Christ Consciousness energy. So this had been with me all these years without me really knowing about it. It was only now, during personal development and awakening that I was beginning to put the pieces together of this puzzle.

When these Unicorns came to me during healing sessions and sometimes at night, they had begun to ask that I bring through Unicorns in my meditations. I sometimes facilitated short meditations for small groups of people I knew when we shared our healing skills with each other.

This request was awesome, but I was still very timid about it. I felt like I just didn't have a clue what I was doing half the time. I often had no idea what to say once everyone was comfortable, but then once I asked for guidance and I began to speak, words flowed completely bypassing my brain. It was a strange phenomenon for me, but when this happened the love which could be felt in the room was incredible.

Most people saw their own unicorn beside them or they would fly with their unicorn and receive guidance or healing during these meditations. I decided to start connecting more often with these Unicorns, to find out what exactly they wanted me to do. So one evening as I lay in bed ready to settle down for the night I asked the Unicorns to come to me. I saw two Unicorns. Each of them placed their energy spiral into my chest, one either side of my heart and I felt I was lifted high above my bed. Their energy spirals were through my body and looked like they were protecting or healing my heart. I wasn't too sure at the time but it felt incredibly special.

I was also occasionally experiencing quite severe headaches, almost like a migraine, sometimes with visual disturbances and nausea. One evening I had such a headache. I went to bed earlier than normal and I asked the light beings if I would benefit from some healing.

"Yes."

I asked if this could be done for me and I became aware there was a presence in the room. I asked if they were able to do the healing or would I need to help.

I heard, "It can be done without your assistance."

I was relieved, lay back and I drifted off to sleep not long afterwards, though I was keen to see what happened. When I awoke the following morning my headache had nearly gone. I was still a little confused with these guides and helpers who kept popping up. I wasn't really sure who to ask for what. I felt sure they each had their own special gifts or skills and wished I knew a little more about them.

Weeks rolled by, I settled more with the new energy within me and 'chatting' to guides and visits from my Dad became more frequent. They spoke kindly and lovingly back to me, no harsh words or lack of patience and it felt very comforting. They seemed to be gently nurturing my gifts and giving me more confidence to go with the flow of working with clients and my family during healing sessions. This felt really good and natural, though at times I wondered what I was doing and sometimes I would receive a few words as a message for them.

This meant absolutely nothing to me and I was extremely timid at first about sharing what I had been asked to share, but I found that if I didn't share the words, all I would hear in my head would be "Tell them" time after time until I spoke up. The intriguing thing was that every time I did share a word or a phrase, it would mean something very pertinent to the other person. This gave me growing confidence to trust in what was coming to me during these special moments.

During a Raindrop Technique workshop one of the women, Jane was receiving treatment and her back began to turn red in small areas - they looked like little bites. She said she felt fine, she felt no heat at all. The redness gradually merged up and down the spine.

Then, as I looked closer at her back a figure '8' appeared in white on the skin. It was very clear. It was over her heart area on her back. The other two women saw it also and as we watched, another '8' appeared near Janes shoulder. At this point she began to weep. This was overdue, she so needed this release of emotion which was bottled up inside. We kept working, one woman gently touching Janes feet.

I had asked for guidance about what the 8 meant. When I asked that question, a '3' had appeared on her shoulder, but then completed to become an '8'. These weren't '8's but infinity symbols.

Words began to pop into my head and I wrote them down quickly. I was to tell her that the love for her from the Universe is infinite. She was to begin to allow this love to enter her and allow it to flow through and around her. This was a reminder to her that this love is infinite - it never ends.

As I was writing this down, a third '8' appeared. Once I finished writing the words down for Jane, all three signs disappeared. I shared the words with her and with her permission, I shared them with the group once she got up from the table. It was a very special message for her, but one which we all needed to hear.

After experiencing feelings of inadequacy throughout my life and often during these times of personal growth, this was very special and a huge sign that what I was doing was right on track.

In the days following this workshop I had heard the words, "You are a child of God, you are very, very special."

We are all special and all children of God, and I didn't understand. I was out in the garden at night and heard again, "You are a child of God. You are very, very special."

This time I started up a conversation in my mind, thinking it might be one of my guides.

I said, "I know I'm a child of God. Everyone is, so we're all special."

"That is true, but you have great work to do here on Earth."

I said, "So has everyone."

"But not like you."

Puzzled I asked who it was, muscle testing to confirm that my 'ears' weren't deceiving me. Was it Flies with Pony, my guide? I heard bubbly laughter and "No."

I asked if it was my Dad? Again laughter. "He is here also."

I stopped breathing for a few seconds and asked, "Are you Source?"

Huge peels of laughter and, "Yes, I am Source."

I was a little shocked. I then saw the image of that first Sekhem initiation with Vicki when I saw a massive light being and two people at either side of it. I asked if that was him 'appearing' to me – "Yes."

My goodness had I been one of the people at his side? I felt I must apologise for not conversing with him much and I heard laughter again.

"I have always spoken to you and guided you. You were just unaware of your connection to me. I am not angry with you. You have much to do here on Earth and it is time for you to accept and acknowledge your importance. You are bringing through the Christ Consciousness and other energies to many so that compassion can enter the souls of all you touch. It is what you are here to do and I ask that you do it with the love which runs through you."

"But that's so hard to accept," I said.

"I understand. But you must accept, for it is what and who you are. When the tree spoke to you, Yvonne, I was speaking through it to tell you 'welcome' and yes, we have been waiting a long time for you to evolve to the light-being you now are. You have infinite love, wisdom and power within you. Through the energy teachings you are learning how to use it. Through them you will learn to advance even more and access other things you will need."

I returned to the house and began to write what was coming into my head. Where was this coming from? It was a little spooky that these thoughts were entering my head and were being typed so fast. I was tingling and I wanted to ask so many questions, yet they seemed so unimportant.

I heard, "They are. You know what I say is true. I know you are feeling that tingle of truth. You must look deep inside and not worry about material things nor what people say. Your work will help change the world for all time. You have the strength, I will make sure of it. No matter what, I am here. Great beauty lies within you and you are loved beyond measure."

I was reeling and wondering what had just happened. I was seriously doubting my sanity. I felt weird, like I wasn't really there in my body. My body felt strange and my sight had been a little peculiar during this experience. It was like someone else was typing, though I was aware of my fingers moving.

The whole experience had lasted only twenty minutes or so. Sometimes I wondered if all of this was someones huge joke. A spirit connecting with me to have a bit of a laugh. I wasn't too sure of what I was being told, yet at the same time I knew it was about loving my 'self', something I still found challenging despite the healing I had done inside and the help from other wonderful people. Yet I also felt a calmness amidst the mind chatter, questions and doubt.

I spoke with my friend Amy, who had been very supportive of my 'weird' experiences. She was a down to earth person, very grounded and her support meant such a lot to me. She felt that I was going through huge transitions and healing and that these experiences were all part of me getting to know my 'self'. Beginning to learn to truly love my 'self', warts and all. She felt I was opening up to so much more and that it would take time for this to feel normal to me. She asked if I would perhaps do a remote healing session for her and I agreed.

This was very different to what I normally did. When I entered my treatment room I was asked to remove my slippers. I raised my hands to my chin to begin the blessing before sending healing energy and my body began to tingle. The energy flow was very strong. I was asked to stand still, with my hands gently by my side and slightly in front of me. It was a familiar Chi Kung stance. I heard that I was to completely use my mind, my heart. I wasn't to make any arm movements but use only thought.

This made me a little nervous, but I complied with the wishes expressed, knowing that this must be for a reason. I connected with Amy immediately. I stood to her left side and I could see something wasn't right at the back of her neck. It seemed blocked. Guided, I used an etheric hoover (this is a tool used by energy workers to remove blockages and substances preventing good flow of energy) and all of a sudden the substance started to flow quickly from her neck. Within seconds I removed the hoover as the substance turned from grey to white.

I then held my hand out and a ball of liquid gold was placed in the palm. I gently placed this at the back of Amy's neck and I watched as it flowed into her neck and throughout her body. It was amazing. I could see her soul lift and stand straight as the heaviness left her. I could then see her wings, beautiful white delicate wings. I watched as she filled with love and light into her very core. It was complete. The healing was done. Within five or ten minutes of starting.

I still couldn't quite believe how fast this energy was. Amy reported back to me thirty minutes later that her headache was shifting, her throat felt better. I hadn't known what was wrong when I started. All she had asked for was some healing because she wasn't feeling very well. Again I was stunned that what I had seen was exactly what she was experiencing.

I returned to the garden. I asked about these healing gifts. "Are they real? I'm not imagining them?"

"No, you are not. You didn't imagine our conversation earlier either. You may think you are going mad, but you are not. Quite the opposite."

"Everyone is special," I said in my head. "So are you trying to say that some are more special than others?"

"No, all are equal. Some have come to do bigger jobs, that is all."

"Oh. Am I one of those people with a big job to do?"

"Yes. You must begin to accept what you are. Integrate and let it flow. It doesn't matter what you did before. It is gone, in the past. The love is still within you, even though you have denied it for so long. The love you had for Jesus then, you have now. It is in your cells, your soul. It cannot be denied any longer. Accept this to be true. Accept your truth. You know truth, you know what it feels like. Look inside and ask if it is truth. Only then will you have the answer."

Oh, inside. I had no idea what depths I would have to travel to know and feel this all to be true. The history and experiences from my many lives which I brought with me to this life, how did this tie in with my life now?

There was much confusion, I couldn't seem to make sense of any of it. It ran around in my head over and over. I didn't understand what effect me teaching a few people about Reiki and energy healing was going to have on the planet. I am only one. What could I do to make such a difference?

I heard gentle laughter again. "Touch that inner place and you will know."

I spoke at length with my Mum during this time, sharing some of what I was experiencing with her. She was supportive and loving, and didn't bat an eyelid at what I told her. She accepted my experiences straight away as completely real and truthful. This made a huge difference and helped me to accept these strange events.

During the periods of self acceptance I felt calm and peaceful and this was something I truly wished to feel more in my life. In 2008, Vicki and I discussed my progression onto the advanced level of Sekhem. We both felt it important for me and she was running a course in early July. I didn't have to think about it too much, it felt right and so I travelled to Aboyne. Her home felt like 'home', it was comfortable and welcoming and I felt a strong bond with Vicki as well as her home.

Our first day was about aura cleansing and learning to use our skills at sensing any disruptions or blocks in someone's energy field or aura around the body. I was working with a woman, trying to see energy with my eyes open. We were working outside, it was warm and sunny and it felt right to be outside in open space and nature.

There was a pale lilac blanket across her and I was wondering how I could 'defocus' to see the energy. Vicki had explained the technique, but I wasn't having much success. I got the urge to remove my glasses, as everything is then defocused without any effort.

I looked towards her and after a few moments I began to see the weirdest thing, especially around the blanket area. It looked like tiny white or silvery tadpoles whizzing in circles all around her. The whole of the lilac blanket was awash with them.

I looked away thinking I was imagining it, but when I looked again they were still there. I couldn't believe it. All along all I needed to do was remove my glasses and stare. As simple as that. I felt joyous and was laughing inside.

I stayed that evening for the crystal meditation and was so glad that I had. I had a great deal of respect for the healing potential of crystals but this was a whole new experience with them. Each member of the group was asked to 'introduce' themselves and their 'chosen' crystals to the rest of the group and explain why they had chosen the particular crystals they had brought along.

I described how I had wandered round the house asking my guides which crystals I was to take for this course and showed the group my fairy wand, the small piece of Moldavite I bought a year ago and the quartz crystal points I had brought.

Vicki just laughed out loud when she saw the Moldavite and said, "Now why does that not surprise me?" She told me that I would find out more tomorrow about its significance.

During this meditation we asked each of our crystals for permission to enter them. Each of our crystals had been chosen or rather had requested to be used in our crystal healing grid. It would seem that we were communicating at a higher level with the crystals so that they could impart knowledge and understanding of their power and healing gifts.

The first crystal I picked up was my small piece of Moldavite. I was taken inside this crystal instantly, without having time to ask if I could enter. Inside it was so beautiful, glowing pale green as light from the outside shone through its structure. Inside I met several light beings who blessed the work I would be doing with this crystal.

Though I was inside the crystal, I watched as it was placed in the centre of a table. Three 'lasers' pointed towards it. I asked what was happening and was told that the lasers were etching an intention into the Moldavite - that this had already been done when the crystal was formed and they were just showing me the significance. It was so beautiful and peaceful inside that I really didn't want to leave when it was time to greet the next crystal.

I selected my fairy wand. When I entered this magnificent structure there were fairies and angels inside. I wasn't sure what I had expected, but it wasn't that. We floated around together inside the crystal for a while, I felt the love and fun all around me. They too blessed the work I was doing and when I asked the crystal if it was happy to be used for the grid work, I began to feel very hot and received confirmation that it was happy to assist.

As I picked up each crystal after this I became hotter and hotter. I then picked up each of the six crystal points in turn and entered inside one at a time. Inside one was a whale and we swam around the ocean, it was peaceful and serene; in another crystal there was a turtle and as we descended to the ocean floor I felt as if I had turned into the turtle. Waiting below was the most beautiful white unicorn (though I did wonder at the time how it could possibly breathe under water), which I greeted and was immediately enveloped with love. My heart was filled with love and I thanked the crystal for such a wonderful experience.

This was such a simple exercise and yet so awesome. It was so easy to connect to each crystal and they all had such different and equally wonderful energies and spirits about them. They felt so alive. I went to sleep that night smiling from ear to ear, so happy that I had decided to come on the course. It was exciting and I drifted off to sleep wondering what the following day might bring.

The next day was another magnificent sunny day and the group connected in a circle before starting the days work. Vicki showed us how to anoint with sacred Lotus essence in Sekhem tradition. What an emotional experience it was. I allowed each emotion to flow through me and asked for it to be released and transmuted. Tears came and went several times. I had no real understanding of what was happening, but felt a deep connection to something so very beautiful and profound.

As we stood at the end of this short ceremony, just absorbing the energy, I was asked to place my hands behind my back, palms facing upwards. I could feel beings around me, clearing, cleaning and sweeping dense energy from me and light into me even before Vicki asked us to imagine it. Then a giant golden key was placed in my hands. I later realised that it wasn't an actual key, but a golden ornate staff.

I heard, "You have the key."

The key to what, I had no clue. I was overwhelmed with tears again, struggling to understand the significance but knowing it meant something important. There was time only to absorb, not to think.

After such a beautiful opening ceremony, I didn't think the day could possibly improve. I knew before I went into the room for the initiation that my Moldavite crystal was to be with me. There was such a strong pull and a 'knowing' that it must be present.

I sat down, placed it between my feet and closed my eyes. I could see golden Egyptian figures in the four corners of the room, one in each corner. The two in front of me were holding long golden staffs with a hooked or curved end and each were unwavering in their stance throughout the ceremony.

As Vicki moved around me, an energy spiral began to form. Heat began to slowly move up the core of my body. As the heat rose I became aware that I was in the centre of the spiral, on my chair, going up the central core of myself.

I saw us inside a stone room. The Egyptian figures were there and I was lying on a stone table. I looked like a golden sarcophagus, body shaped. A golden figure which I presumed was Vicki was dancing at my feet slowly; beautiful swaying moves.

I could see the heart of the figure on the stone table. It rose and fell, in clear sight and it started to come 'alive' - hovering just above the prone figure. Tremendous heat began to spread in the centre of my chest, slowly travelling up to my throat. Vicki began to move around me again, slightly faster and I could see the spiral continue up my body and I experienced even more heat. It was intense, yet comforting.

All of a sudden the figure on the table came alive, jumped from the stone table and joined the dancing golden figure, mirroring her moves exactly - face to face in a tribal and ancient dance to the Gods. The golden dancing figure suddenly became an Aztec woman, with dark curly hair almost waist length. Her skin was shimmering in the sunlight as she performed her tribal dance to an initiate before her.

After this vision I felt as if the top of my head opened and it started to feel so full. I could see a column of light pouring in through the top of my head. My third eye area began to heat up. A huge eye was staring at me, blinking occasionally but unwavering. Then I felt hot liquid gold touch the skin of my forehead. I was shown what was being placed there, some form of golden shape. My third eye began to pulse.

I then saw three triangles coming towards me surrounded by the universe with thousands of tiny bright stars shining. The triangles then melded into one triangle. Following that image I saw a 'chain' of three dimensional triangles and they arrived looking like a gunmetal grey triangular chocolate bar. 'Ching-chung-chung-chung-chung', so fast like a speed train arriving. As they arrived there were gaps between each three dimensional triangle, but once they reached their destination they became one long triangular three dimensional tunnel.

Then the lotus of the Sekhem symbol became a golden plate - like a golden smile. On it was placed a piece of Moldavite and a huge golden staff. It was very ornate, and I realised it was the staff that I had been given that morning as we opened the circle.

I sat on the golden plate and I travelled, faster and faster, from warp to super warp speed. So fast the stars were going past in a streaky blur. Then out of the tunnel and into the light. Blinding yet comforting light. So bright after travelling through dark space. It was so beautiful there. In the next moment I was back, seated in the room.

More pyramids appeared. It looked like hundreds. Then I saw that in each one of the triangles an initiation was taking place - my initiation. Not just here but in all other dimensions - I saw only a couple very clearly; one was a native American; one in a temple pyramid. Each triangle had two small figures inside busy with the ceremony. Then each pyramid lit up and became one. It was totally cool.

I was taken up the triangular tube again, this time in a split second and as I emerged into the light I was astride a huge crystalline dragon. Only its head was visible, its body was almost smoke-like as it appeared out of the tube.

Vicki placed my hands onto each shoulder, crossing over my chest. She placed her hands over my hands from behind me and

I could feel a pulse starting in my body. She left the room then and I placed my hands into a triangle shape over my heart.

An 'Ohm' sound came from my lips. I had been shown this in a vision last week. I had thought I was shouting in the room at the end of the vision. Again the Ohm came from my lips, stronger this time. The third and final time the Ohm went on for ages. I didn't know I had that capability to breathe for so long. It was an Ohm unlike any other I had ever sounded. As the sound emerged from my body it changed and evolved into something quite wonderful. I became emotional at this point and let the sobs come and go for a short time. Then it was gone.

I thanked all the helpers and guides who had joined us for this ceremony. I left the room and sat outside for a while in the sun. My head was buzzing, my body a little wobbly. I placed my hands on the trunk of a tree. It felt so good. Tears began rolling down my face, I think more relief and gratitude than anything else.

As the day progressed and Vicki shared teachings for this level, I could barely take some of it in. I had been shown things during my initiation exactly as she was showing us now.

She explained a little about the technique where two practitioners can spiral the Sekhem energy between the head and feet of a client, with a practitioner at each end of the client. I realised that I had done this before, me and my Dad, though not with this energy.

There was so much to integrate and during the following few days I found myself in quiet contemplation. I was finding the world very brash and invasive. I withdrew into myself a little, just needing some quiet time to let things settle. I had no desire to interact until I felt ready.

I felt small. Not small as in insignificant. Small as in compact. It was a new feeling for me to be experiencing, not unpleasant but new. I tried not to think too much and just allowed things to settle into whatever form they were to take. After the last few initiations and attunements I had felt an expansiveness of myself and it felt strange for it to be so different this time. It felt there had been a condensing of myself.

My treatment sessions began to flow more than they had, in a gentle and loving way. I found that I became very warm and the energy which flowed through me seemed more intense. At times an image would appear in my head and I would ask for guidance. Often the reply came back that I knew already. I would laugh inwardly, thinking it was good to know they had so much faith in me. This kind of encouragement helped me to go with the flow and my inner 'knowing' developed during these sessions. I really wanted to feel this 'connected' in my daily life and not just during these wonderful treatment sessions.

Chapter Twelve

In May I received a call from my friend Lorna. Her son
Jonathan had been killed in a car accident, her daughter
Rachael injured. Jonathan was eighteen years old. I was
shocked and stunned. I had met him briefly during a couple of
recent visits to Lorna's home, but I could imagine how I might
feel if it were my son.

I visited her a few days later, offering any help I could. Her
daughter had received minor injuries and was already home
from hospital. My heart was breaking for her. Yet she was
holding up well. Much better than I thought I might have in the
same situation.

We chatted for a while and Lorna told me about the day
Jonathan was born. A friend had come to visit her and as she
admired Lorna's beautiful child, Lorna had said he was so
lovely but she knew that she was only looking after him for a
while.

Her friend had reminded her of those words after Jonathan
died, asking her if she knew deep down that she wouldn't
have him in her life for long. Lorna told me that she felt she
did know. Somehow this hadn't come as a great shock, crazy

though that may seem. He died days before his sixth year exams. Only a few weeks before he had said to his mum that he had completely lost interest in school subjects. He wanted to focus on enjoying himself, being with his friends and playing his music. Lorna looked at me and I knew what she was going to say.

"Yvonne, I think he knew he didn't have long. I know that sounds mental, but Jonathan was really special. His friends are devastated at his death. I've seen the comments on his Facebook page and I had never realised how much he helped others until I looked at it. He talked to other kids and helped them through their stuff. The love which is pouring from these kids for him is incredible. You can feel it, it's so huge."

I was fighting back tears. Here I was, listening to a dear friend explain how wonderful her child was and she was trying to understand the bigger picture of his life. I wondered if she was perhaps in shock, but the longer I sat with her I realised that she was being held in pure angelic love. The love she shared with everyone else surrounded her and was supporting her.

I spoke with Lorna over the coming days and she asked me to come along to the service to celebrate Jonathans life. I was happy to offer my support in any way I could.

When I arrived, there were already dozens of people there. Many young people, some in school uniform; some of the girls wearing fluffy angel wings. The love surrounding the place was immense. I stood quietly and observed.

It was a magnificent sunny day. The the cars began to arrive and Lorna and her family got out. Her father, ex-husband and two other family members were wearing silly hats and carried

Jonathan's casket towards the chapel. The hats were a tribute to Jonathan - he had loved silly hats. The casket was oval, formed from recycled paper and was bright red with the most magnificent golden sun design on the lid. White feathers were delicately emerging from the join of the two halves. It was beautiful.

I sat in the chapel and listened to his friends and teachers speak about what a special boy he was. Youngsters everywhere were sniffling. The chapel was packed and some of the young people were seated in the walkways and any other available space.

As some of Jonathans favourite music played on the speakers, I closed my eyes. I could see vast numbers of angels inside the chapel and even more outside. My eyes were filled with tears as I connected with their divine love. Then I saw a figure. It was dancing on the ornate stone archway above the casket. I began to smile inside. The figure was playing a guitar along to the music which was playing. I knew it was Jonathan. He seemed really happy and having a blast.

I shared my vision with Lorna a few days later and she laughed so much. She knew me well and I was able to share many of my experiences with her. I was grateful that I knew she was open enough and she valued that I had shared this with her too. She knew he was okay, she could feel it.

We kept in close contact for the following months, sharing our news, our hopes, our fears and many tears. People felt that she would eventually just break, that she was in denial of Jonathans death. I wasn't so sure. There was an inner strength which Lorna had and her family was loving and incredibly supportive.

I learned such a lot from Lorna over those months. I watched as she remained loving and open, helping Jonathans friends through their grief and supporting Rachael as she healed and came to terms with the loss of her younger brother. It was another reminder that life is too short to muck about. Every day counts. Each day to be lived with love and laughter, not moans and nastiness. Our loved ones are what really matter, whether they are blood relations or friends.

By August I realised I had pushed myself beyond my physical limits. I had been extremely busy at work, taken very little time off and had been creating a patio in our garden. I had overworked myself.

I visited Lorna, and we talked for hours. After our talk, she gave me the most beautiful hot stone massage. I hadn't received one before and this was blissful. My body had felt tight and locked. Lorna was concerned for me as she had sensed that I was running on empty and needed a break.

A couple of days later, I felt like I had a virus or something similar, as I was very hot and then freezing cold. I was experiencing pains in my body and I decided it was time to ask my body what was going on.

The words, "Stop, let go. Holding on too tight," popped into my head.

"Holding on too tight to what?" I asked.

"Everything."

Then, "Too much for everyone else - you worry too much about everyone else."

It was true. I was focused on my sons and trying to ensure my Mum wasn't overdoing things and there was very little space in there for me. Little wonder then that my body was complaining.

The next weekend we spent the day at the coast enjoying ice creams, having a leisurely lunch and a walk along the beach. It was good to hear the waves and have the sand under my feet and it was just what I needed.

I was still in a strange place emotionally. I was unsure of where I was in my life. All kinds of things came to mind, my relationship with my children and my mum. Was I focusing too much on my work and not enough on my family? Where did I go from here? What were my desires to create the life I wanted? And perhaps most importantly, what sort of life did I want? I was in mild confusion, not really knowing my focus.

I made a decision that if, by the end of September, my workshops were not that well attended I would step back from the teaching for a while. It was an immense amount of work and perhaps what I had to offer just wasn't that interesting to people. Was this what the Universe was trying to tell me?

I didn't want to give up my healing work. I enjoyed it very much and felt much more fulfilment from that than from my office job. But for the moment things just weren't working and I couldn't figure out why.

My mind drifted to questions which I recalled asking myself as a young teenager. Who am I and why am I here? "That old nugget," I thought.

I had reached a point where I felt I couldn't go on until I knew

a bit more of what I was meant to do in this life. I was fed up.
I had felt a real desire and push to do these Sekhem and energy
courses; to teach others about the Raindrop Technique. Yet
something was still missing. I wondered if I hadn't opened my
eyes or ears to what I was being guided to do. If that were the
case, I requested that things were made a lot clearer for me.

There were quite a few people I knew who seemed to already
know that I had an important part to play. But important how
and a part to play of what? I found this so difficult to believe
or understand. My 'day job' which kept us going financially
didn't fill me with much excitement, but perhaps I was meant
to be there to keep a low profile. One friend had suggested that
to me. But, Lord, it wasn't easy. My other work with oils and
energy was where I felt completely 'at home' and comfortable.
It excited me and filled me with wonder and awe. I truly
believed that this was where my path lay. I felt such joy inside
and felt like I was glowing when I did this work. It felt right.

I was aware too, that this questioning was completely natural
and normal. I had experienced a huge transition during the last
course and was discovering new parts of myself. I was going
through a stage of deep questioning about my inner feelings
and the way my life was right now, looking at everything to
see what did and didn't feel right any more. It was a little
unsettling.

During this time I would often ask for some healing from the
angels and my guides. During each day I spent many hours at
a computer and as a result my body would often feel very tight
and sometimes very painful around the right shoulder blade.

One day in particular, this pain became so bad that I thought,
"Enough is enough, what's going on with this now?"

I decided to lie down, relax and figure this out. I placed my hands over my solar plexus, breathing slowly, evenly and deeply, allowing my body to relax completely. I asked if I could be shown or told what the pain in my right shoulder blade was trying to tell me.

As I closed my eyes I became aware that there was a figure at the foot of my bed. It was a black man with gold coloured clothing. It looked like some kind of ancient Egyptian outfit. He had a headdress, a gold 'tattoo' on his forehead and was holding a long gold staff. He created a beautiful healing cocoon around my body. At that point I could see tiny white energy squiggles. It was amazing.

Shortly after this, in my relaxed state, I became aware that I was looking at myself lying on my bed from the doorway of my bedroom. This felt a little strange. A figure seemed to get up from my body and stood on the left side at the foot of my bed. It raised its right arm and there was a gun in its hand. The gun fired and then the figure disappeared. I felt no pain or anxiety, just calm observation.

A female figure then got up from my body. She was blond with shoulder length hair, wearing some kind of suit. She stood in the same position as the previous figure. She pointed a sword or a stick and this fired something. She then disappeared. Then another figure got up from my body. I couldn't see this one at all clearly but it seemed to have a sword. It raised the sword and stabbed me.

I knew that each of them had shot or stabbed me in the upper right chest area and that each projectile or sword had gone right through my body. It was quite a strange experience and I wasn't quite sure what to make of it. Perhaps these were just to show me some past life experiences, yet I wasn't too sure how I felt about past lives. I believed in them but I wasn't sure what their significance was on my life now.

At that moment I asked Dominic to come to me and when he appeared, he was pale green in colour, looked a little peculiar and he seemed to have small lumps all over him. I felt that he was drained of energy. I hugged him and poured gold loving energy into him. I apologised to him - I had forgotten that I had sent him to do some healing on someone and hadn't asked how he was getting on nor checked on him at all. This was a big lesson for me. I had to ensure that I checked on him regularly when I sent him off to do healing work on others, especially in these early stages of our development and evolvement.

He lay beside me on my bed and the energy cocoon appeared around him also. Gradually he became the clear crystal Dominic I had become familiar with. I was so relieved.

I got a little insight about the visions I had just had as I watched Dominic rejuvenating. It seemed that I had been killed or injured many times in past lives with the right side of my body particularly affected. I settled down to go to sleep and in the darkness of the room, with my eyes open, I could see tiny light squiggles everywhere.

I closed my eyes and looked again - they were still there. I was thrilled. I was really beginning to see energy with my eyes open as well as through my third eye. I felt so much better the following day, empowered and happier.

Chapter Thirteen

It was the eve of what would have been Dad's birthday and my
family were all feeling his loss. The boys were a bit on edge.
I felt reminded again that the most important thing in my life
was my family. I was tearful and felt grief stricken. For my
Dad and for the life I so wanted.

I wondered if together Dad and I could have made it work
better. Mum and I had trusted, moved again when things
seemed to be looking up and to try to develop my therapy
business. That decision felt wrong, workshops and clients were
non-existent. Life seemed to move along quite nicely for a
while then we hit a brick wall. This happened time, after time,
after time and we were both fed up of it.

I wished to be successful in my life, yet felt a failure. As a
mother; a provider; a happy role model for my sons. I felt that
much of my judgement thus far seemed to have proven poor,
and I was feeling extreme self doubt on all fronts. This scared
me a little, considering I had so recently been in a place of deep
joy and blissful being. What had changed? Why such a painful
place now? My whole being knew that most of this was grief
reaction, but I was beginning to wonder if something else was
getting in the way.

I missed my Dad so much. I was so blessed to have such a good connection to his spirit, but I missed not being able to talk to him face to face and hug him.

As the days passed, these feelings subsided. I was learning to go with the flow of these emotions, to fight them and pretend that they didn't exist just didn't work. I had learned that I must acknowledge them as they appear and if I needed to cry, I would cry. If I needed to be in quiet space, then I would arrange that for myself. I gradually worked through this episode of deep emotional hurt to a place of quiet joy within myself again. This felt much more pleasant and I was noticing that these contented periods were lasting longer.

I had set aside some time to treat each member of my family. I treated my mum first. I selected the oils for her Raindrop treatment and she was deeply relaxed very quickly. This allowed me to work easily and it was a real pleasure to be able to help her.

Next, I treated Callum. He had an ache in his lower back and he was almost sleeping throughout the session. He reported that his back felt great after the session.

Lastly, I treated Glenn. He had his prelim exams the following day and was looking for a session to help calm his nerves. I used Peace and Calming essential oil on my hands and cupped my hands above his nose during the first few minutes of the session, asking him to breathe in deeply. I then used the oil of Harmony on the solar plexus reflex on his feet.

I became aware that there seemed to be a different energy present. As I held both his ankles gently I saw a pale blue watery cocoon appear around him. It was beautiful and delicate. I also saw a strange 'light' thing moving around above him. It was like some of the creatures you see at really deep ocean levels on television. It was brightly lit, like it was plugged into electricity or had its own power source, delicate and pulsating. I wasn't quite sure what this was and what I should do. I heard that I wasn't to concern myself, that what needed to be done would be done.

I relaxed and let my instincts guide me, working my way up his body and simply allowing the energy to do what was needed for him. I completed clearing and energising his seven major chakras and felt drawn to return to his feet. I held them gently for a short while and was shown that I needed to cross his arms over his chest, which I did.

I was almost holding my breath by this point, bowled over by what I had experienced. I then saw a sort of hoop or circle at Glenns feet, around four feet in diameter. It then started to shimmer in the centre - a circle full of liquid energy, moving, living energy. This slowly moved up from his feet, his body appearing gradually through it. It looked like someone was performing one of those magic tricks whilst the body is suspended in mid air.

After a few minutes I was taken down deep in water and saw Glenn reunited with a unicorn under water, it was beautiful to watch. The circle had moved all the way up his body and as his head appeared, the circle vanished. I knew this session was very nearly complete and placed his arms down by his sides again.

Glenn asked me afterwards what I had done and he explained that it had felt very different compared to other sessions of energy work he had received. It was an extremely special session and he had enjoyed it immensely. I knew that I had been shown something wondrous, something new and it felt really exciting.

As I grew in confidence with each session of energy work I did, I experienced more 'visions'. During a craniosacral session I received, a message came through to me.

"You are to believe the visions you see."

At times I had a difficult time doing that, believing. This all seemed rather surreal when trying to live a 'normal' life with a day job in an office. It often felt like two completely separate worlds and my main challenge was how I could either keep the two separate or how I could integrate both aspects of my life. I asked that I receive some guidance about this and perhaps some idea of what my role really was. Was I meant to be doing sessions with people, sharing the gift of healing?

A few days after this, a friend and I spent an afternoon chatting and doing a treatment share for each other. This was always a special time when we shared our gifts with each other.

Danielle's treatment was wonderful. I had another vision during this session. I could see a huge double doorway. It opened as I heard "let us show you." I was looking out onto scenery from a hill. I could see for miles and yet couldn't make anything out with any clarity. It meant nothing to me at the time and I hoped it would become clear. It somehow felt significant.

I had arranged an appointment with a young man who had been recommended to me. He worked with angels and Archangels and from what I understood he gave a combined session of healing and information from the Archangels specifically for that client. It sounded lovely and I had been gifted this session with him by a friend.

When I met Rae, I felt an instant comfortable connection with him. The room felt loving and Rae commented to me that the Christ Consciousness energy was all around me. I settled myself in a chair in front of Rae and closed my eyes. Instantly Archangel Michael came in and removed cords, particularly one connected directly from my heart chakra to my base and sacral chakras. Apparently these were from the past dark times in my life which were still having an affect on me now.

Archangel Gabriel came forward and said he would assist with the flow for me to do the work I need to do. This will be in all ways including financial, so I was to call on Gabriel to assist me. My Nana suddenly barged her way through the angels. She was my maternal grandmother and she was asking me, well it was more of a demand for me to start connecting with her so that she can help me.

Jonathan then appeared for me to pass a message to his mum, Lorna. He wanted her to start taking care of business inside herself, heal herself. She was to stop worrying about everyone else, Rachael would be absolutely fine.

My white unicorn guide came forward then and connected the energy horn from his forehead to my third eye, to help me see more clearly. This felt wonderful when he connected.

Jesus, or Lord Sananda as Rae referred to him, came forward. I liked this name for him. It felt right to use it. He appeared out of a long trail of energy which was zooming towards me. He stepped out of the ball of energy and we hugged. I was asked to breathe in all the love he has for me. He then started to open my wings. Apparently this had been done before by someone else but it hadn't lasted.

"It will this time," Rae told me. "You will know when they are locked in place."

My upper back felt warm and tingly as this was being done.

A nun came forward - a hint that I have been a nun in a past life and it would seem that the negative ties and energy from this life needed to be cut.

Mary Magdalene and Mother Mary were both in the space then. Mother Mary came forward and stood in front of me. Her hands opened and in her palms sat a dove. The dove flew into my heart centre and Rae asked me to breathe in the energy from the dove. It circled round and round my heart, filling it with golden energy.

Rae was shown daffodils, hundreds and hundreds. I asked if this was my Dad. At first he wasn't sure but confirmation of this came swiftly. My Dad showed Rae hundreds of rabbits. We weren't sure of the significance of this, but perhaps it would make sense at some point in the future.

Merlin came forward. Rae was told that I will be connecting with his power and I must start to connect to him to prepare myself. Rae explained that this energy was massive, it was almost overwhelming him. As we chatted about this it became apparent that I had felt Merlins energy before during a meeting at work. That energy had left me reeling, so I had an idea what he was talking about.

Archangel Michael stepped forward again to do more healing. Rae explained that he often worked very closely with me, very much liked my humour and willingness to simply get on with the job at hand. I found this quite amusing and Rae and I had a good laugh about it. Archangel Michael removed small black 'ribbons' from my knees, right hip and then they started to fly off all parts of my body. He placed a blue ball of energy into my throat.

Rae told me that Archangels Ariel, Uriel and Gabriel were all around me. A large padlock had appeared in front of me. Rae asked me to close my eyes and focus on the key which was being placed in the padlock and it sprung open. Energy poured into my heart centre.

After this beautiful connection, Rae explained to me that I will wake up one morning and just possess a new energy. No human initiations involved. This was news to me and an unexpected turn. How wonderful. Rae was also shown a silver sword, pointed downwards and spinning. As it spun it emanated vast amounts of light. It seemed to signify something for the future. A rocking chair appeared to Rae, but this didn't seem to have a significance at that moment to either of us.

Archangel Gabriel stepped forward again and placed a green cloak around my shoulders. It flowed down to my knees and gradually became like a second skin. It was very soothing and we were told that it would remain with me for many days.

An energy ball was also placed around me, it felt huge. Rae told me that I would find the energy in my workspace to be different and as I discovered upon returning home this certainly turned out to be the case.

The session with Rae was amazing and very beautiful. It wasn't what I had expected at all and I was taken aback at how intensely I had felt the Archangels around me during the healing. I hadn't experienced anything like this before. It had been a very intense hour, though enjoyable and I was fascinated by some of the things which had come up during the session. So we had rabbits and a rocking chair which we couldn't figure out and I hadn't known that I had wings either.

Later that night I experienced some extreme pain in my right shoulder blade area and after a while I realised that I could see huge tall wings reaching high up behind me. They were beautiful clear glass-like wings, but not solid. They were flowing and 'alive'. I could really feel them. This was a new and strange experience.

For two days after the session with Rae the name Nexus kept popping into my head. I was unsure if it was the name of a guide; something to look out for in the future or perhaps this was the name of the energy to come. Only time would tell. I still felt an unlikely candidate for all of this. What did I know about how this was all going to work? Yet I knew that when the time was right, it would all be as it should and I would just know.

I began to pose questions to my guides. I am inquisitive by nature and I wanted to know more. My life was turning into a really bizarre chain of events and I was trying to adapt to it all as best I could. So I asked, "What am I here on Earth to do?"

"To help heal yourself and others."

"What do I need to do to help me fulfill this?" I asked.

"You are coming to a special time soon, and you will know."

"What do I need to do to learn the lessons or find the knowledge from the unresolved lives so that I may move on?" I asked. The words just spilling from my mouth.

"That is what is being dealt with."

"What does that mean?" I exclaimed.

"What has been done today will assist this process." I probed some more about this last answer given to me, but very little was forthcoming. I had to be content with what was offered to guide me, frustrating though that was.

I was looking forward to attending Rae's workshop. I hadn't been to an angel workshop before and after his healing and reading session I was really excited about what I might experience. I was keen to release any old baggage, anything which didn't serve me any more and which might be holding me back so that I could fulfill my potential.

The workshop was wonderful. In the very first meditation I recognised the form before me and was told that it was Lord Sananda. Tears were flowing down my cheeks, the love was so enormous. He enveloped me in his wings and I was shown the triangles again. The same ones which had appeared during the Sekhem initiation.

I was also shown the doors again. This time I saw people coming up the hill towards us. Lord Sananda was holding my hand showing me all these people. "They are here to see you, be healed by you", he said. I recall thinking that he couldn't possibly be meaning that. Why would they be coming to see me?

I saw us standing in the centre of a circle of triangles. He was pointing at the triangles, telling me something. Then the circle started to rotate around us and stopped. Another different triangle appeared in front of me. Finally the circle rotated faster and faster like a Catherine wheel around us, energy pouring from its extremities.

The final mediation arrived and immediately I lay down I felt pain in my right shoulder blade area. That familiar pain that I had come to know so well and yet dread. I couldn't focus, each breath in was painful as the muscle began to cramp.

After a while we were directed by Rae to reach out when we could see a golden crystal in front of us, take it and place it into the middle of our chest, our heart centre. Suddenly I could see something in front of me as his words mirrored exactly what I was seeing. The golden crystal appeared in front of me, almost octagonal in shape. It became clearer and clearer until it looked 3-D.

I knew this to be the exact moment I was to physically reach out my hand and take it. I grabbed the crystal most unceremoniously, but the pain in my back was fairly intense by then and I apologised for the lack of manners. I pushed the crystal into my chest and immediately the pain in my back subsided. Within seconds the pain was gone.

In the days following Rae's workshop I experienced moments of great heat throughout my body. This wasn't unpleasant, nor overwhelming but I recognised this to be a shifting and releasing of emotions and energies which no longer served me. Though it was a little uncomfortable at times, I welcomed these signs. I was moving into another state of being and knowing. These times always invoked questions within me. I questioned my purpose, my life here on Earth and again I found myself asking for these questions to be answered.

I asked about this book I had been encouraged to write from that first meeting with Mary when I bought the picture of my guide, Flies with Pony. What purpose will the book serve? Was there really any point? I was told that it will serve to show others the way; to help them guide their own lives towards their truth and purpose; to help them understand that they are not alone in this journey and that what they seek is within, as it is within all of us. It wasn't something from outside of us.

I felt concerned about what elements of my life and my journey that I was to share.

"You will know what to share."

"But how?"

"You will just know. Be guided by what you feel in your heart."

My life had taken on a completely new dimension. No longer was it all about doing the shopping, going to work during the day, coming home in the evening and organising things for the boys. It hadn't been that way for a while, but now there was a depth of discovery which I hadn't expected.

I had taken the step onto a path of self discovery and through walking that sometimes painful path, I was beginning to appreciate that there really was much more to life than the things we can see with our eyes. Perhaps because this concept wasn't as widely accepted as it could be, I found that I tended to keep these experiences to myself and only shared them with close friends and family.

I think because of my experiences, having been admitted to a psychiatric hospital, I felt that people would think I really was crazy if I started talking about what I was now experiencing on a daily basis. I knew that I was a little fearful of being labelled again, as I once had been. I was fearful that I would be judged and ridiculed for believing in this non-physical world. I had been ridiculed before and the words still stung when I remembered them.

However, as I gradually opened myself to these new experiences and as I became more comfortable with them in my life, I worried less and less about what people might think or say. People were coming into my life who also believed and experienced similar things, and this helped me realise that we weren't mad.

These people were ordinary and led ordinary lives (just like me) and yet they too had conversations with 'spirit' or saw energy or sensed things with a deep knowing that they couldn't explain. I was so fortunate to have these people come into my life as they helped me to relax into my self and gave me a renewed enthusiasm to keep going with my journey.

I had developed a routine each morning in the shower where I would spend a few brief minutes in silent meditation and connecting with the light energies. It was my way of setting up my day. It was a wonderful way to start the day and a time when I had no interruptions. These days though, I couldn't guarantee this - some mornings I would become aware that a guide had appeared before me in the shower.

"For goodness sake, I'm in the shower!' I would mutter, "Some privacy might not go amiss."

I suppose that I was partly embarrassed, as I presumed they could see my naked form. Though after speaking to a friend, she explained that all they see is our true light form, the body means something completely different to them than it does to us humans. I was very glad to hear it.

A whole variety of healing, clearing chakras and conversations went on whilst I was showering. At first I was a little peeved at these visits from light beings, but I soon became used to it and if I wasn't in the mood that day I politely asked them to leave and come back another time.

Sometimes at night as I lay in bed just before sleeping I asked for healing from my guides and any angelic beings. I often saw light and could feel many beings working around me. Several times I saw the doors I had been shown before. I was still unsure of their significance, yet felt it had something to do with my purpose here. One moment this purpose would seem so clear and the next it was lost. I had an impression that it felt like a vast task and yet I still didn't really know what the task was, it was still eluding me.

Rae had explained to me in a reading that I was being guided, but it took the form of a 'carrot and stick' kind of guidance. I wondered if this was to ensure that I didn't walk away from it all. That each small piece of the puzzle which was provided got me excited and wanting to learn more. Yet at times I felt fed up of it all too. I was confused and frustrated. It felt like I knew and then didn't. I likened it to catching smoke. Just when you thought you had it, you opened your hand and there was nothing there.

One day I felt that I had been visited by Merlin. When I asked about it I received confirmation. But was it really Merlin who had come to me in the shower? Rae had said his energy was powerful and yet I had felt little in the way of that energy when we connected. This alone made me doubt my vision. I was told then that this was because my own energy was of a high vibration and strength now that I hadn't felt an immense energy when we had connected. All was being integrated and I was to trust all I saw and felt.

A few days after this I met up with my friend Megan. We spoke of the energy connections and how, though it would seem I was connecting with Merlin, I didn't feel the energy as massively as when we had first connected. Megan explained that this was because I already knew the energy. I had integrated it on that first 'meeting' of myself and Merlin. This made perfect sense. Her explanation felt right. So I continued to connect to these guides and angels on a daily basis and my treatment sessions with clients, friends and family became more profound.

In early January I awoke feeling very tired. The previous night, just as I had been ready to turn off my light and go to sleep I was prompted to place my Moldavite crystal beneath my pillow. Apparently I was to receive healing during the night and need do nothing, just to go to sleep. This sounded rather good. As I was drifting off to sleep, I was enfolded in love, comforted and supported by beings around me. That was all I could remember.

I had a busy day in the office with little in the way of breaks. At midday I went outside, enjoying the coolness of the air and the respite from constant phone calls, emails and demands on my time. The squirrels in the grounds were leaping through the branches of a tree into some bushes, making them shake as they ran through them. I laughed out loud, as the bush looked like it had a life of its own and was dancing.

As I began to walk back to the building I began to sense changes within and around me. I felt calm and centred, despite my hectic day. That name or word 'Nexus' kept popping into my head. I received a text from Megan. She needed to speak to me. I let her know that I only had a short time before I had to go into a meeting. She called me immediately. She told me that she had a message from the Universe:-

"Love and accept yourself for who you are now, because who you are now is exactly who and what you are meant to be."

I was stunned. This was exactly what had been coming to me for weeks. That I must accept myself for who I am. Yet I had found myself constantly drawn back to look at my other lives and didn't know why. I didn't know much about any lives I may have had and I had heard many people say that you must find out about past lives to help you heal things which remained unresolved.

I was beginning to appreciate now that despite what I felt about these past lives, despite what felt like huge hurdles to get over those experiences from the past, they were showing me my gifts, as well as showing me what I had previously endured. Perhaps these small snippets were even giving me some clue what some of those life lessons had been and perhaps where I had got things a little wrong and the areas which I still needed to work on. I knew inside that I mustn't dwell on them but at the same time they intrigued me.

At times I ached to know more. The Universes idea of the 'carrot and stick' was my idea of purgatory. Sometimes though these things cannot be rushed and no matter how much I wanted the answers, I was being taught a lesson in patience and the answers wouldn't arrive until the timing was just right. I thanked Megan for calling. I needed to stop analysing and let things 'be' for a while.

After the meeting at work, I went outside, attempting to clear my head. It had been stuffy in the room. It was such a beautiful day and again I got a feeling of new 'stuff' being around. Things just felt different. Suddenly I began to wonder if the 'new' energy had arrived?

I asked and heard a 'yes'.

"Wow, when did that happen?" I thought. I got a quick flash of memory. I was asked last night to place the Moldavite under my pillow. That was the catalyst or channel for it. I felt the truth of this very strongly. I was so excited I could barely focus for the last hour at work. I wanted to get home and really take some time to connect with my guides about this.

I had a client in the early evening, a lovely gentle woman. After giving her a session of Reflexology I began to do a little energy work. I stood at the foot of the treatment couch and heard "Ask for Nexus." I did just that and saw a huge rush of energy coming towards me, round and bright, like a Catherine wheel firework. It stopped and I watched as it began to move, spiralling slowly up from her feet to her head. It was magnificent to see and I offered immense gratitude for this gift of sight through my third eye.

I became aware that there were smaller versions of this energy coming out of each finger as I pointed my hands towards her. The heat was building and I was told that I need do nothing.

The energy knew what to do. I was there to hold the space for the energy to work.

After a little while, I moved to her head and cupped it in my hands gently. There was a pulsating beat there. I stayed in that position for ten minutes or so and then I moved down to her feet again. The heat subsided a little at this point. From my position at her feet I could see Flies with Pony with his white unicorn behind him. The unicorn placed the energy spiral into her heart area. It was glowing gold and light was beaming out from that area.

When she came round from the deeply relaxed state she explained how incredible the treatment had felt. She had felt an energy working up her body from her feet after I had finished the Reflexology. I was advised later that evening that the spiral energy working up the body was the 'Nexus Spiral'.

I initiated a few people with the Nexus energy. I was keen to have feed back from people I trusted and who would also keep this energy quiet for a while until it was time to share it with other practitioners. I wasn't sure if that was ever meant to be, but the others found the energy incredible to work with. Most were finding that during treatment sessions, their clients were more deeply relaxed and the effects of the session were more profound.

On one occasion, we worked in a group on a man who had been in a car accident some years ago. His hip had been badly damaged and at age forty-nine, he limped heavily and was in pain most days. His consultant had explained that he was too young for a hip replacement and so he seemed resigned to waiting another few years for some relief. We asked him what he would particularly like to receive during this session, as the

Nexus potential was limitless. He asked for a 'new' hip joint.

So we began. As the energy built, the heat in the room was immense. I began to see his hip joint completely change inside and seemed to eventually become a liquid silver colour. I was told that it was complete, his hip joint had been energetically replaced. I had no idea how, but knew something very special had happened. I asked him after the session to let me know how things developed over the next few weeks.

I heard from him some weeks later. The pain in his hip joint had subsided and he was limping far less. He had been able to do more exercise and as a result was becoming fitter and stronger. His demeanor had improved, having been quite low in mood before the session. He was delighted with the effects of the treatment, as was I.

This was what I had been told the energy could do. It was capable of replacing; regenerating and rejuvenating organs, systems and parts of the body. This was something I felt was possible, without any doubt in my mind and over the coming months, this energy proved to me that it was very special indeed.

At the very end of January 2009, these words found their way to me:

"The holographic blueprint consciousness of the new Earth is being created NOW for the future melding with this physical Earth we inhabit. Every time a healing event occurs here, we each add to that conscious blueprint, so creating and energising the holographic threads of light. By not using the talents and gifts you have right now, you lessen the potential for that blueprint.

Consider this. You were drawn to energy work (or to read this book) for a reason. You were 'called' or 'awakened' by your higher knowing to step forward to assist in the conscious awakening of the planet. Such things as energetic replacement or rejuvenation of body organs, systems and structures; taking them back to their original blueprint of health is possible RIGHT NOW.

This challenges current ways of thinking for the majority of people, but the light workers, those who work with beautiful energies to help raise the consciousness, know this is possible. In fact it is happening right now, here on Earth. The more people work with their beautiful energies, the more awareness is added to this conscious blueprint ready for it to meld when the time is right.

It is now time to recognise and acknowledge the calling to your higher knowledge and join with other light workers to work together in groups of two or more. To access the greater healing potential of the group energy. It is time now to access your true 'power', recognise that within you which can do ANYTHING once you connect to the higher vibrational energies beyond those which you are working with at this time."

I was awestruck at these words. I had felt for a while now with the energy work I was doing that so much more was possible. Almost that something was missing from the Reiki energy. Perhaps not quite missing. It was more that people were most definitely not of the same vibration as when Reiki was brought to the world by Mikao Usui.

I felt that the world had moved on and that new energies were required to support them and help them in greater ways than Reiki was able to provide. It had served an enormous purpose and was a beautiful blessing to be the catalyst for even more wondrous energy to emerge when the time was right.

My own experience with the Sekhem and now the Nexus energy had proved that to me beyond any doubt. People needed higher vibration energy to help them shift much deeper issues or ailments which were stuck inside. One of the ways to achieve this was to work in groups. This facilitated a much higher energy and all the gifts and talents of the group were available all at once to enable deeper healing. I discussed this with a few of my friends. who very much supported this way of working.

A few weeks later Lorna contacted me to let me know she was running a Karuna Reiki course shortly and she asked if I might be interested in attending. I hadn't considered it before, but when I sat with the idea for a while it felt right to do.

I had wondered for a while why I was being guided to attend these workshops and courses. I was shifting and moving with each course. I felt an urgency to my personal journey, but didn't understand why. With each course I attended I knew that I was healing deep wounds and hurts. Without healing these and letting them go, we cannot move on.

Sometimes I felt that I didn't want to move on anymore. Sometimes my healing was intense and painful. Yet something inside me was pushing me on to do more. I had gained greater understanding of myself over the past four years and knew from some of my teachers that I was on a 'fast track' of learning. Why I was on this fast track, I was yet to discover.

I had found that each time I felt weary and in need of rest, someone had come into my life to help motivate and support me. Somehow I kept being drawn back to this path of energy work and self discovery and it really was a blind faith of sorts. I had no idea where it was leading me, yet the choices I was making felt right at the time.

I was learning very quickly that this was all I could ask of myself and was learning not to analyse or judge my choices. Coming from a fault finding scientific background, this analytical mind set was a challenge to put aside at times.

I felt very drawn to attending Lorna's Karuna course, like an urge to be there for my own growth and that of the bigger picture. Some people had told me that I didn't require any more tools to do what I need to do, yet I was drawn like a magnet to further my expansion of inner knowing and healing.

Lorna had also invited me along to sit in on a Reiki Master class she was running. I was keen to go. Seeing how other teachers share their knowledge and experience is always useful and no matter what, we always learn something from others, no matter how small that something is.

I spent the day with Lorna and her students. One of the first meditations was to connect with our Reiki guide. Lorna began the meditation.

"Picture yourself in your living room at home. Feel comfortable and familiar with this space. You may picture it exactly or just know you are there. Now take yourself into your garden or into a park or place in nature where you are comfortable and at peace. In the centre of your garden a ball of energy emerges slowly, turning into a ball or column of mist....."

Lorna continued speaking and I was vaguely aware of her words but began to drift through a beautiful experience. This is my account of it.

"I see a mist. In it I see Flies with Pony, my guide. He is dancing and twirling inside the mist. It is so very clear. He emerges from the mist and beckons me to join him. I step inside the mist and we are standing facing each other. We begin to rotate inside the mist and then spiral skywards together.

I see his unicorn. Our unicorn. He is so beautiful, white and shimmering. I lean against him, feeling the love pouring from him and enveloping me. I am safe and warm. Together Flies with Pony and I appear on his back and we fly higher and higher.

Now I can see Flies with Pony and I, standing side by side, our hands entwined. We begin to walk and I can see a band of light before us stretching into the distance. Slow steps at first, which begin to quicken. I see us from a great distance and realise we are walking on a huge sphere of some kind.

It soon becomes clear that this sphere is Earth. Faster and faster, we seem to be running, still hand in hand and the band of light is going round and round the Earth until we begin to fly around it. I see Earth with light all around it. It seems to be glowing pure white. We are hovering now, watching the Earth and I feel the 'job' is done."

Questions emerged in my head.

"Were we healing the Earth? Were we helping to prepare it? Preparing for the merging?" I thought.

This was so similar to other 'visions' I have had for some time now. Was I being shown what I am to do or what I am doing?

It was an amazing experience, very beautiful and though I seemed to have no clue what I am doing, I realise that I am doing it. I am bringing light to this Earth and helping to heal, balance and ascend those people who live here, as well as the Earth itself. Each time I did a healing session for myself or someone else, I was adding to the healing of all.

That felt really wonderful.

After this meditation I picked a card from two different packs which Lorna had on a table. Each card had the same message. 'Speak my truth.' I laughed inwardly. I knew this meant to speak it to others, but also to myself.

Later that morning, I was given a Reiki attunement from Lorna. I hadn't expected this. I was there as an observer, and this was a lovely surprise. I sat down in her tranquil treatment room and could feel Lorna working behind me. I felt gentle energy touching the back of my head.

As I relaxed completely another vision began to play in front of my eyes. I was escorted by two people up a set of steps into what looked like a temple. We were all dressed in white robes. There was a long table in the temple which had what looked like very soft leather or chamois draped across it.

On the table there were many items laid out on the cloth. I could see crystals, books and feathers amongst the items. I felt I was to pick something up but I was told "no."

In front of me the table covering was rolled up, with all items inside. The roll of cloth seemed to shrink right down. I knew there was no way all those items could become so small a package in this reality, but that was how it appeared. The roll was given to me.

I heard, "Yes, you do need to speak your truth. But it isn't quite time. Nearly. Nearly time to do the work you are here to do. I will speak to you and guide you. I am here always and know it is work of pure love."

I emerged from the temple. I seemed to have a golden crown on my head but it then changed from the crown into a head-dress of feathers. I was wearing the same golden cloak with jewels and colours that I recalled seeing when I received the attunement sixteen months ago from Kiannaa. I felt immense love all around me.

I told Lorna what I had seen during this lovely attunement from her. We both felt that it was showing me that all the tools I needed were all there. They had been given to me. Then perhaps I wasn't meant to attend the Karuna Reiki course. If I had all the tools I needed, why then would I need to go on this course? I was a little confused, yet still felt drawn to go.

A few weeks later I was involved in a minor car accident. A car reversed into mine at a junction which was blocked by another vehicle. The driver hadn't seen me behind them waiting to turn. There was some damage to my car, but no injuries either to myself or to Glenn.

I wasn't even angry or upset. No-one had been hurt and after all, they were only cars. It did cause some extra hassle in my life whilst I sorted out the repair, but beyond that I felt I was fine. Yet a few days after the accident I began to feel exhausted, numb and tearful. I kept telling myself that there was no reason for this. It had been a minor accident, but I soon realised that I was in need of some assistance.

I was blessed that Danielle, a friend and colleague, was able to do a treatment for me and as she began to settle my energy, I felt a rising of emotion to the point I thought I would cry and then it was gone.

I felt muscles cramping in areas of my back, which was intense but short lived. As Danielle laid her hands on my back, with each movement the pain moved further down. She was drawn to my right shoulder blade area and asked me to describe what was there. Immediately a hollow triangle appeared to me and I told her what I could see.

Immediately the triangle started to rotate and spin, faster and faster. Then another triangle, upside down, appeared and joined the other triangle to form a 3-D star. This then rotated faster and faster. Shortly after this faces began to appear to me, very clearly and in human form. Each one looked me in the eye and seemed very close.

Each one said to me, "It's not your fault. You aren't to blame."

I felt much better after the session and I asked my guides later that night for an explanation or hint as to the meaning of what was said to me during the session. "You are not to blame for humans not listening."

I wasn't sure what this meant either. The more I thought about it I wondered if it was to do with my teaching work. I had been trying to help others and yet was faced with apathy and fear from some of them, making the work with some almost impossible. I felt that I was reaching only a few.

I had always reasoned that reaching a few was better than none at all. Perhaps I was trying too hard. After all, we each have a choice what we do and what we choose to hear. Perhaps it was time to really step back and look after myself more. I had been a little remiss in that department of late and decided to book a Raindrop treatment with Danielle.

I was looking forward to this treatment. I hadn't received a Raindrop for many months. I lay down on the couch and before Danielle had even picked the oils for the session, I was aware that work had already begun on me.

I could see my body being separated into two halves, with a gap up the spine. Each side of my body was pushed apart and ash like material appeared in this long gap and I could see hands pushing the ash or powder out of my body and off to one side. It fell off the couch.

"Being swept clean," I thought.

The experience was wonderful, with huge shifts and tremendous heat in areas on my back. When I sat up, I was wobbly and it took me a while to come back to the space without feeling like I would fall over. I had obviously received some very deep healing and I felt vastly better physically; calm and centred emotionally.

I met a young woman, Karen, a few days later who was learning to use her psychic gift. She offered me a reading and I accepted. She had the most intense blue eyes and her reading proved to be very interesting.

She saw a pregnancy, but that there were two babies, yet only one was born. My stomach lurched. Could this be the pregnancy with Callum? I had always felt that he had been a twin, yet had no medical proof to confirm or deny this. Karen confirmed that my instincts were valid and that one twin had died very early on in the pregnancy. Callum was indeed a twin.

This made so much sense to me. Just the way Callum had been as a young child, his behaviour and actions, all pointed to this being correct. Karen also saw a Buddhist centre and described the interior of the room. Without knowing it, she had perfectly described the room in which Lorna's forthcoming Karuna Reiki workshop was being held. Karen confirmed that it would be in my interests to do the course. She was shown hundreds of rabbits and was told that this was to show the number of people I would be helping in the future.

She was told to tell me to stop shouting. I laughed at this. The angels were telling her that they were taking my healing out to people and working to help these people listen so that they could heal and move forward on their soul path.

The word 'patience' also came through to her. I was to be patient. Things were being made ready. I was to take care of myself as I tended to work too many hours and became tired and my energy depleted.

She turned another card and explained that she felt overwhelmed with a massive and beautiful energy. She said that the job I am to do here is definitely the healing which I was doing, but it was going to be vastly more powerful than I could imagine. I had been hand picked for the job, apparently. This was a wonderful reading from someone just 'learning' and I was very grateful to her.

I made my decision and committed to the Karuna Reiki course. I spoke to my friend Emma about it and told her that I was doing the Karuna because I felt I needed more compassionate energy when I work, she said that compassion wasn't missing from my sessions at all. It was very much apparent whilst I work.

That got me thinking and later that night it came to me that the reason I needed to do this Karuna course was to accept the compassion for myself. This made me well up with tears as I realised the enormity of it. Despite so much work, I still didn't love myself that much. I had broken through and had begun to love myself but there was scope for a whole lot more.

The next morning I was feeling quite emotional. I was thankful yet again for the wonderful essential oils which have helped me to move on from so much pain and hurt. I used Forgiveness oil over my heart centre. I felt 'tender' inside.

Emotions were coming up about Tom; the abuse; the miscarriage. It wasn't earth shattering in scale but I could feel them in my heart and I noticed that occasionally my heart missed a beat. Work was work at the office, as usual. I realised that I was so uninspired by it and that I was desperate to leave. I was almost on the brink of walking out, yet knew it was still too soon for that.

A week later was the first day of the Karuna course. The first attunement was gentle and delicate. I began to feel warm gentle energy around me and as Lorna worked behind me I could see a purple heart in front of me. This purple heart then turned to pink and began to pulsate. I saw a door open a little and light pour through the small opening.

Gentle tears ran down my face as I felt pure love all around me from this light. I could see a face peeking around the edge of the door, but I couldn't quite make out any features. I could certainly feel the mischief pouring from this being. Then, one by one, light beings came through the open doorway and we were hugging.

My heart was pounding in my chest. I felt heavy yet light, all at the same time. The purple came and went with yellow blends on occasions. The purple colour appeared again and suddenly turned into the most electrifying 3D colour, so real I felt that I could touch it. The attunement was complete and I began to feel very hot and a deep 'silence' seemed to pervade every cell.

On the second day Lorna talked us through a meditation. I had wanted to do a shadow self meditation for a while and had no idea what to expect. I saw a ring of fire, then I saw myself standing in the centre of this ring of fire and I began to fly, making a shape in the sky.

Then I was on a beach and I could see what looked like a cup or bowl begin to float down from the sky. As it got closer I could see it was a 'cup' of white feathers with a light coming from the centre. It was mesmerizing to watch as it gently floated down onto the sand. I could see there was a figure in the centre of this feather 'cup' and as the figure stepped forward I realised that it was Lord Sananda. My heart filled with joy and warmth.

We were directed to look behind a rock at our shadow self. It could take any form at all or have no form. Lorna directed us to just have an open mind to what you saw or sensed behind the rock. I could see my shadow self. It took the form of a small being, very light in colour with beautiful large eyes.

I was not alarmed by this at all, somehow almost expecting this form. My shadow self wanted me to help heal the anger. The being held a baby in its arms and I was told this was the twin I lost whilst I was pregnant with Callum. I was sobbing quietly, tears flooding down my face. I could feel Lord Sananda using this 'cup' of feathers all over me, helping me to heal on all levels and helping the healing of my shadow self.

My shadow self asked me to step away from the workplace I was currently in. It was too damaging to my soul. It asked me to work with energy and share my healing gift. We hugged and held each other and I was so grateful for this opportunity.

A few hours after the shadow self meditation and it was time for the second attunement. As Lorna began her preparations, we were all seated in a circle with our eyes closed ready for her to begin. I realised that I could see bright light emanating from the centre of the palms of my hands and as I observed my hands with my eyes still closed, I could see that there was a round hole in each palm. Through the 'holes' was a long rod of white light stretching out to either side of me as far as I could see.

I couldn't quite believe what I was seeing. I settled myself more comfortably and could feel Lorna working behind me. It felt loving and light. She moved away, to work on another person and I began to feel heavy and a little nauseous. I could see skaters drawing shapes on the ice with their skate blades. There were two separate triangles. I began to feel waves of pulsating energy.

During this attunement I found myself so deeply relaxed that I was slumped over in my seat. This was most unusual for me. I had experienced a variety of attunements, but none had felt

as intense as this. I saw my 'self' lying on a floor then saw a
pair of arms lift the figure from the floor and place it into what
looked like the ocean. The waves were gently rolling near
the waters edge. This was repeated over and over to me and
I didn't know why. I began to feel that there was much more
happening than a simple attunement, though I didn't know
what that might be.

The attunement was complete and as I opened my eyes, I felt
different. My vision was strange and I felt a little unsteady. I
lay on the floor for a short while then felt the need to go outside
for some air. I walked out onto the stone steps at the entrance,
my bare feet on the cold stone. This felt really good, but each
time I was upright and walking I felt unsteady and slightly
queasy. I began to feel very cold, a sure sign that I was healing
or processing at a very deep core level.

I sat in a chair with a blanket around me shivering. My skin
was warm yet I felt ice cold. Lorna directed me to lie down on
one of the therapy couches, as I was in need of some treatment
and that was the next stage of the workshop. Oh, how I
welcomed the thought of lying down for a while.

As I lay on the couch with my eyes closed, the whole scene
started to play out in front of me again. I saw the arms
outstretched and the figure being placed into water. This played
two or three times and each time I could see the picture more
clearly. The arms placed the figure into what looked like a
bath and eventually I could see that it looked like a bath of the
crystal Selenite. It was beautiful and delicate.

This scene played another few times until I realised that I was
the figure and it was me who was being placed in this Selenite
crystal bath full of water. As I lay in this bath, I became aware

that the shape was oval and I could see two light forms, one on either side of me holding each of my hands.

My stomach lurched as I became instantly aware that I was 'home' and this scene was my 'birth'. I was overwhelmed with feelings of love and joy and yet knew I was being shown me leaving this place of love and light. I didn't want to leave this place, it was so magnificent.

The treatment was complete. I had been aware of all sounds and movements around me, yet I was unable to move. I had been very deeply relaxed. Lorna came over to the couch and all three practitioners who had been working on me were gently urging me to return.

As I slowly returned, the tears were running down my face. I began to sob, feeling so homesick. Why did I have to come back? I didn't want to be here. I explained to them what had happened during the treatment, that I was home. I had just seen my 'birth' from that place of light. I was so overwhelmed by the experience. On the one hand I was very sad and yet I had been shown a wondrous thing.

Lorna explained that this was an inevitable stage in my evolvement and she wasn't at all surprised at what I had just experienced. Yet it had never crossed my mind that I would see this. I rolled into a ball on my side, sobbing for a few minutes just trying to accept what I had experienced and letting the emotions flow and release.

Within a short while I felt able to get up and I began to feel such strong energy pulsing through me. All sadness gone, I was in awe of what had occurred for me today and I was ready now to move on to the next stage. I assisted with a healing treatment, knowing it would help to focus and ground me. I felt wonderful afterwards.

On the drive to the course on the third and final day, my friends Christine and Danielle were discussing how much they were enjoying the course. I felt a deep shift within me since yesterday. It was such a very different day.

The final attunement was in complete contrast to the previous day. It was gentle and loving with the purple heart again. This time it changed from a heart to a 3-D square, back to a heart and then to a 3-D pyramid shape. It was fascinating to watch.

We worked with 'sounding' and I could feel the heat of the Karuna energy flow through me as we made the sounds. I loved it. I felt it was a compliment to what I was already doing and I could feel a great deal of anger had dissipated from me over these past three days. There was an inner calmness which seemed to be at my core.

I openly thanked all the angels and masters and any light beings who may have helped during these three days. It had been a wonderful experience. I was looking forward to using this energy when I was working with people and looking forward to its nurturing effects for me.

Chapter Fourteen

It was early August 2009 and a new part of my life had emerged. My eldest son, Callum, had received his final exam results and had passed all the subjects he required to go to University. I was delighted for him and so proud.

He had experienced his own challenges along the way and there had been times we wondered if he would turn things around enough to follow his dream. He had and I could see a new spark of confidence in his eyes. It was a time of celebration for the whole family and I looked at this young man of eighteen and wondered where those years had gone so quickly. I'm sure every mother has thought the same thing and can remember the day their child was born.

Those eighteen years seemed to have flashed past. My heart filled with love as I recalled memories of those years. I had done a good job after all. I had doubted my ability as a mother at times, as I am sure many mothers do. Yet I looked at my son and realised that I had helped nurture his growth in every way. I had helped him become the lovely young man he was, simply by loving him.

This was another turning point in my life. Callum was an

independant person now. He was having to take responsibility for his own decisions and choices, something I had always encouraged. He knew that I was there to support and love him, whatever his choices were and I felt stronger than ever that I was letting my little boy go. It felt good yet was tinged with a little sadness. Perhaps there was a little grief, an ending of the old relationship and the beginning of a new one.

This was exciting too, I realised. I watched as he set about making his own preparations, with a little bit of guidance, to begin this next stage of his life.

Glenn had passed his fourth year exams, achieving much better results than even he had imagined possible. Both my boys were doing so well and I was immensely proud of them.

An older gentleman came to me for a session of Raindrop, primarily to see if this could help him relax and relieve his muscle aches. He had stomach cancer and his doctors had given him little hope of a recovery.

I gave him a Raindrop treatment and during this was able to connect with his higher self. We had quite a chat about things and his higher self explained to me that though he wasn't ready to leave at a human level, his higher self knew it was time. This wasn't unusual for me. I had been able to connect to people's 'higher' self, their soul, for a while and was often guided for the client's highest good.

Stewarts higher self asked me to clear him energetically as much as I possibly could, which I did after the Raindrop. He felt much better after this treatment reporting that he had several pain free days and generally felt more well.

I saw him again two weeks later for another Raindrop and was asked again to clear him. I had a feeling that he didn't have long. I discussed none of this with Stewart, his higher self asking me not to. Stewart and I had built a cheery relationship very quickly and I think he knew that his time was limited.

I found out a few weeks later that he had passed away. I had a 'feeling' this was the case three days before being told. Later that evening, during a quiet time in the garden, his higher self came to me briefly and thanked me for what I had done.

This was a very humbling experience. I was told very clearly that part of my 'role' is to clear people of their past baggage and issues so that they may pass more easily and with a 'clean slate', if you like. This allows the soul to be able to ascend on the other side free of, or less bogged down with, generations of emotional and spiritual baggage.

It was a moment of great clarity and understanding which I hadn't quite been able to put into words before. Far from being a depressing thought, I think this is a wonderful gift to be able to give to a soul, to help clear their past baggage so that they can move on. This tied in with the phrase I had heard before about me helping people to 'ascend.'

Little by little, these small pieces were coming together so that I could see where I fitted into the bigger picture of life. This role tied in with my role as a mother too. I had worked very much towards nurturing my sons ability to look inside themselves for answers and inner strength, knowing that this would benefit them greatly in their lives as they grew into young men. I was also becoming aware that tied in with the ascension role was another dimension of awakening people.

As I drifted off to sleep one evening, the words 'I facilitate awakenings' popped into my conscious mind and remained in my mind the following morning.

We humans call it healing, which of course it is, but it is the awakening which so many people ('lightworkers') here on Earth are helping to facilitate. I had been told by guides that I help people ascend, and of course for people to ascend, they must first awaken.

During the writing of this book, I had contemplated whether it was necessary at all. Though part of me was unsure of its value, part of me understood that it might help others awaken also. Awaken to the fact that there is more to life than a nine to five job, shopping, cleaning the house, mundane jobs and most importantly to awaken to see themselves for the beautiful beings that they are inside, no matter what form their exterior.

As I was going through my own 'awakening' and with each workshop I attended, I understood more what this meant. I had begun to experience small things from past lives. Whether this was 'past' as in human timeframe or whether this was a life which was being experienced simultaneously, I didn't know.

My brain couldn't cope with trying to figure that one out. All I knew was that I was being shown things from other lives I had experienced and at each workshop or during healing sessions, similar pains or wounds were coming up to be released.

At first I had thought these wounds or pains were the same ones coming back time after time. But I began to realise that they were different wounds from different lives. They may have been in similar places on my body, but they were from different lives. I wasn't sure why this might be, but the more I thought about it, the more it felt right.

One such experience happened after a beautiful workshop in 2009 facilitated by Rae. I had really enjoyed the workshop and felt the immense energies which were present. I had a strange headache after the workshop. It felt like I had something stuck in the top of my head and when I closed my eyes I was convinced I could see the handle of an axe out to the right side of my head. As the day wore on, the headache became more severe and my energy felt like it was draining away. It was most peculiar.

I contacted a friend and asked if she could help me shift whatever it was. She worked remotely and removed an axe from my skull and a dagger from my shoulder. She could see that my head had been split in two. What came to her was that I had been attacked (in a past life) by an Indian Chief who had felt threatened by me. I got the feeling that the Indian Chief may have been my ex-husband, Tom, though I wasn't sure. It seemed that we had shared many lives together in a variety of roles.

Within an hour my energy began to return and the headache disappeared. Much as these seemed very crazy experiences, they were happening regularly. Far from feeling frightened, I saw these as opportunities for me to let go of deep and formerly unresolved 'stuff'. Each time I let some 'stuff' go, I felt better and much more at peace.

My family were always supportive and I think they had realised that as I was releasing my 'stuff' they too were benefitting. I was a lot happier and this filtered through to them too. This is also what my various teachers had referred to as taking responsibility for one's own healing. I was seeing first hand the effects of me addressing and sorting out my issues, both physical and emotional.

One day I thought to myself, "Just think if every person on the planet took responsibility for their own choices, lifestyles and healing and stopped looking to blame others - even if half the people did that, it would be a very different world."

An email from Vicki arrived in my inbox. She was running a workshop I had been waiting for and I responded immediately that I would like a place on it. I had no idea what it entailed but it was a single day of training.

I was excited about seeing Vicki again. The day of the workshop arrived, the sun was shining, it was such a beautiful day. Blessed yet again with such wonderful weather for the workshop and it was great to see her brown Labrador Teddy again. He seemed to have remembered me even though it had been a year since I was last here. I could hardly believe that so much time had passed since my last visit.

Vicki was looking well and on good form for the workshop. Our first of two meditations was wonderful. I was a little reserved and seem to find it difficult to relax fully. I was lying on a fluffy blanket with another one on top of me and as I relaxed throughout the meditation a band of freezing coldness slowly worked up my body. By the end of the meditation I was shivering and feeling like a block of ice.

As the day progressed, and ancient Egyptian schooling was discussed, it became clear to me that I hadn't 'graduated' in this human existence before. Vicki explained that there were many reasons for this and part of the reason for the workshop was to find out why you didn't graduate, release that and move past it so that we could graduate now.

During group sessions we discovered that in previous times, initiates were placed into a sarcophagus and left there to either 'get it' or die. I knew I died, more than once. I didn't know how I knew, I just did.

It became apparent that one thing which had stopped me graduating before was me sacrificing myself for others. I was being trained in the healing arts and was very good, trained by an immensely gifted and powerful healer. I agreed to sacrifice myself for the good of all, and so never graduating.

This left me feeling angry and frustrated in many lives afterwards. I had been 'on track' and doing what I was meant to do, but that had all stopped. I recognised the feelings which had filtered through into this life and suddenly it made more sense. The anger and frustration in this life wasn't just about this life.

I asked that during the workshop these emotions and traumas be released and healed. It was ancient history now. It was time to heal and move on.

I couldn't recall much of the afternoon meditation. I was much warmer this time and was aware that I was seeing very quick images. They were so quick that only a few were really visible or making any sense. I felt like I was floating, I was convinced that I could feel my bottom begin to leave the floor slightly, my head also. The lightness of my body was intriguing. It was all very fast and I was experiencing feelings of immense love. I was smiling from ear to ear.

We were being guided by Vicki to begin to return to the crystal steps we had been directed to climb at the beginning of the meditation. I hadn't heard many of her other words. As I descended the steps, I got a quick glimpse of the crystal crown I was given a while ago in another meditation and again I saw it melding into my head and it disappeared.

I caught quick glimpses of the temple steps I climbed to receive all the books, tools and artefacts rolled into a fine leather cloth. I smiled at the remembrance of it. The meditation was coming to a close and part of me was a little disappointed - I hadn't seen or been shown so very much in this meditation. I told myself that was okay, perhaps it just wasn't time to see any more.

Then, suddenly I saw myself stop at the bottom of the crystal steps and a flowing cloak was placed around my shoulders. I knew it was crystal, yet it wasn't solid. It was like liquid quartz crystal, flowing, floating, soft, yet made of crystal. I wasn't sure this was possible, yet I knew it was a quartz crystal robe. It was very beautiful.

I turned to leave the steps and was told to stay where I was. In front of me I could see a pale purple head. As I focused on it more, I saw it was an amethyst crystal skull. My heart began to thump in my chest. I saw my hands outstretched and the skull was placed gently into them. I wasn't sure how I felt, excited and in awe. I held the skull for a few moments, unable to completely focus on it to see it fully. I held the skull out, to hand it back, grateful for being able to hold and connect with it. But my hands were pushed back towards me, still holding the skull. Was I to keep it? I knew instinctively that I was and I felt tears welling up in my eyes.

As I gently returned to the room as the meditation ended, I

felt that I had to go outside. My heart was so full of love I was sure it would burst. As I stood on the decking of Vicki's house, looking onto the hills with the sun beaming down, I realised that I had just graduated.

Unsure of exactly what I had graduated in I questioned this feeling. Surely not? Yet in my heart I knew I had. I wanted to shout and dance, yet out of respect for the others gently coming back from their meditation experiences in the room behind me, I remained silent.

I walked down into the garden to the trampoline and began to bounce, higher and higher and then let out one single, loud 'Yeeehhhhaaaaaaa!!' It reverberated around the hills, a joyous expression of this special occasion.

As I sat on the decking, to write a few words about my experience for my journals, I looked into the sky. There right above us was an upturned half rainbow. A rainbow smile in the sky. It was right next to the sun, shining down on us, blessing us with great warmth and energy.

I pointed out the rainbow to the others in the group and we couldn't believe what we were seeing. I had never seen a rainbow in that shape before. Then as I watched, this disappeared and two round balls of light appeared on either side of the sun. These balls were also rainbow colours and over the space of a few minutes it almost seemed like the sun and the two rainbow circles were making a perfect elongated oval shape in the sky. Like a flying saucer shape. We were all awestruck at this sight and I remember wishing I had brought my camera. However, the sight is etched in my memory.

I was so amazed at these latest discoveries and new

understanding. I felt I was in uncharted territory. It was both exciting and a little overwhelming. I was ready, in ways I did not understand, but I was ready. For the next step, the next stage of my development and of my divine purpose.

However, I experienced an intense letting go of the old. Much to my dismay this took the form of a friendship coming to an abrupt end. I had felt for a few weeks that our relationship had changed. I wasn't sure if that was because I was changing or if it had just run it's natural course. Sometimes we aren't meant to be friends with people forever. It hurt at the time, our friendship had meant a great deal to me. I spoke with my friend at an etheric level, wished her well from my heart, and hoped she found peace inside soon.

I had been helping Mum rearrange and decorate her bedroom. She had been clearing out an old cupboard and came across a few items left over from the custody battle of the children ten years ago. I hadn't remembered that she still had these and I roared with laughter when I saw them. They weren't in the least bit amusing at the time, but now years later with much healing done and time passed I could see the funny side of it all.

I met with my friend Emma and for some reason showed her these items. This led on to a long conversation during which I realised that it was time to let all this stuff go. I was holding on to it, and for what reason? The boys were both over sixteen and the child custody paperwork was no longer valid. There was no reason to keep it.

In fact there was no reason to keep any of the paperwork. I could feel the truth in her words. I recalled telling another friend earlier that year that I felt I still had something to either let go of or heal before I could move on more fully. I hadn't realised until now that this was part of that letting go. I had done so much to heal my broken heart and spirit since Tom left and was a very different person to who I was then. Thankfully. I felt that I was a better person because of it all.

After our chat Emma and I did a treatment swap of Raindrop for each other. I called in the Nexus energy and Emma could really see it this time. I could feel it like never before. My hands could feel the liquid energy cocoon around her and it felt so incredible.

I lay down to receive my treatment and within moments of Emma placing the oils onto my back, I could feel a letting go. A gentle releasing. I could see a large cocoon of liquid energy around me and what looked like tiny bubbles of air coming from my body.

As they reached the outer surface of this energy cocoon I could see and hear them. 'Pop! pop! pop! pop! pop! pop!' It was the most bizarre thing. Almost like bubbles rising to the surface of a fizzy drink in a glass. By the end of the session, I felt light and content.

There was a drive within me. I knew what I must do to help myself move on, to help my family move on.

Once Emma left, I looked out the two box files of legal papers from the divorce, child custody hearing and the bankruptcy. They had been pushed to the back of a cupboard. I set about sorting through the pile created on the floor, sifting through the papers. I didn't read anything, merely checking to ensure that nothing of great importance was left in the pile.

The pile for destroying was quite large. Two box files worth of paperwork. Two box files of bickering. Two box files of hurt.

I was in a state of elation. I knew this was absolutely the right thing to do. The boys didn't need to see any of it. I didn't need to keep it any more. I went out into the garden and started to burn all that paperwork. I was so happy to be doing this. It took a while to burn everything thoroughly.

I couldn't help feeling as I watched the words burning through, that in keeping it all, I had held Tom back from moving on too. I was genuinely sad to realise this. That was never my intent.

I spoke out loud. "I am sorry if I have held on to you too long. I release you now to enjoy your life and fulfill your purpose too."

And in so doing, I released myself to do the same............

Chapter Fifteen

And so the universe responded to that shift, the releasing of my ex-husband Tom and a few months later I received an email from a friend introducing me to a woman called Joy.

She explained that Joy was looking for someone to organise a venue for her workshops and she felt that I might be able to help her with my local knowledge. I decided to look at Joy's website, as I wanted to ensure her work felt right for me to promote and assist with. It all felt good and I emailed her to introduce myself and arrange a convenient time for us to chat about her requirements.

When we started to talk, I felt like I had known her my whole life. The conversation flowed freely and we shared a similar outlook and I found it easy to talk to her. After this long conversation I felt comfortable assisting her. She gave me some possible dates and I set to work arranging a venue for a few of her courses alongside working on my own business ideas.

I had been making plans over the months to develop my business but these had unfortunately fallen through, much to my dismay. Mum was annoyed and upset for me. She had seen the amount of work I had done and the level of commitment

I had. I was disappointed too but pointed out that she would only hurt herself with this amount of anger and it really wasn't worth it.

We did some work to help her release the anger. It helped a little but she was still fuming at the injustice of my situation. A few days after this I returned home from work to find Mum very unwell. I didn't know what else to do for her. She was struggling to breathe properly, was very unsteady on her feet and had been feeling nauseous all day with a stabbing pain in her chest.

I felt that this had probably been building for a couple of weeks and was directly related to how annoyed she was feeling. I had explained to her that when we get so angry or upset about things we hooked into that negative, destructive emotion which then allowed even more denseness to come to us as well. It's like becoming a magnet for all sorts of denser energies to get hold and I had often thought that it was a bit like throwing yourself into a tar pit.

She went to bed early and I looked in on her a little while later to see how she was. When I saw her I sensed that her whole aura was very grey and that her energy was disappearing. It came to me then that she had been so wound up that this was a classic case of drawing a psychic attack to you. I felt sure of it.

She had been so angry that this emotion had lowered her own energy levels and as a result had opened her up for all sorts of dense energies to attach to her. This denseness was depleting her energy now. I did some work to clear as much of that dense, heavy and dark emotional baggage from her and her aura brightness improved.

We chatted the following morning and it became clear that she was beginning to understand that once we start going into the emotions of anger or frustration, our own personal energy lowers in vibration. There are many books available which explain the energy vibration of thoughts and emotions and I knew from personal experience that when I got angry or upset about things in my life I felt unwell or 'out of sorts'.

Mum felt a little better and I did more work with her later that day. My friend Lynn called just after I had finished. She explained that Dad was very concerned about her and this psychic attack or dense energy around her. Lynn explained that I could help by placing a web of light in my front doorway so that every person walking through it was cleared of any dense energy instantly. This felt right to do and would benefit myself and my family, so I did that straight after her call, asking the Archangels to ensure it was completed properly.

A few days later Mum and I were able to talk more fully about her experience. She acknowledged that she most definitely needed to keep herself more in balance so that she didn't draw this kind of dense energy and negativity to her. This is what some of my work is about - to help educate people about what their thoughts can do, how powerful they are if used nastily or used without an appreciation of what these thoughts can do to others. Negative or nasty thoughts are like darts fired at other people and they find their 'target' with ease. Nasty or negative words have an even greater impact.

I knew it was important for people to begin to understand that there is so much more than the physical body we walk around in. I wanted to show others that it is normal to see auras or energies, that this aspect needs to be accepted in our society instead of tucked away in the 'loony' or 'eccentric' corner.

I met people every week who were discovering these gifts within themselves, people who were just as frightened as I had been when my gifts began to emerge. These gifts aren't as widely accepted as they could be and a lot of the people who are 'awakening' feel that they have no-one to talk to about their experiences.

After our conversation I did a brief massage for Mum and once that was complete I knelt at the end of the couch lightly holding her heels. I felt a huge pulse of energy and watched as five light orbs came towards us. These turned into five magnificent white unicorns with an angel on the back of each. The angels dismounted and began to work and I watched as a unicorn stood at Mums head and two unicorns stood at either side.

They bowed their heads and placed their energy horns under her body. Tears were rolling down my face at the sheer beauty of the feeling which was so strong beneath my hands, wave upon wave of divine love and healing energy.

This was a lovely gift, especially as I had felt a bit low the previous night. I went out into the garden pondering my experience and in my head I heard the words, "Look what you can do."

"It's not me, it's just my ability to channel," I replied.

"Yes, but it is this ability which allows us to do what is needed."

I hadn't really thought about it much, just as I hadn't thought about my third eye (etheric) vision. A friend had said to me that she wished she could see what I see. When I mulled over what she'd said I suddenly understood a little about why I see what I see, why I had been given this gift.

One reason was that I had excellent third eye vision in previous lives and I had been able to access this gift more easily this time. I felt I was also being given a test of faith. Because of my life experience thus far I was having to trust in these 'visions' to guide me during the healing work I did and as each 'vision' proved to be correct, this was building my trust in myself.

I began to ponder about this gift of sight. I thought about the 'things' (energy) I had seen moving on the floor during my 'breakdown'. These were labeled as 'hallucinations' which left me feeling mad and not 'normal'. But I had seen those things. I knew that now beyond any shadow of a doubt.

So many times I'd had to face the doubt about my visions because of that labeling years ago, because of others judgements, because others didn't understand or were a bit frightened by this gift. I had known the truth deep inside then, but at the time I was in too much emotional pain and was too disconnected to believe it. So I had believed those judgements and ignored my third eye vision.

It had been a long and rocky road back to that belief in myself. In that moment I expressed my immense gratitude and acknowledged the support and gifts I had been given.

Later that month I had another profound vision during a beautiful meditation led by Rae. There were several of us setting time aside to connect remotely and work as a group. During this work we would receive assistance and healing energies from the Archangels.

I lit a single candle and put on some gentle music. There was a full round moon shining through patches of light cloud and I sat in my treatment room on the floor facing the window, the light of the moon shining on my face. I closed my eyes and could feel the presence of loving beings close to me.

There was some tension down the back of my neck and across my shoulders, which became tighter. I dropped my head forward and let the weight of my head stretch my upper spine and muscles. I held this position and felt sensations along my neck and shoulder muscles.

I focused on the back of my upper body and could see what looked like tiny diamonds being placed into my skin. The skin looked a bit like modeling clay. These diamonds were pressed gently into the modeling clay on either side of my spine at the base of my head and then down my neck and along my shoulders. They were glistening with light.

As I watched, these diamond lights also appeared up the back of my head and to the centre of my forehead and down each arm in a glistening line of white sparkles. I could see wings of light from beneath each arm connected to my waist, like delicate shimmering fabric. It looked so flimsy, yet I knew these were incredibly strong.

I was shown many more of these tiny diamonds, this time they were dropping gently from a hand and glided into my skin, all over my body, forming flowing lines of light.

Then I appeared to be skating on a huge rink of ice, without any boundaries, my arms outstretched and the lights clearly visible all over my body as I glided and moved over the ice. The outstretched wings caught the light and they appeared to be alive, the colours moving and changing constantly.

I raised my head to discover all tension in my neck and shoulders had gone. I wasn't quite sure what had happened, though I felt calm, energized and glowing. The experience had lasted about fifteen minutes, yet it had felt like hours.

I spoke to Rae about my experience and he felt that I had received some kind of extra assistance or boost for my spiritual growth. If this were the case, I was very grateful.

After this I was looking forward to meeting Joy even more. I didn't know why but I felt she would somehow be able to help me find my way. My way where, I wasn't exactly sure but I felt she had a vast amount of knowledge to share which myself and others would greatly benefit from.

We had kept in contact by email and I had found a venue for her first course in Edinburgh, Diamond Inguz LiGHt Healing in April 2010. Joy had also asked if I would be interested in joining her on a visit to the Isle of Arran in March to do some Earth clearing work. I had no idea what this might entail but was intrigued and felt drawn to accept her invitation. I was looking forward to finally meeting her in person.

The morning of the trip to Arran I got up early and made sure I had everything I needed in my bag. Joy arrived early to collect me. We were catching the ferry to Arran and were on a tight schedule for the day.

When she emerged from her car, we hugged as if we had known each other our whole lives. I instantly warmed to her and during the drive to the ferry port we chatted openly about what we would be doing over the next two days.

Our 'job' was to clear some rather dense energies on Arran, a residue from years of ancient battles and skirmishes which had left their energetic mark in the ground. The earth takes on the emotions of people who inhabit it and if this isn't cleared, the emotions and issues seep deeper and deeper into Mother Earth. Just as we humans can become clogged and weighted down by emotional issues, so does Mother Earth. This is why some areas that you might visit can feel quite uncomfortable to be in. Just like with buildings, where the emotions and issues seep into the very fabric of the structure, earth also takes these on board.

I had trained my Reiki students to be responsible with any dense energies which came off their clients and not to put these into the earth or throw the remnants around their treatment rooms. All dense energies should be transmuted so that it doesn't get passed on to others. If everyone placed this dense energy into Mother Earth it was no wonder she was having a hard time.

The day was nonstop. We boarded the ferry at Ardrossan and sailed across to Arran. I stood silently for a long time whilst I watched us getting closer to Arran. I visualised that as the ferry got closer to land, an opening of light appeared so that we could dock in safety and in complete protection.

Once we docked in Arran, we drove to the small jetty to catch the ferry to Holy Island. All along this roadway I could see angels and beings of light lining the road on either side. I was overwhelmed in that moment with love and joy and my eyes were brimming with tears.

It was a beautiful sunny day, the boat was loaded with eight passengers and some supplies for the Buddhist centre and we began the short journey across the water. As we left Arran behind, I was becoming excited at the prospect of visiting Holy Island.

There were two Buddhist monks in the boat, one was wearing a bright yellow knitted hat. He had such a happy face and calm disposition. One of the other passengers addressed him as 'Lama' and I discovered later that he was Lama Yeshe Losal, Chairman of Rokpa Trust, Abbot and Retreat Master of Kagyu Samye Ling and Executive Director of The Holy Isle Project.

I was delighted to have such an impromptu and unexpected meeting with him. After visiting Samye Ling last year, this was a real bonus. Especially as I realised days later that he had conducted the ceremony on the day I had visited Samye Ling. Synchronicities at play again.

Lama Yeshe invited us to the centre to use the facilities and showed us a walk which he recommended on the tourist route map. He showed us around, obviously very proud of the centre he had helped to create and quite rightly so.

We decided to go on our walk first and return afterwards for a cup of tea before the ferry returned to collect us at 3.30pm. Before we left, Joy stopped to speak with Lama Yeshe.

I waited outside with the other woman on the trip and when Joy joined us she explained that she had said, "I was a student of yours in another life."

Lama's response was, "That was many lifetimes ago."

I felt he knew exactly why we were there, helping to put right some awful things which had happened over the centuries. What we managed to clear would help many, including those souls who had died as a result of the battles, fighting and disputes.

We walked along the shore line. It was sunny, the wind was blowing and it was quite cold on the exposed side of this tiny island. I found the walk refreshing and was enjoying the sea air. We sat for a while before we reached St Molaise's cave.

We began the clearing work and I used my singing bowl to increase the vibration of energy around us and into the earth below. I saw men lining the ridge above us, perhaps those lost in battle years ago. Within minutes the denseness which had been around us began to disappear and when I looked at the ridge the men were gone. We stood in silence for a while, waiting until the energies felt settled and calm and light.

We walked a little further up the path and came across huge stones which had paintings on them of Buddhist masters, one of which was of Kuan Yin. It felt very serene and peaceful in this spot. We returned to the centre and warmed ourselves with hot tea whilst we waited for the small ferry boat to return to collect us.

I was still a little shy about sharing what I could see and sense with people I barely knew, but I soon realised that I could share anything with Joy. This helped me to relax, allow my intuition to guide me and revel in the experiences I was having as part of the group.

The journey back to Arran on the ferry boat was a little choppy and cold but I felt a sense of satisfaction that we had completed the first stage of our clearing work here.

We drove to the next site, the ruin of Kildonan Castle. It was

privately owned and surrounded by fencing so we couldn't
gain entry. However, we walked a little way down a small road
towards the shore line and realised we were standing inside the
ruins of the castle. This was perfect and we stood silently in
concentration.

I looked up to the castle ruin. For some obscure reason, I raised
my arm and placed my finger as if touching the castle with it. I
began to clear the dense energies within it, as if I was rubbing
them away. I started to feel tingles throughout my body and felt
the denser energy begin to clear.

I turned to face the sea and Ailsa Craig rock. I focused all my
attention on it. Much to my amazement, with my eyes open,
I began to see an orange glow all around the rock. I closed
my eyes and opened them again thinking I had perhaps been
staring at it for too long. But the glow was still there. This
orange glow shifted quickly to one side and then disappeared.
A few seconds later the same thing happened again, an orange
glow around the rock for a short while which then disappeared.

I was still staring at the rock, in awe of what I had just seen,
when I began to see tiny spiralling 'tadpoles' of white light in
front of me. There must have been hundreds of them dancing
and spinning in front of me. It was beautiful. I was choked with
the emotion of how beautiful it felt and I could feel my heart
centre glowing.

From this site we then drove up the coast towards the 12
Apostles cottages and the Kings Cave. We arrived at the car
park for the Kings Cave late in the afternoon. We hadn't
realised until we looked at the map in the car park that the
Kings cave was quite a walk. +

Joy had been driving all day and was tired, so Gail and I set off, whilst Joy remained in the car. She would easily assist us from the car by tuning in remotely. It was quite an arduous walk and I could feel a large group of angels behind us, spurring us on.

We reached the shore path, having manoeuvred our way down steep tiny pathways. There was a sense of urgency, a time limit for us to complete this stage of the work. We opted to go to the Kings cave first but knew we also needed to go in the opposite direction, a secondary area needed to be cleared afterwards.

There were three caves. I stopped at the first one, Gail continued on to the next. As I entered the long low cave, I could feel the denseness. It was a cloying, damp feeling. I felt like I was walking through treacle. I used my singing bowl and began to feel the changes in the cave instantly. It took only a few minutes to clear and felt light and airy when I was finished. I moved into the second cave and cleared this one quickly too.

I made my way through a third cave which was open at both ends, a 'passageway' to the Kings cave. I cleared this as I walked through it, asking the pure light energy I held to enter the rock structure and I touched the stone briefly. It immediately felt calmer and much happier, almost sighing with contentment.

I could hear a deep humming sound and saw Gail standing at the entrance to the Kings cave. I wondered how she was making that amazing sound. However, the closer I got I realised it wasn't her making the sound but someone playing a didgeridoo inside the Kings cave. I felt the vibration in my body as it reverberated around the cave. All density was gone.

I searched the darkness of the cave and finally managed to

see inside. There was a young man, sitting at the very back of the cave playing the instrument. We knew that his sounds had cleared the cave for us. It felt wonderful, so light and 'alive'.

We left the caves and returned along the pathway heading towards an outcrop of rock. We realised we didn't have enough time to walk there and return to the car in time for the next area to be cleared. I spotted a long low rock on the shore and suggested we could perhaps clear the large outcrop remotely from this rock. It looked like the spine of a creature.

Gail said, "It looks like a dragon's back."

"How appropriate," I thought to myself.

I immediately asked all my guides, but particularly Dominic my dragon guide to assist us to complete this next stage of the work. We reached the rock spine. It had two flat parts which looked like seats along the spine and I laughed, thinking, "How wonderful! Sitting on the dragon's back as we work! Just as I have done so many times with Dominic!"

I breathed slowly and deeply, focusing on the ridge to our left. I became aware that I could sense and see the vibrations from the didgeridoo rippling along the ridge of the hill leading to the large outcrop at the end. But the vibration stopped at a particular place.

I focused on this area and again used my finger like an eraser, working up and down this area until I saw the vibration waves carry on along the ridge.

There was a second pocket of density. As I concentrated on this area of the ridge, I could see men running down this hillside, dressed in kilts. I realised this must have been an area of much fighting. I could feel the fear and anger which had seeped into the land all around us. I cleared this small area too. I then asked if the ridge was clear and received confirmation that it was.

I focused my attention on the end outcrop, playing the singing bowl and occasionally toning with my voice. I watched the outcrop, staring at it for what felt like many minutes. I thought it would never clear. Suddenly I saw an orange glow just surrounding the outcrop. It shifted up and to one side and then disappeared.

I checked to ensure our work was complete and received confirmation. As we climbed the path back to the car park, the sun was beginning to set behind us. It was beautiful and I wished we had the time to stay there a little while longer to see it.

When we returned to the car, Joy explained that she had felt the clearing of the land from the car and was very satisfied with what we had been able to accomplish. I was very relieved as I didn't fancy another trek down those paths to do it all again.

We set off in the car in search of a particular standing stone. By the time we found it, it was dark. But we entered the field where the two stones were situated, laughing at the absurdity - three grown women wandering about a field in the dark. It seemed ludicrous.

We positioned ourselves around the two stones. I was standing at the back of the second stone. I felt a deep sense of sadness coming from it which was quite overwhelming at times. I touched the stone and began to talk to it in a language I was becoming used to speaking and I felt it beginning to shed the denseness.

I moved to the larger stone and did the same. I felt I was reassuring it and saying, "Welcome back". Joy had connected to both of the stones, standing between them with her arms outstretched working on levels I could only begin to imagine.

We returned to the car, it was late and we decided it was time to find our accommodation. The road for our direct route was closed. We looked at the map and the only other option was to drive around the rest of the island to get to the B&B. We were all a little tired, but as we would be passing Lochranza Castle on the way, we decided to stop and complete its clearing.

As I looked up at the castle, the stars were shining brightly above it in a jet black sky. It looked like a beautiful dome of stars. At first, I felt such dense, dark energy within the stonework of the castle. But as we all worked, I could feel it clearing rapidly.

It felt happier now, more settled and contented. I knew that this sounded ridiculous to my brain. But when I thought about it more clearly, I realised that if buildings and places took on the energy of what was around them, all the battles and anger and fear had seeped into the ground and buildings here, as with so many other places. Centuries of disputes, fighting and killing.

I knew I had felt this type of thing before during visits to areas where there had been battles or wars and knew that by clearing these old stuck emotions, it was allowing the area to feel calmer, be free from that damaging resonance and this would allow much lighter energy to flow.

We eventually found our way to the B&B, ate late at a local restaurant and it was nearly 10pm by the time we were settled for bed. It had been a long day and I was looking forward to sleeping.

During the night I dreamt that I was meeting different clans or groups who were in opposition. They wanted to fight, but I explained that was over now, it was long ago and it was time to move on. After a while the clan members shook hands and an immense sense of peace descended.

The next day we had a more relaxed start to the day and a good breakfast. We had another day of clearing ahead. It was a pleasant day once the early rain stopped and the sun began to shine.

We parked at a view point surrounded by trees right next to the sea shore. There was a mountain behind us and the scenery was magnificent. I stood facing Gail and Joy and began to use the singing bowl and my Tibetan cymbals. I felt the shift of energy, a sudden lightness to the atmosphere around us.

I used the singing bowl again, feeling the vibration rise higher and higher. The area felt different now, happier and less intimidating. Joy began to tone and sing and within moments I felt a huge welling up of love inside and around me. I had seen a few faces peering at us through the trees, guarded and suspicious. Elementals. As the area cleared I felt these guardians of the surrounding woods relax and when I looked again, they were smiling.

We left this beautiful place and returned to Brodick to buy some food for lunch. As I waited outside next to the car for Joy and Gail to return, I felt Dad close by. When I focused on him I could sense that he was wearing the white robes I had often seen him in. I felt great comfort knowing that he was so close and assisting us.

It was almost time to return on the ferry to Ardrossan.

I couldn't sit indoors, it felt too enclosed. I needed to be outside in the air as my energy felt more expanded and I felt uncomfortable inside the ship. Outside I felt happy and free and open in the elements. I needed this time and space for me, to integrate the magical yet intense two days on Arran before setting foot back on the mainland.

After that weekend I was becoming very excited about the Diamond Inguz LiGHt Healing course with Joy. I wasn't even sure why, but knew that in some way, big or small, it was going to change my life. I asked that this be for the greatest and highest good and prayed that it would somehow move me away from feeling stuck in life. Life had, without a doubt, got better but there was still room for improvement and any improvement would be gratefully accepted.

I turned up on the first day not knowing what to expect. I had attended quite a few workshops over the years and was open to whatever might happen. I had experienced some of the most beautiful and amazing feelings and connections at some of these workshops and was grateful for every one of them. I hoped that this workshop might provide me with some direction or at least some hope that I was indeed on my path, despite some outward appearances to the contrary.

This workshop was different. For the entire first day we cleared and repaired damage to our main seven chakras, damaged from deep emotional wounds in this life as well as previous lives. This felt really, really good and I loved the visualization which Joy used.

She explained to us that in many healing methods the chakras weren't cleared sufficiently prior to receiving the energy connection. This meant that the recipient wasn't as clear and open to receive the most optimum level of energy that they could be and sometimes people were overloaded and felt unwell as a result.

This made perfect sense to me. How can you receive the very best light energy level available if you are clogged or blocked in some way? I couldn't recall any of my previous teachers explaining this to me quite so clearly, but perhaps I hadn't been ready to hear.

Joy led us through a meditation to open the heart centre. I had done quite a bit of work on this area through the Chi Kung practice, knew there was more work to do yet wasn't prepared at all for the experiences I was about to have.

As Joy guided us through clearing our heart centre I saw my heart like a flower with a spinning diamond shape at the centre of the flower. As the flower opened to reveal beautiful petals I could see myself kneeling in the centre of this soft place brushing away ash from the centre of the flower. I was using the softest brush, it was feather-like.

This took a little while and I could see all the ash disappearing and the flower being cleansed and polished. After this my heart centre felt huge, almost like it was ready to burst and my chest felt expanded out into the room. It was a very moving experience, particularly when it struck me that this beautiful heart was inside of me.

Later that day, Joy led us through a connection and opening of our sacred heart centre, which lies behind the heart centre. I hadn't even known we had more than one heart centre and was very excited. All these amazing things lying hidden away inside us and we didn't know.

I saw a beautiful shell shape when I connected to my sacred heart and it appeared to be white or colourless, I wasn't quite sure. When I drew the shape afterwards it felt very familiar.

A little while after this connection we received the Diamond Inguz energy. There was no human attunement and no symbols. I was pleased about not having symbols as I hadn't really been drawn to using them and each time I had used them it felt like my brain was getting in the way and stopping the natural flow of my intuition during sessions.

The attunement was done by Kuan Yin and I could feel her energy as she entered the sacred space which Joy had created. During this attunement, I became aware that I could see a bright red open top Chevrolet beside me.

I can recall thinking, "What's that doing here?"

It felt so out of place and made me chuckle inwardly. I felt myself running alongside this car, faster and faster. It wasn't a race, but it was as if the car was encouraging me to go faster and we kept pace with each other.

Afterwards I shared my experience with the group. I was rather embarrassed as it seemed so out of place during such a beautiful and gentle energy connection.

However Joy smiled at me and said, "Fast-track, eh?"
At the time I didn't understand what she meant fully. It was probably just as well, as the months to follow would be busy and full.

On the second day, we were shown how to work with Selenite crystal wands to help clear out old emotions, dense energies and blockages from the body. The wands were lovely to work with, very gentle and they also assisted to rebalance the energy flow and create better energetic connections. During my session I felt lines of energy rushing up my body to my neck, then this energy moving quickly sideways. It felt wonderful. My head began to feel very full and tight and then it subsided.

I could hear my guides telling me to 'let go'. So I surrendered to the experience and immediately travelled up a tunnel of beautiful light, so fast that I felt a little nauseous. I was aware that my head was gently moving and my body swaying slightly in the chair.

As I emerged from the tunnel I was met by the most serene female figure. She had long fair hair, which was slightly wavy. She looked like a mermaid. When we met I felt an enormous wave of love from her. I moved closer to her and she gently embraced me in her arms. I was engulfed in love and nurturing. I felt so safe; so comfortable. Home.

Tears were running down my face, it was such an immensely joyous moment. The practice session was over and I said goodbye to this beautiful being, though I didn't want to be parted from her.

Joy was standing beside me and asked how I felt, she had realised that I had been on a journey somewhere. I explained what I had just seen and felt. She smiled and asked who the female was.

Without thinking about it I said, "I think it was me, my soul." Joy nodded her confirmation.

It was quite a realisation - me, ordinary me, my soul, was

that beautiful. It went against everything I had believed about myself, yet it felt right to my newly expanded heart.

Over the coming weeks I connected to the Diamond Inguz energy and the light grid surrounding Earth every day. I had loved the Reiki energy, it had helped me a great deal. This was something else entirely. Each day my heart expanded more and there was a glow in my heart which spread throughout my whole body as the days went by.

I felt the connection to Mother Earth more strongly than before - she supported me and I was helping support her too by simply connecting with this energy grid which was connected to her very core. This energy was loving, gentle, nurturing and yet very strong. My core strength felt much more solid and negativity was clearing from my body every day, which was an immense relief.

I woke up most days smiling and feeling really happy and content inside. I felt more in balance than at any other time in my life and I remember wondering how long it would last. Other healing energies had not been able to sustain this feeling, it had subsided after a while and many other practitioners had expressed the same thing.

Surely this calm and balanced centre couldn't be maintained. "Was that even possible?" I thought. "Was it really possible to feel this good every day?" If so, bring it on, I wanted to feel this way for the rest of my life - calm, centered and happy. It was fantastic.

A few days later Joy ran her first six day School of Life course in Edinburgh. This was an inspirational and life changing six days for everyone who attended. It was interspersed with interactive hands on and energy work, as well as a multitude of information explaining about the way our experiences in life mould how we respond and live our lives.

I was familiar with much of the information already, but the way Joy explained it gave me even greater understanding and insight. We had class discussions about the material and learned an enormous amount about ourselves and the six days were packed from beginning to end.

I had some wonderful personal experiences and as each day went by I felt myself becoming lighter, literally as if a weight was being lifted from my shoulders.

We did more intensive clearing of the chakras and on the first day I discovered that my base chakra seemed to be leaking energy - it was no wonder that at times I had felt tired and not able to control my energy levels better.

We were shown how to seal any leakages in our chakras and by the end of this exercise, I looked at my body and could see all seven of my chakras, front and back, pop open from the base to the crown like a flower quickly bursting into bloom. I felt energised and balanced.

I had felt this before, but somehow this time it was different. It felt much more permanent and solid. The main thing I learned from that first day was how vital the chakras are to our health. I had already known this at one level but the way it was explained and focused upon gave me new insight to their worth and importance.

I wondered why I hadn't taken this information in before at this level, that the energy system, the chakras and the aura are vital for our physical well being. A simple daily routine of clearing the chakras can have incredible effects to our physical energy and health and I began to include that within my morning routine when I connected to the Diamond Inguz energy. It took so little time to do it was easy to incorporate this into my busy day.

It was my forty-eighth birthday on the second day of the School of Life course. I had decided to keep it to myself, that this was my time, an honouring of me without fuss from anyone else.

We started with a heart meditation. Joy asked us to tell her how many petals we had on the flower in our heart - the number 5172 came into my head immediately. I was fascinated how easily we were able to blurt out an answer to a question. How would I know how many petals were in my heart centre? Yet I seemed to know, my soul knew.

I saw my heart centre like a puffy dome, but when I looked closer I saw that the petals were so slender that they looked like fingers of a sea anemone. As we released the pains, hurts and traumas from past lives all the way back to Atlantis, these petals opened - the anemone shape opened.

The love within me just got bigger and bigger and bigger. I began to have indigestion type pains in my heart centre, which I didn't normally experience, and then they gradually subsided. I saw a hand appear and gently drop Rose oil onto the flower. The flower was then placed into my sacred heart shell shape and I immediately saw the numbers 8134. That must be the number of petals now.

"Wow, how superb was that?" I thought.

I could feel a gentle yet enormous expansion of my sacred heart and I thought that perhaps the shell shape couldn't hold the flower, but I was shown the shell slowly expanding to accommodate the flower and then the whole thing began to glow. This felt amazing and delightful. I was moved to tears with the sheer beauty of it.

During a session where we worked at clearing the chakras I could see my guide, Flies with Pony and our unicorn. A spiral of energy was spinning towards me from the unicorn and I felt like I 'lit up'.

I felt my third eye at the front of my head tingling and I could see many shades of purple. At the bridge of my nose I felt intense tingling and vibration and the top of my head felt massive. Then I saw my 'self' really clearly, almost in 3-D. I saw beautiful fair hair flowing behind her, almost curly. A set of wings were outstretched in a fan above her, body slender and shimmering in rainbow colours which changed constantly. Magnificent. It was hard to accept that she is me, inside; in all my glory and divine magnificence.

During that week Joy and I had arranged for me to receive a one to one session of DARE from her. Joy explained that she had developed this treatment technique called DARE (Dissolve and Resolve Emotions) over many years to meet the needs of people at this time. Other modalities just weren't going deep enough nor were they clearing emotional impacts that the soul had endured. DARE was able to do just that.

I was intrigued and wanted to check it out for myself. I asked if we could work on some of the abuse issues I knew I still carried. As Joy worked I became aware that people had come forward (etherically) to return parts of me that they held.

Joy explained to me that when we have traumatic experiences we leave parts of ourselves behind, energetically speaking. I felt the anger and pain which I had held in my body was slowly dissipating.

I hadn't experienced anything like this before, the session had felt like it was fairly straightforward, almost as though nothing much had happened yet when I sat up I realised how intense it had been. I felt a little wobbly and unable to stand for a few minutes, but more whole somehow.

I knew this was how I wanted to deal with the remainder of my emotional baggage - it was fast and got to the root cause, dispelling emotions, trauma and shock faster than anything else I had experienced. I had received counselling, trained in EFT some years previously and this DARE technique left them standing.

There was no need to go into the emotion of these experiences as you are encouraged to do with counselling and other methods. Though it is a recognised way of dealing with personal issues, talking about these issues can sometimes be just as traumatic as the actual event itself. I had personally experienced this and sometimes going over events can even add to the trauma.

With Joy's technique, the issues are addressed but in a very different way and without going into the emotion - this way the trauma isn't compounded even more. You still had the insights into what these issues were about, just no traumatic emotion. I liked the technique a lot.

Joy also explained that because life can be tough and because of the suffering people endure, it is common to find that their hearts are closed down as a form of protection from any more pain. This was quite understandable but it is one of the major reasons why people feel so disconnected.

Many people believe (as I had) that because they do things from a place of love that their hearts are open. I have learned that this is far from the reality. Yes, they may be loving and nurturing, but if you tune into their heart centre it can literally be broken in two or shattered into tiny pieces from life's traumas or locked away in a box with a padlock, with them working with a small percentage of their true self, their true inner love. I had been in exactly that position and my inner work was now focused on freeing my poor battered heart.

The following day I arrived at the venue early and sat in the gardens. It was a lovely day. During the session the previous evening, we had dealt with some promises and vows I still had at play from previous lives.

That one session with Joy had helped me understand instantaneously how these promises and vows, made in a life hundreds of years previously, were still affecting my life now - simply because they hadn't been rescinded and the ties and/or links removed completely. They had served me well enough in that life, but were definitely not serving me in this one.

I was eager to get on and free myself of these types of things which were still affecting me and preventing an easier flow through life. As I sat in the morning sunshine I decided to complete some of the work regarding these vows and promises. Perhaps I was a little too eager.

Suddenly I had hundreds of souls all around me. They each had a tiny part of me to give back and I had a tiny part of them to return. I could feel pieces returning to me, pains in my heart, tingles around my body and emotions welling up as these were returned. As each piece was returned to the other souls I watched them shoot into the sky, like a tiny shooting star in a blaze of light. I felt my heart settling and calming, peace descending. This had all happened within five minutes.

In those connected moments I felt sublime and wonderful and relaxed. The centred feeling that I desired in my life, which I knew I'd had in previous existences, could be attained in this one too.

This process of 'getting back to who you really are' was like settling into a comfy bed and snuggling into the duvet. Comfortable and reassuring. I could hear my heart laughing and chuckling and sighing with pleasure all at the same time. This was just the beginning of this deeper journey, I felt sure of that.

My family saw the changes in me. Over the months to come there were a few blips, as deeper unresolved issues came up to be addressed and sorted out, but I had fully expected this. Unresolved issues can't stay inside forever, they do so much damage and don't serve us when we hang on to them.

I knew I had many depths to these emotional and spiritual impacts and I was fortunate to have a supportive group of friends and with Joys assistance and support I worked my way through these other issues using and being treated with the DARE techniques.

I sensed an urgency within me to attend the next DARE course which Joy was running in Wales in June. I had attended the School of Life course in late April and this was the prerequisite for attending. She had said that she thought I would prove to be a good DARE practitioner and the training would really help me to pare away more layers and baggage.

I had very little spare money, yet this felt absolutely right for me to do. I felt like I was 'on a mission'. Perhaps I was without knowing it.

So in June 2010 I drove to Wales and spent a week with Joy and another student learning the techniques in the foundation level of DARE. The weather in Wales was kind for the seven days and most of the course was done outside in the sunshine, much to my delight.

It was an intense seven days and each day we worked on each other with these techniques. I learned so much that week, some wonderful techniques which were new to me but I also learned why I did some of the things I do during treatment sessions.

I found that my instincts and insights were actually very good. My biggest problem was trusting in them.

"Trust and Faith - that old nugget," I thought. There seemed to be layer upon layer of trust issues going back hundreds of lives. I was keen to be rid of it and as the week went by this trust in my self did improve. I felt more at ease with myself at another deeper level.

One of the techniques we learned proved to be extremely beneficial to me. On the first DARE course the focus is on limbs and organs. After a session during which my legs and knees were treated, I was amazed to discover that much of the injuries and traumas to my knees from accidents and surgical operations in this life were still held there, let alone damage done in past lives.

The shock and trauma were locked into the cells. Once this was released during a session, my knees felt stronger than they ever had and have been excellent ever since then.

I also discovered that the head traumas I had experienced in this life, from a variety of accidents, were a direct link to the severe migraine-like headaches I experienced at times. Shock, trauma and the emotions I felt (mainly fear) when these accidents occurred were all still held in my body.

These head injuries were in areas which had been injured in previous lives through battles, fighting and a variety of other accidents. It was no wonder that my head had always felt a very sensitive area. With the healing and repair work done during the DARE course, my head sensitivity lessened and the headaches I had experienced throughout my life subsided. Miracles do abound.

Throughout the summer months I worked on my family and friends as case studies. With each case study my experience and confidence grew and I was enjoying using the techniques. The changes in people were nothing short of dramatic.

I had seen vast changes in people using my other therapies but this healing was different, it was deep and more profound. Tension dropped from peoples faces as their baggage was removed, they looked years younger after one session and the calmness they felt astounded them.

They were enjoying the 'new' me also. It was all excellent feed back and I was thoroughly enjoying myself being in student mode again.

Joy organised the advanced level of Diamond Inguz, called Opalescence, in Scotland in October. It was being held in a lovely retreat venue, very quiet and it suited our three day experience perfectly. A group of us gathered and had a wonderful three days with Joy and making new connections to this higher vibration energy.

I found that with Opalescence, whenever emotions came to the surface, the moment I started to feel these emotions, my heart centre became very hot and felt like it was 'buzzing'. I felt myself then being gently drawn back from the emotion to a place of calmness.

This was something completely new. Diamond Inguz had been brilliant and helped so much, but this put a whole other meaning to 'living in the heart'. Once connected to this energy, I felt a depth of subtle strength and support I hadn't known before - regardless of what the human experience was showing me.

This did seem a little ridiculous, considering there was a variety of difficult things going on around me, but I knew if I observed and didn't get drawn into the drama, I would certainly have a far better perspective to be able to make informed decisions as well as being able to help those going through the traumas.

At times this was certainly not easy, but this was my challenge. I was being tested, sometimes to the very edge of despair. Each time a challenge presented itself and each time I stayed calm and focused, life flowed smoothly and I felt content inside all the time.

Occasionally I slipped and got entangled in the emotion of these dramas and I felt quite unwell. So I focused even more upon staying within the stability of this heart energy. I was delighted that (for the most part) when these challenges appeared I managed reasonably well.

My connection to the energy and supportive light grid got faster every day and felt more secure and solid as time went by. I felt more aligned. A few days after receiving the Opalescence energy connection I had begun to see loops of golden energy around my body the moment I thought about Opalescence.

A thought popped into my head shortly afterwards, "I am Opalescence" and I felt my heart respond with a glowing sensation. The energy was there surrounding me, within me every moment of the day.

I was even more determined to continue with my training, as with each step I took I was becoming lighter inside. At a physical level I felt less weight on my body and at an emotional level I felt calm most of the time and didn't enter into anger or anxiety like I used to.

I had done vast amounts of work on this, yet there had been a hint of it creeping back into my daily life at times before Diamond Inguz, much to my dismay. With the connection to these energies I was finding a new way of living.

I began to experience the energy in a more subtle way, it felt almost imperceptible. It was there all of the time it only needed my focus to see it. I knew from discussions with Joy and other light workers that we assimilate these energies to a point where we don't feel them the same way as the first time we connect. It isn't that they aren't there - our body has adjusted to integrate it. One day, two weeks after the Opalescence course, I saw pastel coloured rays all around me. I could see golden threads within these pastel rays - fine, subtle and glistening with life with a power and strength which took my breath away. Every day there was something new to experience as this energy built in strength, I hadn't had this much fun in a long time.

I attended the second DARE course in November. This time the focus was on relationships and learning techniques for negotiation and removal of attachments. It was a fascinating course and provided a spring board for me to let go of lives of poor self esteem, abusive lives, lives of suppression and, interestingly, lives of suicide.

I found this information intriguing and it helped to explain my experiences in this lifetime and how the patterns from those lives had still been working within me in this life.

The attempts at suicide in this life, the self harming, all began to make sense. I hadn't felt as if it was 'me' during that time and I now realised that it most definitely wasn't 'me'. Mostly it was the patterns ingrained into my cellular structure which were still working away, interfering with my functioning, my progress and holding back my full awakening.

I hadn't fully understood why I seemed to go into these self destructive patterns of thinking until this point. Then during a session on the course, I literally saw and felt them within my body and then felt them being dissolved as the work was done. Areas of my body which held these patterns were a little painful and as the patterns disappeared from my physical body, the pain went with them.

We were able to eliminate the trauma of these lives and the detrimental effects they were still having upon me, and thus eradicating the downward spiral of negative thinking which did pop up now and again when I least expected it. I was delighted.

As these patterns left my body there was more space for my confidence to grow. I had a deeper trust in myself and with each passing week, these positive feelings were becoming more and more prominent in my life.

During this second DARE course I also discovered that my fast track of learning was mainly because I had been closed down spiritually for so long. I should have been 'awake' in my mid teens, but with the death of my Grandfather and not enjoying school life, the grief and lack of fulfillment had been too much and I had closed down instead.

So I was on a fast track now catching up on all the years I had missed out on of my learning and spiritual development. It made perfect sense to me when I scanned back through my life and could see the nudges and pushes I had received to encourage me to look beyond the day to day human living. I knew that at times this fast track wasn't an easy route, but I had little option if I wanted to be free from the past influences which were still affecting my life. I most definitely wanted to set myself free.

After this second DARE course, Joy and I travelled to Belfast. A health fair had been organised focusing on women's and children's health and we had been invited to take a display stand. We decided that whilst Joy promoted her new book, 'Pregnancy and Birth - A New Generation' I would offer taster sessions of my Raindrop Technique and the Diamond Inguz LiGHt Healing.

It was a wonderful though busy day and I was very sure that the Opalescence energy served me very well in the environment. Both Joy and I could feel some of the heartache, shock and trauma which people were still carrying after years of the 'troubles' and as I worked on some of the people who had booked taster sessions I was very aware that I was removing shock and trauma as a result of the emotional impact of those times. Some of that shock and trauma was immense.

Many of the visitors to the fair were interested in what Joy and I could offer and after the health fair we organised dates to return in the New Year to run courses.

These past months had been an interesting, if a rather accelerated path of self discovery. Joy had become a mentor as well as a teacher and our friendship was blossoming. I hadn't expected this at all when we first made contact. I was content to receive training in these new and exciting techniques, to have a friendship on top of that was like icing on the cake and I was hugely grateful to her for all her efforts to assist me.

I was invited by Joy to join her and a small group on a trip to Egypt in December 2010. This was my first experience of joining with a group of people to do some planetary work for a whole week which would assist to balance energies for the highest good of all occupants of Mother Earth or 'Gaia'. It was an exciting venture and I was delighted that I had the opportunity to make a difference. It was what I had come here to do.

I left Edinburgh mid morning in the final days of December 2010 and drove to Manchester airport, our flight was early the following morning and I was glad of the rest before we set off. I slept reasonably well and was ready to leave by 7.15 the following morning.

The airport was busy, with people heading away to ski resorts or sunshine holidays. The flight was uneventful until we began our descent for Luxor airport. With around ten minutes to land, the turbulence from a sandstorm which had blown in from the desert buffeted the aircraft and made for a very fraught landing. I was very relieved when we landed safely.

The air was warm as we departed the aircraft. The airport was busy as we collected our visas and made our way through security to collect our bags. The other members of our group were waiting outside for us to arrive and after greeting each other, we boarded a bus which took us to our hotel.

The hotel was very pleasant, plush and clean and I was sharing a twin room overlooking the Nile with a view of the Valley of the Kings and Queens. This was lit up in the darkness and was an impressive sight. We packed a small overnight bag, as we were leaving early the next morning to catch a train from Luxor to Aswan.

The following day we spent several hours at the station waiting for the train to arrive. It had been due at 9.30am and by 12.30 we were becoming anxious and very tired of waiting. We needed to get to Aswan and despite having bought train tickets we decided to arrange for a small minibus to take us to Aswan and we left the station. It all felt a little surreal, like we had been in a holding space on the platform of the station all that time. Literally going nowhere.

The drive to Aswan was quite long and arduous and it had been a long time since I had experienced this kind of driving, which was a bit like a massive game of 'chicken'. We arrived in Aswan safely and boarded a small taxi boat which took us across the Nile to a small island situated in the middle of the water where we would be staying at the Isis Island Hotel. It was lovely, with beautiful grounds and felt very peaceful compared to the bustle of Luxor. We enjoyed a meal together then met up to discuss plans for the following day. During this meeting Joy facilitated a gentle release of any personal issues we still held from previous lives we had each had in the temples we would be visiting. This would help us remain clear and focused for the work we were each to do.

I slept reasonably well, though awoke early and was unable to go back to sleep. I went for an early swim in the heated outdoor pool which was a blissful way to start the day. There were three sites that we would visit - Philae, Kom Ombo and Edfu and we were all excited. We had some breakfast, though for some reason I wasn't very hungry at all. We alighted the taxi boat and returned to the jetty at Aswan where our bus was waiting.

It was a reasonably short drive to Philae Temple and our bus driver was a cheerful man who pointed out local places of interest with a little of their history. Here we were shown to the jetty where we climbed aboard another small boat which took us on a ten minute trip to The Temple of Isis.

We explored the temple in the warm morning sun and as we walked around the site we were clearing and collecting ready for the next temple visit. Whatever we were clearing was very old and at times I felt as if my heart would break with such deep sadness for some of the events which had taken place and were linked to the site, but it felt good that we were able to assist this dense energy to shift and go. We sailed back to the mainland, waited in the sun for a short while for our bus to arrive and then headed off to the next temple, Kom Ombo.

Here we did more clearing work, some of which was an emotional experience for others in the group. I began to appreciate how much some of the previous experiences at these places were still held within me. I had never been to these temples before in this life and yet a visit could evoke such emotion.

If we have experienced something sad or unpleasant in another life whilst living or visiting in that area, when we return to that place those unresolved emotions are triggered, coming to the surface to be released and resolved. Sometimes this emotion can come from nowhere and I recalled some of my family holidays to various parts of the world and how I felt quite emotional in some places and hadn't known why.

I felt blessed that we were there with Joy, who could assist those old emotions to be released allowing us to be finally free of them.

It was a hot day and we decided to have an ice cream after the visit to the temple, buying these from a small shop on the site. The vendor opened a new container of coins to give us change and I remarked at how beautiful the EGP 1 coin was - a beautiful image of Tutankhamun.

The Egyptian man serving us took a coin and handed it to me saying, "For you, Madame".

I was surprised and touched at his generosity, the coin was so striking. I thanked him and we returned to the bus. I felt like I had a piece of Tutankhamun with me and felt a strong connection to him. I recalled that I had watched a television documentary when I was a young child, sitting next to my Dad on the sofa. The documentary was about Tutankhamun and I can remember watching the pictures on the old television screen, mesmerized and feeling as if I knew him already. That memory made me smile now.

Our next destination was that of Edfu Temple. As we travelled the road I became aware that many of the rocks on one side of the road were shaped like Hathor faces and some of lions. Bit by bit I pieced together the shreds of information which were coming to me as I relaxed on the bus, until I had the full picture of what I needed to do at this next site.

When we stopped at Edfu and walked towards the site, I felt great resistance within myself and I wanted to turn around and go back to the bus. As we drew closer to the entrance I really didn't want to go into the temple and didn't know why. I knew I was there to help clear the past emotional and spiritual scars which were held in and around the temple so returning to the bus wasn't an option.

I found Edfu a distressing place to be, I could feel the pain and suffering of some of the people who had been there without really knowing the details. There seemed to have been very little love there, or if there had been, I couldn't feel it. I felt that I had had a very unpleasant time there.

In one room there was a small hole in the stone wall and as I looked at it more closely I could 'see' a metal ring through the hole with a chain attached to it. A shiver ran through my body as I realised this was where people had been chained up, I got a quick picture of someone slumped against the wall. I knew somehow that I had been one of those people and that I had died here.

I was glad once we had completed our work and we could leave. As I walked away from the temple it became apparent that I was also transmuting for a huge group of people who had suffered as I had there. I felt such grief and sorrow. It was never meant to have been that way, my life there felt like it had been quite brutal at times.

Joy assisted me to release these emotions and within a few minutes I began to feel better. However on the drive back to Luxor I began crying quietly in the darkness, tears streaming down my face as the emotions emerged and then released.

I was keen to have a little space to myself to process the events of the day and the last thing I wanted to do was go to the New Years Eve party which was being held that night after we returned to the hotel. I was persuaded to go, however, and I'm glad that I did. When I arrived at the party Joy took me aside and explained she thought I had handled the emotions well which had come up for me during the day. She had felt my pain and yet I had remained focused on what we there to clear and not let it overwhelm me.

I didn't think that I had handled my emotions at all well, they had come from nowhere and I had felt a little overwhelmed, but she insisted I had managed just fine. She explained that the personal emotions I had felt combined with transmuting the pain and heartache of all the other people who had suffered there had been an enormous amount to release and transmute.

I had a wonderful time that evening and it was exactly what I needed after an emotional day. We celebrated as 2011 was welcomed in. By 1am I was very tired. It had been a long day and we returned to our rooms for a well earned sleep.

As I drifted off to sleep I was mulling over the events of the day and started to feel the acceptance filtering throughout my whole body of how well I had managed during that day. After all, I was still a novice at this Earth work and had much to learn.

We slept late the following day which was very welcome after all the travelling and clearing work we had done. We spent a relaxing morning in the sun and enjoyed a gentle Felucca boat ride on the Nile later that afternoon. It felt strange to be relaxing in the sun on New Years Day, a day normally spent at home with my family.

That night I had a fitful sleep and when I awoke just after 6am my room mate was also awake. I drew the curtains aside to open the balcony door and above the Valley of the Kings & Queens opposite our balcony were nine hot air balloons in the dawn sky. Their colours glowed in the dawn light and it was a breathtaking sight.

After breakfast we took horse carriages to Luxor Temple. Joy specifically wanted to visit the temple of Sekhmet and asked a group of Egyptian men for directions. A man stood up and offered to show her the way. He spoke little English. His legs were malformed and his feet flopped as he walked. As he led the way towards the temple of Sekhmet he took Joys arm and gazed at her. The adoration poured from him and as I watched them and tuned into the energies around them I began to realise that they had had a life together.

As the time wore on I had more clarity and insights and it became clear that Joy had saved him as a very young baby or child. It seemed that he had been abandoned because of a similar deformity or injury which he still carried now, he had his foot removed and she had saved his life, quite literally. He had been enormously grateful and this is what shone through now when they met again in this life. It was a very touching meeting.

We were shown the temple of Sekhmet and afterwards carried on with our visit around the temple. I was particularly drawn to the ceremonial pool where I felt relaxed and comfortable and even saw a few light orbs darting about in the water, which made me smile.

The next day we had a three hour journey to Abydos. Once we bought the entry tickets and entered the temple grounds I was guided to walk on the central flat portion between the steps. When we reached the top of the long entrance of steps we realised that we had passed the toilets and we were all in need of a comfort break.

When we returned to the base of the steps they felt different this time, as if we were in a different time zone or something. We all felt it and this time when we retraced our footsteps to the temple entrance it felt more ceremonial somehow.

As we walked around inside I occasionally saw some of the glyphs on the walls rotate or move as our energy presence unlocked them. It was most bizarre. Some areas I was more drawn to than others and I stood for many minutes at these places until I felt the urge to move on.

When we gathered in the room of Osiris we felt his presence strongly. I was tingling all over in this room and we each received gifts from him. We then moved to the Isis room and we each received a gift from her. I couldn't believe that we were being given these energy gifts. It felt wonderful and not something I had expected.

The third room was that of Cobra and for some reason I felt tearful as I stood quietly in the room. We were each gifted strength and courage and I later realised after speaking with Joy that I had left my strength and courage there. It had taken me a very long time to return to collect it and that was why

I had been tearful. Apparently this return of my strength and courage would ensure that I had the will to carry on with the light work I am here to do.

I felt strongly that I had also died here in a life, as my body felt as if it was getting older and older the longer we stayed there. My footsteps became more heavy and I felt as if I was slightly hunched over. Once I was outside, all of these feelings disappeared, much to my relief.

We left this site and drove for two hours to Dendera. It felt a very gentle and relaxed site in comparison to the other temples. There were only a few tourists.

As we approached the entrance to the temple, instead of walking straight through the enormous archway, I was gently pulled to my right to walk around a small stone structure about twenty feet square.

As I walked on the path surrounding the structure a small lizard appeared in front of me, out of the stonework and began to run in front of me. It felt like it was leading the way. I walked behind it, chuckling inwardly and as I approached the main entrance it disappeared.

For me this was a time of gathering. Everywhere I went I seemed to be gathering things that I had left behind during a life there. Most of the time I had no idea what these 'things' were. When I looked up at the temple wall I saw three Hathor carvings below a stone line and three above. There were also three lion statues along this wall higher up and as I collected something the lion carvings appeared to turn.

It was an amazing sight and I could really feel the change of energy around me, tingles throughout my whole body as these carvings turned and moved. I began to feel like I was in the middle of an Indiana Jones movie. I felt content being here, it felt like a homecoming and it was fast becoming a game of treasure hunting as I collected all the things that I had left behind.

We had two hours at Dendera, an hour passed before I was ready to go inside the temple. The interior was relatively dark and I felt there wasn't as much for me to do inside as there had been outside.

We followed a narrow dark passageway to the roof and as I passed some of the carved figures in the walls they appeared to move. When I entered one of the rooftop sanctuaries it smelled of death, but not gruesome horrors like I had felt at Edfu. This was more of a natural passing over of people, in the natural cycle of life.

As I spent time in this room it became apparent that there was a sequence in which I was to visit each corner and then move to specific cartouches on the walls. These areas on the walls were very small, sometimes only one tiny etching in amongst the whole cartouche and I wondered how I knew which ones to stop at.

My eyes were scanning the whole time and I would be drawn to a particular area. When I stared at that area something happened each time. One image rotated; another moved into the wall and a different one emerged; another would blend with some other characters and on this went for many minutes. Quite strange, yet I seemed to know what I was doing.

The sun was beginning to drop low in the sky and it was time for us to go. It was a beautiful sunset and as we left the site we stood in the car park and looked up at the sky. There had been planes high above us and they had left vapour trails behind.

There were three trails and when I gazed at it for a few moments I saw that these vapour trails had formed into an elongated Hathor head and I laughed out loud. I pointed it out to the group and in that moment we could feel the Hathor love flowing through us as we stared at the image high up in the sky.

We all felt very contented after visiting Dendera, I could have stayed there for longer it felt so peaceful and welcoming. However it was time to return to the hotel and enjoy our last evening meal together as a group. We shared a lovely meal, enjoying the company and laughter before retiring to bed. It was to be another early start in the morning.

The following morning we met in the reception of the hotel ready for our visit to Hatshepsut Temple. The drive was uneventful and our driver stopped at the viewing point which had been the original temple gates. We got out and looked over to the hills. The temple was set into them, and I could see little caves dotted around. We took some group photographs, got back on the bus and were driven to the temple car park.

As we walked the long road towards the temple site, I looked at the stone hillside around us. I could see faces in the rocks around the site, though this wasn't obvious at first glance. The temple was busy, full of tourists and it was a struggle to stay together.

We cleared areas as we walked around the site and energetically collected a variety of things and once Joy ensured that everything was completed we left. As she looked back, she explained that she could see all the stone figures turning gold, a sure sign that everything had gone according to plan.

On our return to the hotel we retired to the decking for some much valued relaxation time. The day was warm, the sun was shining and it felt wonderful to relax in the sunshine before our final visit that evening to the Luxor Temple light show.

I watched the sun go down over the Nile. It was slightly chilly and I was glad that I had brought a warm wrap with me for the evening trip to Luxor Temple.

During the light show a man walked out from an opening in the wall, smoking a cigarette and calling 'Mohammed' to someone on the other side of the courtyard. The crowd laughed, it was so out of place. A few moments later, in the dark sky, a single shooting star appeared. I tingled all over and the crowd gasped in surprise. It was beautiful and I felt sure it was a very positive sign that our work was going well.

One member of the group was taking pictures and in each one there were dozens of light orbs visible. They looked like snow. She was so excited that the camera had captured these beautiful images and I wondered why my camera didn't seem to show orbs very often.

I heard an instant reply which made me smile, "Because you don't need the proof".

I felt the presence of all of these light beings and my heart warmed and expanded as this love surrounded us all. We received confirmation that our work had gone well at Luxor and I was mightily relieved. It had felt quite intense at times during the show as we worked to clear dense energies and then bring through new light energies here.

The following morning I woke early. The soles of my feet were burning hot and I instinctively knew there was something I had to do before breakfast. I was repeatedly shown images of the decking at the rear of the hotel, so I quickly dressed and went outside.

It was a chilly but magnificent morning. No guests were around yet, only a few hotel staff cleaning and preparing the area for the day. I stood on the decking which was suspended above the Nile and a large white bird landed on the boat in front of me. Its feathers fluttered in the breeze and I felt it was there offering protection while I completed this stage of my work.

Energy began to pulse through my body, the soles of my feet tingling and hot. This energy built to a crescendo and then suddenly was gone. I saw golden energy move quickly along the Nile and within minutes that whole stretch of the Nile was gold.

As I watched, the entire valley of the Kings and Queens lit up, the rock shimmering gold. It was so peaceful and loving and tears were slowly sliding down my face. I felt relief, my part complete before going home and yet I didn't want to leave.

As the time drew closer to leave for the airport I was becoming excited about seeing my family again but I was torn. I wanted to remain in Egypt to assist Joy as she was staying for another week to complete her work. But I couldn't stay as I had no more holiday leave left to take. With her support during the week long trip my skills and trust in myself had blossomed beyond anything I could have dreamt of and I was grateful beyond measure.

The flight home was delayed and I had a long drive from

Manchester Airport to Edinburgh, arriving home at 4am. I was extremely tired by then and on the journey I had pondered the events of the past week.

Back in the UK it all seemed so long ago already. For years I had grappled with my personal experiences of visions and feelings, often thinking that there was something wrong with me, that I was weird. Having spent an intense week working each day with guidance from Joy and a number of non-physical light beings, I had seen some truly amazing sights and been a part of something quite magical.

This brought me full circle, once again, to the 'knowing' that my experiences were very real. Just because they were felt or seen through senses other than the physical eyesight, didn't make them any less real.

Many times in the past friends had reacted with laughter or blank looks when I had said something which was completely normal within the context of my life but which they didn't understand or hadn't experienced. It had made life challenging at times and just days into 2011 I was already wondering where these gifts and insights would lead me.

I knew what I was hoping for. I knew that I had the abilities to help people turn their lives around and I really desired the opportunities to be able to do just that on a more full time basis.

I was keen for my own personal baggage to go, all the things holding me back or preventing me from being the success I was meant to be. I was considering renting or buying premises to use as a training and treatment base. How this was going to work was anyones guess and I was asked to 'trust' this would happen. This seemed to be my test of strength and resolve, to trust that everything would work out exactly as it was meant to and that my dreams for the future would come to fruition.

In the New Year I found that my family life was more relaxed. Both my boys had attended a Diamond Inguz LiGHt Healing workshop and I watched them grow with this energy. I could see benefits to them straight away and they shared their experience of this energy to me.

They explained that they felt greater calmness and more able to deal with the things that life throws at every one of us. They didn't get angry the way they used to, which was a huge bonus for us all.

Once we understand that when we release those fears which cause anger and therefore allow the traumas long held in our very cells to be released and healed - then we can live in a much happier place.

Through learning about myself, I was more able to share this knowledge with my boys - when they wanted to listen, of course. They were both teenagers, after all said and done.

I recommended to two of my clients that they might find the Diamond Inguz of great help to them. They had come to me through recommendation and each of them, because of life experiences, had come to a point in their lives where they felt they didn't want to be here any more. They had literally had enough of taking on others issues and pain as well as their own.

Through the techniques I had learned I was able to remove much of the weight of these issues they had taken on. They each attended a Diamond Inguz workshop with Joy and were astounded at how they felt, the grounded calmness that they felt and which filtered into their family life.

The skills they learned on the course were easily applied to their daily lives. They had begun to understand, too, that our daily interactions with people were very much dependant upon what our past experiences had been.

Unpleasant or antagonistic interactions they were having with people now turned out to be remnants of discordant past lives with those people. When we cleared the past discord during a session, they each found that the discord with those people in this life completely dissolved. It was exciting for them to experience and for me to facilitate.

I watched these two women glow with renewed energy and happiness after the workshop and I was delighted to hear from both of them that despite them thinking that it couldn't possibly last, they were being proven wrong and were feeling more contented and energized as each week passed.

From my own experience and that of others I knew that this was most definitely the way forward in healing terms. The 'sensitive' clients that I was blessed to work with were loving that they felt better in such a short time, how quickly these disconnections within themselves could be addressed and how quickly their lives improved.

So what I had learned on this 'Journey of Life'?

I had learned that there is no need to fear - fear only cripples growth, development and transformation into personal joy. Fear had been in my life for far too long and I was enjoying the freedom which grew and developed as those fears were removed. This transformation into joy was magnificent.

Sometimes this transformation is by taking small steps - I started by appreciating the smallest things in my day. Seeing a beautiful sunset; a butterfly nearby; the sound of birds singing or someone's laughter; another car driver acknowledging you have stopped to let them pass. Small things which, little by little, helped my pathway to joy emerge day by day, small step by small step.

I looked at people in a new way. Though I had shown compassion to others and their struggles, I had a deeper understanding of why they were facing these struggles and was able to really do something to help them in ways I hadn't dreamed would be possible.

I had learned through my work with Joy and speaking to others that there are many people on planet Earth who are 'sensitives'. These people, adults as well as children, have highly attuned senses. Some can see energy and spirit forms clearly, some see life through geometric and mathematical formats, others are empaths who can feel and sense others pain. Some people have a mixture of some or all of these senses.

They can have a really hard time with the harshness of the human environment. I have had many people tell me that they don't like to be around other people, that they sense negativity which others carry and find it quite 'toxic' to be around. Sometimes they feel nauseous or start to get a headache.

I am one of these people and through Joy's work and the energies she is here to share I am finding that life is much easier to deal with as a 'sensitive'.

I have always wanted to be able to wake up each morning and feel content and happy, no matter what. Most days I wake up smiling and every day I express heartfelt gratitude that I have been given another chance at life, that I have finally connected to someone who could make a vast difference to my life and that of others.

It is April 2011. It is almost a year to the day that I began the 'Journey of JOY'. I am happier and more content than I have ever been in my life.

We live in an ever changing world, constantly evolving, new energies coming in as we evolve. Learning to live with love, grace and compassion. This is not the same for everyone, each one of us has our own path, our own destiny and only we know when we are in our state of joy. What works for one doesn't necessarily work for another. You will know what works for you to keep you in that special place and allow the flow of the universe to come to you and help create your beautiful life.

Every one of us can choose joy over misery and fear. It is easier than you might think when you begin to release the old and accept yourself as you are and come to love yourself for who you are. Little step by little step.
Try it - I think you will enjoy it.

As I continue to free myself of all past ties, I am holding more of the essence of who I AM. My true essence.

I have been astonished to discover that the essence of 'me' is truly awesome. I had never believed that I could ever begin to feel this good, this centred, this calm and this whole.

With love and many blessings for your brighter future.

Love is all there is.

I view my truth through the heart of someone who was lost,
Someone who found her way back to her core of love
- where all things become 'ONE',
Where all things merge to create light and love.

Yvonne Jevons 2008

Useful References:

Pregnancy and Birth - A New Generation by Joy Wisdom

Shell of Soul by Joy Wisdom

The Bodymind Workbook: Exploring How the Mind and the Body Work Together by Debbie Shapiro.

Your Body Speaks Your Mind: Understand the Link Between Your Emotions and Your Illness by Debbie Shapiro.

Feel the Fear and Do It Anyway by Susan Jeffers.

Many Lives, Many Masters by Brian Weiss

Same Soul, Many Bodies by Brian Weiss

Heal Your Body A-Z: The Mental Causes for Physical Illness and the Way to Overcome Them by Louise L. Hay.

Love Yourself, Heal Your Life Workbook by Louise L. Hay.